The Rising Tide

*The Leading Minds of Business
and Economics Chart a Course
Toward Higher Growth
and Prosperity*

EDITED BY JERRY JASINOWSKI

John Wiley & Sons, Inc.
New York • Chichester • Weinheim
Brisbane • Singapore • Toronto

This text is printed on acid-free paper.

Copyright © 1998 by The Manufacturing Institute
Published by John Wiley & Sons, Inc.

Library of Congress Cataloging-in-Publication Data

The rising tide : the leading minds of business and economics chart a
   course toward higher growth and prosperity / edited by Jerry
   Jasinowski.
      p.   cm.
   Includes index.
   ISBN 0-471-19213-9 (cloth : alk. paper)
   1. United States—Economic policy—1993– 2. Economic development.
  3. Competition, International. I. Jasinowski, Jerry J.
  HC106.82.R57   1998
  338.973—dc21   97-29024
                                                   CIP

Printed in the United States of America

10 9 8 7 6 5 4 3 2 1

Contents

Acknowledgments

In theory, this is a book that could have, and should have, been written years ago. After all, economic growth has been central to our country's prosperity since the dawn of economic study. But somewhere along the line the idea that noninflationary growth was limited to something less than 2.5% became ingrained in our thinking. And, unfortunately, attitudes among economists, policymakers, and even the business community change slowly.

That's why I'd like to thank, first and foremost, the contributors to this book. They were among the first to shake off the yoke of status-quo thinking to embrace the notion that higher, noninflationary growth was possible. I'd also like to thank them for their patience. It takes a long time to coordinate more than two dozen separate articles.

I am also indebted to a number of individuals, especially Robert Hamrin. I've known and worked with Bob for nearly a quarter century. In 1995, he and I coauthored *Making It In America*, an important book detailing the keys to business success in the new economy. His role in *The Rising Tide* was equally significant. Bob was instrumental in shaping the book's structure and performed admirably the sometimes Herculean task of wading through and editing the first drafts. Bob deserves much of the credit for ensuring, as much as possible, that *The Rising Tide* speaks with one voice.

Special thanks is also due Jeanne Glasser, editor at Wiley, who believed in this book and kept it on track, and David Shapiro, executive director of the Manufacturing Institute, who, as much as anyone, was my collaborator on this project. Finally, I want to extend my appreciation for the contributions of Michael Baroody, Amanda Carnevale, Graham Vink, and Claire Huismann.

Jerry J. Jasinowski
September 16, 1997

Foreword

During 1995 and 1996, most experts on the U.S. economy were convinced that the annual growth rate could not, and should not, exceed 2.3%. Anything higher, they argued, soon would create shortages, pressure on plant capacity, and rising costs for labor and financing. Inflation would accelerate. Bond yields would soar and stock prices collapse unless the Federal Reserve Board moved to push interest rates higher and cool the economy. Economic growth above 2.3%, they argued, was perilous and damaging to the long-term prospects of businesses and living standards in the United States.

I disagreed. So did many of my colleagues at the National Association of Manufacturers (NAM), the nation's biggest industrial trade organization with 14,000 companies as sponsoring members. In addition to my full-time job as chairman and chief executive of Tenneco, a $7.5 billion (sales) global manufacturer of packaging and automotive parts, I was chairman of the NAM from late 1995 through the first nine months of 1996. From the outset of my tenure, the NAM executive board, myself included, and Jerry Jasinowski, NAM's president and leader of its talented professional staff in Washington, made a commitment to assemble and present new facts about how the production of goods and services had changed and improved the U.S. economy. Our objective was to widen and popularize the policy debate about the potential for raising the rate of economic growth to 3% or above without a corresponding jump in inflation. We think this is both highly desirable and achievable.

As leaders of manufacturing organizations large and small, we know how much has changed in our factories and organizations in a remarkably short period—fewer than 10 years. We wanted to describe the policy implications of these changes. For manufacturers alone, the stakes are huge. Our sector of the economy contributed about $1.1 trillion, or 21.8%, of the gross domestic output in the United States last year. We employ 18 million people, or 16% of the total U.S. workforce. (As these statistics attest, manufacturing is one of the most productive sectors of our economy. Output per employee in manufacturing rose 4% in 1996, and has averaged an increase of 3.2% a year since the early 1980s.)

We also wanted to build a majority view among opinion leaders in Washington, Wall Street, and Main Street that faster economic growth was (1) achievable without reigniting inflation, and (2) necessary to help ease the difficult transition for our society from an industrial economy toward a knowledge economy.

To a great extent, we succeeded. There is a new acknowledgment among the Fed, policy makers, the media, and the public that we can grow faster. This book is an important next step. It examines many aspects of the economic growth debate with considerable scope, precision, and sophistication. Our fundamental goal remains: To encourage policy makers and lawmakers to take the many steps noted in these essays to substantially improve living standards and the quality of life in our society.

Many influential newspapers and magazines, radio and television programs developed numerous prominent articles or features on growth throughout the summer and fall of 1996. Their timing typically was linked to an approaching decision by the Federal Reserve on whether or not to increase interest rates. For a few months, the presidential election campaign added more fuel to the fire. All the while, the journalistic search for speculation, forecasts, and opinions provided us the opportunity we had sought to make this a front-burner issue.

Monetary policy is one of many issues this book analyzes for its impact on growth. In 1996—and throughout 1997—it was the issue that consistently drew the most attention of the news media. Was the economy growing too fast? Was consumer confidence too high? Plant capacity near its limits? Stock prices too far into the stratosphere? Labor markets too tight, with costs pushing higher? Was the core inflation rate about to break out of an unusually tame phase? How would the Fed respond? How should it?

Each time, we argued against raising interest rates. Our positions were rooted in the real world of today, not in theory or statistics from the past. The old analytical assumptions no longer fit very well when they tried to measure growth, unemployment, and inflation. Yet the inflation-hawk pundits who opposed us persisted in pointing to statistical trends of the past. According to their interpretations of these trends, any growth above 2.3% per year would inevitably produce either rising inflation or aggressive action by the Federal Reserve to tighten credit, raise rates, and head off inflation.

Many critics among the inflation hawks were quick to dismiss our views as self-serving bluster from business leaders more concerned about the threat of higher borrowing costs on this year's profit than the longer-term health of the economy. Worse yet, some of us were stunned by the number of people with hostile attitudes about economic growth. They consider economic growth not as a logical path toward more investment, greater global competitiveness and, ultimately, higher living standards, but as a suspect means toward an evil end. They see economic growth more as a plot created by greedy corporations and wealthy capitalists of the world to turn the United States into a plutocracy, a society governed by the wealthy. This kind of dangerous, divisive ignorance must be confronted with reasoned analysis. This book is just that kind of response.

After a small increase in March 1997, the Federal Reserve left interest rates unchanged. While difficult to prove, we are confident our efforts to describe the new economy had an impact on the Federal Reserve's conclusions and performance. Also during this time, a few other influential opinion makers, notably editorial-page editors at *Business Week* and the *Wall Street Journal*, were echoing our call for restraint by the Fed. Both publications featured several major articles on economic growth and Federal Reserve monetary policy, as did *Fortune*, the *New York Times*, *Washington Post*, *Barrons*, and *USA Today*, among others. Meanwhile, a few of us from the NAM met privately during the year to present the argument to leaders of the Federal Reserve, the Clinton administration, and the Congress.

We knew from the difficult lessons taught in the global economy of the 1970s and 1980s that we were competing in a new business climate. We knew we had to keep costs low, customers loyal, and earnings growing to remain competitive in our markets. We also knew, as a consequence of these new factors of the 1990s, that we were generating higher revenues and profits with fewer employees. This was happening mostly without the benefit for producers of periodic price increases. Indeed, two very simple, very harsh rules of the markets were the driving forces behind much of the corporate upheaval of the '90s. They were: (1) if you raise prices, you lose customers, and (2) you must raise productivity, or lose profits.

We told policy makers at the Federal Reserve and others in the halls of government that they continued to overemphasize certain gauges of economic activity, such as inventory levels, capacity utilization, and, especially, the rate of unemployment. The behavior was a misuse and misreading of economic data that did not take into account the impact of computer technology, telecommunications, and global competition, and our production capacity.

On inventories, these policy makers were misfiring because they did not recognize how major changes in supplier-manufacturer relations should have altered their interpretation of inventory statistics. Low inventories used to be considered a signal that capacity utilization was about to rise as production revved up for new orders to replenish inventories. In the new economy, however, manufacturers often can and do order parts from suppliers that can be delivered from nearby plants within two hours or less. This means that manufacturers can make more productive use of their floor space, and they have far less capital tied up in financing large stocks of inventories in their plants.

As an example, our automotive parts business, Tenneco Automotive, is the largest independent maker of shock absorbers and exhaust systems in the world. Its customers include all of the major auto manufacturers. For many of them, we have built or are planning to build parts-manufacturing plants very close to their assembly plants.

On capacity utilization, the Federal Reserve was slow to appreciate the impact of process improvements from countless reengineering and quality projects. Many plants expanded capacity far beyond their original limits, with many of them operating well above "100%" levels. As a result, the Fed understated the nation's available manufacturing capacity and concluded incorrectly that manufacturers had more power to raise prices than they actually had.

Finally, on unemployment, the Fed and legions of economists elsewhere in government, academia, and consulting were suspicious of our conviction that the "natural" rate of unemployment in this economy, the lowest level that would not set off pressures for higher wages and stoke inflation, was much lower than 6%. Others in this book have much to say about the *nonaccelerating* inflation rate of unemployment, or NAIRU. I will simply state here that the notion that the NAIRU in the U.S. economy is 6% has been thoroughly discredited by the events of the past two years.

Fear of losing a job and benefits in an era of downsized companies, globalization of labor markets and competition, staffing flexibility created in new labor contracts. These are some reasons why wage pressures were not rising as the unemployment rate fell below 6% 1995 and 1996, and eventually to 4.9% in April 1997.

During 1996, it was evident to us from many public comments by Alan Greenspan that the Federal Reserve chairman was thoughtfully analyzing our positions on growth, productivity, and inflation. Perhaps the best evidence is that he resisted the clamor for higher interest rates, much of it coming from his fellow Federal Reserve Board governors. In our view, Greenspan clearly exhibited a new flexibility in his views. His actions in 1996 as Fed chairman quite probably enabled the current expansion to continue into what is now its seventh year.

In a speech at New York University in May 1997, Greenspan made a strong defense of the Federal Reserve's policy to raise interest rates at early signs of inflationary pressures in the economy.

The goal, he said, was not solely to keep prices stable, but to sustain and foster "growth in economic activity, jobs, and real wages," a goal we certainly share. Greenspan also observed that new factors in the economy, such as computer technology and telecommunications that we have noted often, were altering the early warning signals of rising inflation. "Our production system and the notion of capacity are far more flexible than they were 10 or 20 years ago," he said. But, he added, cautiously, "(A)ny inference that our productive capacity is essentially unlimited is clearly unwarranted."

To be sure, none of us in the NAM leadership is arguing for the extreme position of "unlimited" capacity for growth. What we are saying is that we have had strong economic growth in the last year, with low unemployment and low inflation, at aggregate levels that were considered highly improbable as recently as a year ago.

Absent some unforeseen political or economic shock, most economists anticipate that the expansion of the '90s will continue well into 1998. With unemployment the lowest since 1973 and inflation remaining below 3%, we can now think realistically of having the opportunity to answer this question from experience: Can the new American economy grow at a sustained rate of 3%, with unemployment at 5% or less, and inflation below 3%? We do not know how Greenspan and other members of the Fed would respond. Many of us, however, are convinced the answer is yes. And if the Fed does not scuttle the current expansion with unwarranted rate hikes, we may have the evidence as soon as 1998.

A related goal for us in 1996 was to promote the debate about economic growth as a worthy focal point of the contest for the White House, as well as for other national and state political campaigns. This was accomplished on many fronts. Biggest of all was Bob Dole's decision shortly before the Republican convention in San Diego to place faster economic growth at the center of his run for the presidency and, then, to choose Jack Kemp as his running mate. Kemp, a longtime advocate of faster growth, presents his arguments in a commentary in Chapter 1.

Today, we see signs that the case for economic growth is more firmly embraced by members of Congress and in academia than ever before. In April 1997, the *Wall Street Journal* quoted House

Speaker Newt Gingrich as saying, "It is unconscionable to have the Federal Reserve system close off economic growth because of some theoretical model. Our goal should be to say bluntly, up front: We want a high-growth, high-income, high take-home-pay, high-opportunity society." Gingrich spoke following a Labor Department report that the proportion of American adults with jobs reached a record of 63.8%, with 1.3 million jobs added in the first three months of 1997.

The same week that Gingrich spoke, Robert Solow, Nobel laureate economist at MIT, typified the supporting voices we are hearing from academia. "Where was it written," he asked, as reported in a column by Peter Passell in the *New York Times*, "that absolute security against inflation is worth sacrificing unknown quantities of national income?"

As I write now in June 1997, the overall tone of the economy, as well as economic statistics, continue to support our basic position: We can generate higher-paying jobs, grow faster than 2.3%, with unemployment below 5% and inflation below 3%. We are in a new era where rules and assumptions from the past about the limits of economic growth no longer hold.

It is obvious to me, yet worth stating plainly, that economic growth is an issue with consequences far broader than conventional political battles or policy arguments among or within business, government, or special interests. Faster growth, without inflation, can generate huge resources—huge amounts of money—that we as a society require to adjust to all the problems related to managing the transition from an industrial economy to a knowledge economy.

This transition, in all of its ramifications, is perhaps the greatest domestic challenge we face in this country over the next decade. Economic insecurity, worker anxiety about potential loss of job and benefits, social displacement and disruption—these are the palpable, unavoidable results of the accelerating technological revolution that has made American business again the unquestioned leader in global economic competitiveness and job creation.

Business restructuring will continue. Corporate leaders realize this is an ongoing, essential task of management in order for their organizations to become or remain successful in brutally competitive global markets. At Tenneco Automotive, for instance, we currently are carrying out a restructuring that includes hundreds of job relocations and hundreds of job reductions—primarily involving management positions—despite just having completed a third consecutive year of record revenues and operating profits. Why did we do it? Because we expect to save approximately $70 million a year in administrative costs, work more effectively together, and preserve and create jobs in areas with growing demand for our products.

Unless we as a nation can achieve growth at levels high enough to generate the revenues that both government and business need, it will become increasingly difficult for our society as a whole to pay for these kinds of ongoing dislocations. We will not be able to pay for the training and retraining we need to equip our workforce with skills for jobs, jobs with a future that deliver something of value for the employer. We will not be able to pay for necessary and effective safety nets for the dislocations and economic hardships. We will not be able to pay for all the new computer systems and other technology that we require to continue raising productivity, performance, and living standards.

This remarkable book is the most thoughtful and detailed examination to date of our assertion that the nation can and should aspire to sustained annual growth rates of at least 3%. In these pages, many of the nation's best economic thinkers and innovative industrialists describe multiple facets of the complex story of economic growth. They bolster our convictions about the benefits and importance of achieving faster growth in the U.S. economy, and the policy decisions that can help us accomplish it.

Dana G. Mead
Greenwich, Conn.
June 1997

Introduction

Growth in the New Economy

JERRY J. JASINOWSKI, PRESIDENT OF
THE NATIONAL ASSOCIATION OF
MANUFACTURERS

Why economic growth? Because it is only a slight exaggeration to say that nothing matters more when it comes to economic progress and an improved quality of life. Growth ensures that the economic pie gets larger so that no matter how it is sliced, everyone can get a bigger piece.

Pundits and policy makers alike acknowledge the importance of economic growth, yet some insist that we are stuck in a period where growth is limited to less than 2.3%. The usual way to estimate potential output—the highest growth rate that can be sustained without causing inflation to accelerate—is to add together the growth of the labor force and the historical trend in productivity. With productivity potential estimated at only 1.2% and population growing at 1.1%, the conventional wisdom says long-term growth cannot sustain a rate of more than 2.3%.

There is more and more evidence that the conventional wisdom is not correct, particularly with respect to manufacturing. After pundits in the early 1980s declared manufacturing unable to compete globally, American industry reinvented itself and made a remarkable comeback. Innovating in every aspect of operations and applying technology to production and processes, manufacturing productivity has been rising at a rate of 3% for several years and increased by 4% in 1996.

Following the lead of manufacturing's revolutionary changes, the service sector and other elements of the economy are also making the changes necessary to increase productivity. Measures of sales per employee in firms have been rising more rapidly than official productivity measures. More recently, national income has been rising significantly faster than national output, which suggests that productivity for the economy as a whole—and our potential for economic growth—is considerably higher than officially estimated. At the same time, the economic statistics for 1996 and 1997 are far better than conventional wisdom thought possible: real GDP up 2.8% while inflation, as measured by the GDP deflator, increased only 2.1%. It seems that the economy has a larger capacity to grow without inflation accelerating than most people realized.

Whether this conventional wisdom is correct or not is crucial to the future of all Americans whose standard of living is at stake. The articles in this book, authored by 26 leading economists and CEOs, add up to a thorough investigation of American growth prospects. Although there are differences of opinion, the consensus is that dramatic economic changes have increased the nation's capacity for sustained, noninflationary economic growth.

The reason our economy can grow faster is because of the confluence of increased competition in the global economy, a high technology revolution in computers and communications, and the way in which American business has radically altered its methods of operation. These forces have significantly increased private-sector productivity and the country's capacity for growth. This crucial finding was best expressed by Nobel laureate Lawrence

Klein when he said that America has entered a sustainable phase of productivity improvement, which means that an economic growth rate "of at least 3% and possibly as high as 3.5% is sustainable."

This historic economic transformation, which is called the "new economy," is evident first and foremost in manufacturing. Faced with extraordinary foreign competition, American manufacturers invested heavily in productivity-enhancing technology. Today, according to calculations done by the National Association of Manufacturers, manufacturing productivity is significantly higher in the United States than in its major competitors. Manufacturing productivity in Germany, for example, is only 82% that of the United States, while in Japan it is even lower at 78%.

In order to understand the full context of this rapidly changing growth debate, we need to appreciate the benefits of growth, understand the major elements of consensus on how growth happens, analyze how recent economic changes make higher growth possible, and examine the paths to the emerging higher growth rates.

My own view, which is beginning to be shared by a broader group of intellectuals and business leaders, is that we can already see an epochal transformation in the American economy. This new economy is characterized by more intensive global and domestic competition, a reduction of pricing power in product and labor markets, a greater use of technology to increase speed and productivity to compensate for lost pricing power, and a stronger integration of product, people, and process innovation to meet the challenges of continuous improvement to spur a high rate of technological change.

There is also a significant consensus among the writers in this book, as well as others, on the elements that drive faster growth. First, they agree that in the long run, increases in output per person are driven mainly by technological advance. The fundamental insight is that living standards rise mainly because of productivity growth, and that productivity is raised primarily by technological advances.

Second, the writers agree that market capitalism is the most efficient economic system. Entrepreneurs and individual companies competing in a global economy, not only in the United

States, but also in the world are the fundamental source of new economic vigor. With the breakdown of the Communist regimes and with much of the Third World now integrating itself into the global economy, the future for American firms clearly lies in expanding international trade. Several of the writers argue that one of the major new growth opportunities for American firms is to penetrate markets overseas. This would lead not only to faster growth, but also to gains in efficiency from economies of scale.

Third, there is a general consensus among the writers that the role of government should be reduced. There are certain functions that governments should perform, such as using macroeconomic policy to create a stable business climate and supporting areas such as education, infrastructure, and scientific research. There is less agreement on specific policies, such as whether the tax system should be reformed and, if so, what types of taxation would yield the best results.

Finally, there is a sense among these writers that the economic potential of the United States is greater than has sometimes been argued. Over the last few years, there has been an extensive debate over the growth rate that can be sustained in the late 1990s and the early part of the next century. I believe, and some evidence seems to support the notion, that the sustainable growth rate is close to a half a percentage point higher than currently articulated in Washington and on Wall Street. With additional major policy changes in Washington, the sustainable noninflationary economic growth rate could be higher still, which could yield substantial benefits for the nation. The essays in this book, written by some of America's leading economists and business executives, argue that with a little imagination and a lot of political will, Americans can experience a new golden age of economic prosperity and growth.

THE BENEFITS OF ECONOMIC GROWTH

The benefits of achieving a higher growth rate are huge. For instance, if the growth rate were to be raised by half a percentage point over the next seven years, on a cumulative basis, real GDP would increase by $675 billion; direct compensation to labor—

wages and salaries—would increase by $390 billion; the pretax income of the average family would increase by $6,588; and federal tax revenues would increase by $129 billion. By increasing wealth, raising incomes, and providing revenue to balance the budget, higher economic growth would translate into a higher standard of living for the nation's employees and better economic opportunities for millions of companies.

The significance of growth, and in particular industrial growth, can be seen in the history of the advanced economies. Since the midnineteenth century, North America, Europe, and Japan transformed themselves into developed economies with high incomes, stronger industrial bases, and state-of-the-art capital and technology. Prior to this time, economic progress had been slow and halting, with periods of prosperity giving way to periods of decline. The industrial revolution guaranteed not only that progress would be rapid, but that the gains would be permanent. In the United States alone, real incomes per person increased by a factor of more than eight since the 1870s. Side by side with the gain in real incomes, the quality of life improved in unprecedented ways as a result of new technologies. Over the last 40 years, some Third World countries—notably in the Pacific Basin—duplicated this feat, advancing to the level of middle-income nations within a generation.

According to Felix Rohatyn financier, investment banker, and contributor to this book, growth is the only way out of the social and economic problems confronting late twentieth-century America, which he identifies as including job insecurity, significant income differentials, and a deteriorating urban quality-of-life. "Even though each of these requires different approaches, the single most important requirement to deal with them is the wealth and revenues generated by a higher rate of economic growth," he insists in this book. "John Kennedy was right," he adds, 'a rising tide lifts all boats.' Although it may not lift all of them at the same time and at the same rate, without more growth we are simply redistributing the same pie. That is a zero-sum game," he concludes, "and it is simply not good enough."

Former vice presidential candidate Jack Kemp echoes much of what Rohatyn says in his essay. Kemp rejects what he terms "conventional pessimism" and blames government policy and conventional wisdom for sapping American prosperity. "The good news," according to Kemp, "is that today's slow economic growth has nothing to do with the economy's intrinsic ability to produce. The permanent slowdown in production is induced by policy, not growth," he insists. "Hence, this growth ceiling should not be taken as natural or inevitable. We can raise the ceiling on growth by judicious changes in policy." He suggests a number of such policy changes.

GROWTH IN THE NEW ECONOMY

Just as in the past, raising America's trend-growth rate requires focusing on the long-run production side of the economy. Fluctuations in demand over the course of the business cycle have only a marginal effect on our capacity to grow. This long-term path for the economy is determined by the supply-side components of labor, the stock of physical capital (machinery and structures), and technological advance.

It would be a mistake, however, to assume that our fundamental capacity to grow will be determined exclusively by past formulas. Advances in economic research tell us that the ability to innovate is greater than widely assumed. The confluence of the forces of global competition and the revolution in computers and telecommunications has created a new brand and scale of intense competition. This competition in turn reduces price-and-wage-setting power and calls for greater improvements in productivity, better trained and empowered workers, greater requirements for quality and product improvements, and much more emphasis on accelerating both the production process and product delivery. In order to be successful in the new economy, companies must be stronger competitors in terms of speed, productivity, and quality.

This new economy provides greater opportunities for growth. In the new economy, greater emphasis is placed on rapid innovation and technological advance, since it is the best way for firms to respond to changing consumer demands, increase productivity, and manage their business on an international basis. That is why growth is no longer straightjacketed by the increase in the labor supply on one side and the stock of physical capital on the other. Now, innovation and technology play a bigger role in our capacity to grow.

The importance of technology in growth was first recognized in the late 1950s by economist Robert Solow, who later won the Nobel Prize. Solow demonstrated that labor and capital alone accounted for only about two-thirds of growth in output. The remainder—termed *total factor productivity*—had to be coming from some other source, mainly advances in technology.

The major limitation of this model was that it did not specify the source of the technology. Lacking anything better, modelers tried fitting linear trends to productivity to represent technological advances that were thought to occur exogenously. Over the next two decades, other economists looked at several aspects of this issue, such as the extent to which improvements in machinery led to better-quality products, and whether investment in research could account for productivity growth. It was not until the mid-1980s that Paul Romer worked out a formal model in which technology was generated by the decisions of firms. His idea was that firms accumulate knowledge in much the same way as they accumulate physical capital, and that this knowledge would spill over to benefit society as a whole.

This idea led to what were termed *endogenous growth* models—*endogenous* because technology came from within the activities of companies and the economy. In endogenous growth theory, several factors give rise to technology. One is investment in research, which leads to the development of new products and improvements in product quality. A second factor is production improvements made possible by new forms of equipment, such as computers. Finally, technical knowledge is transmitted to the workforce via education and training. Training enables the workforce to make use of the best available technology, and in turn to assist in the development of new products and processes.

The crucial role of technology has been borne out in the 1990s. In fact, technology and innovation in the broadest sense now drive growth and make possible an economy with higher productivity and less inflation. Since the mid-1980s, breakthroughs in microcomputers have made once-unimaginable computing power widely available at a significantly lower cost. The wave of computer investment in the 1990s has been accompanied by new production techniques, which have raised the capacity to produce higher-quality goods and services at a lower average cost.

Some of the contributors to this book build upon and update the work of Solow and Romer in arguing that technological innovation can raise the growth rate permanently and substantially. Economist Lawrence Klein makes the case powerfully in his essay. He believes the United States has entered "a sustainable phase of productivity improvement" and that the economy is "being inappropriately restrained and is underachieving its potential." He argues that the potential growth rate may be a full percentage point higher than currently believed.

For economist Robert Eisner, the chief result of the new economy is the increased competition in labor-market conditions that yield an unemployment rate that can be far lower without triggering inflation. He argues that his research shows that "low unemployment has not brought accelerating inflation," as the NAIRU concept would suggest. Similarly, Joel Popkin makes the case for a more accommodative monetary policy, arguing that the United States is in a period of low inflation. This environment of lower inflation has itself contributed to the potential for faster growth.

Productivity and Technological Progress

Given technology's central role in increasing productivity and growth, the specific dynamics of its contribution are treated in detail by several authors. The technological advances that drive growth in the long run are generated in the private sector and, particularly, in individual companies. Among the writers in this volume, Richard Cyert sets out a model of firm behavior in which technology emerges from specific goals. While the overall goal of the firm is profit maximization, its executives often focus on objectives closer to their particular departments, such as adopting new computer technologies, which may lead to wider changes within the firm. For instance, the use of computers makes it possible to run the firm in a more decentralized way: activities that used to be handled by managers can now be handled by production workers.

In his examination of the factors leading to productivity improvement and changes in employment at the firm level, economist John Haltiwanger argues against the conventional wisdom that the productivity gain in manufacturing was caused solely by downsizing. Instead, many firms were successful upsizers, increasing both productivity and employment. The successful upsizers added almost as much to manufacturing productivity during the 1980s as firms that downsized and restructured. Furthermore, nearly one-third of the productivity increase during the 1980s was generated by construction of modern factories with advanced technology and computers displacing older equipment. Since the late 1970s, there has been a massive increase in investment in computers: business fixed investment in computers and peripheral equipment rose from $1 billion in 1978 to $132.8 billion in 1996. The conclusion is that in order to generate sustained productivity gains, it is necessary to reallocate both labor and capital to the most successful establishments and processes.

Capacity to Compete and Grow

The CEOs of powerful industrial firms provide some detail as to how manufacturing has increased productivity. Tracy O'Rourke identifies several improvements that have made Varian Associates a world-class competitor in high-tech products. One key improvement has been innovation and new product development. Another is speed—shorter cycle times for production runs, faster inventory turns, smaller lot sizes and faster test times. To shorten cycle times, Varian has emphasized running several phases of its operation concurrently. Outsourcing of supplies and components has been used to speed up production. Varian also has adopted an internal strategy based on several criteria: improved customer focus, high-quality goods, and a workforce trained in the use of the latest equipment. The workforce was reorganized into teams, such as teams of engineers that worked on several sets of projects, using new methods such as CAD-CAM. As a result, over 90% of this firm's products have gained market share.

Further evidence for technological advance and increased productivity, particularly in the manufacturing sector, is provided by Frank Lichtenberg. He analyzes two forms of investment in technology: R & D and computers. The rate of return to firms from research is extremely high. Furthermore, the return to society as a whole from new products and processes is much higher than the return to the individual firms or investors. He notes that in manufacturing, R & D has been rising steadily as a share of sales, which has added half a point to the annual rate of productivity growth between the 1950s and the 1990s. In addition, both the use of computers in production and the hiring of computer specialists in industry have raised productivity above and beyond the levels implied by R & D alone.

The government can also encourage technological progress by removing regulatory impediments to private innovation, wisely investing in university and basic research, and enacting tax laws that encourage R & D to enable American firms to keep pace in the modern economy. Also, the federal government's current $70 billion investment in R & D should be spent more wisely. Washington should follow the lead of firms by rationalizing their R & D investments and focusing them on achieving goals that have a chance for a significant payoff. The government also needs to modernize its patent system to protect new ideas and inventions without excessive delays.

Several conclusions emerge from these essays. First, basic research generates increases in the stock of scientific knowledge, but it is applied R & D that translates into new products and processes. Second, there is a strong empirical relationship between various measures of technology and the rate of productivity growth. Third, there is a relationship between certain forms of capital and technology. For example, the advent of microcomputers has made it possible for business to undertake a broad range of process improvements, such as just-in-time inventory control, statistical quality control, and computer-aided design. Increasingly, computer-aided manufacturing and networks tie the whole manufacturing process together.

Going Global

One element of the growth process that has long been recognized by theory is economies of scale. When firms have a comparative advantage in producing certain types of goods—for instance, the use of the best technologies—they can raise their rate of return by penetrating larger markets. With many corporations now operating in niche markets, there is no reason for them to limit operations to the United States. Instead, many have achieved substantial scale advantages by operating globally. Indeed, four years ago the Bechtel Corporation did 70% of its business in the United States. Today, it does 70% overseas.

As Jeffrey Sachs points out in his essay, the world economy today is more interlinked than at any time since the First World War. During the last fifteen years, the countries of the former Soviet Union, central Europe, and much of Asia, Africa, and Latin America have moved toward market economies. Sachs argues that the United States is in a very favorable position in the world economy, that it stands at the cutting edge of critical technologies, such as information processing and biotechnology, and that it has successfully restructured in the face of foreign competition. Hence, America's competitive position is stronger than most of the world's other industrial countries. In the global economy as a whole, the increasing scale of markets will stimulate innovation, since the larger market provides more opportunities to sell new products. International capital flows will rise as a proportion of global saving, while production will be relocated. He argues that the combined effects of technology and economies of scale will raise the long-term growth rate of per-capita incomes by about half a percentage point.

This rosy picture could be threatened, however, by protectionism and regulatory controls over trade. Growth is highest when workers and resources are allocated to a nation's most efficient and competitive enterprises. Protecting inefficient businesses behind a wall of protectionism, or forcing more efficient foreign producers to navigate a maze of regulatory controls, raises consumer prices and prevents the economy from earning the biggest bang for its bucks. A key to America's current competitive success is the rigor of an open market that forces U.S. firms to respond quickly to changing competitive pressures. In her essay Marina Whitman says that if government helped the private sector react to trade pressures by promoting investment in new technologies, a "virtuous circle" would be created. In it, higher productivity generates faster income growth, which increases public support for free trade, which in turn helps raise growth.

Investing in People

Perhaps the greatest challenge to higher growth is improving the quality and quantity of available workers. This is a challenge precisely because it is the least susceptible to short-term improvements. Too often, new entrants to the workforce are poorly educated and lack the skills necessary for the new economy. Nearly one-quarter of the respondents to a recent *Chief Executive* growth poll, sponsored by Deloitte & Touche, cited a lack of skilled workers as their company's main barrier to growth. Investing in new technologies to streamline business processes will do nothing for a company if the workforce does not know how to operate the new systems efficiently. Ideally, firms should set a goal of investing 3% of payroll in training and educating their workforce.

Beyond education and training, successful companies are developing a new employment relationship that stresses empowered workers and the increased use of incentive compensation. Reports suggest that aggressive employee-involvement programs raise productivity, which improves firm competitiveness and further motivates workers. So effective are these programs that roughly two-thirds of our manufacturing firms provide some form of incentive compensation that is often tied directly to productivity.

While the government can help with education and training, our educational system is one of those areas least likely to see solutions at the federal level. Tinkering with the tax code to encourage higher education will do little to raise basic educational skills and may succeed only in providing a windfall for universities and those families whose children would go on to college anyway. Nevertheless, the federal government must not ignore the deepening crisis in education that is sapping the ability of firms to grow. In his essay, Anthony Carnevale argues for an enhanced governmental role in education and training. He suggests that a good start would be the consolidation and reform of the nearly 150 federally administered training programs to make them more responsive to the employment needs of the private sector. Beyond that, the federal government must also consider vouchers, charter schools, and other measures to spur competition in order to improve the educational opportunities for all of our children.

Higher economic growth also comes from increasing the quantity of the workforce. But rapid increases in the size of the labor force, at least for now, is a phenomenon of the past. The size of the workforce is projected to grow at an annual rate of little more than 1%. Tight labor markets in key sectors of the economy, such as semiconductors, may already be dragging down the growth rate. Some help may come from the transformation of the workplace from jobs that require brawn to those that require brains. An acceleration of this trend could bring more women into the labor force, (currently roughly 4 out of 10 women do not work full time), encourage older workers to stay in the job market, and increase legal immigration of skilled labor. Greater flexibility of work schedules and telecommuting may also increase the pool of available employees. Economist Audrey Freedman says that reducing the amount of time the unemployed spend looking for work means more hours worked, which can also increase the growth rate.

A More Productive Government

With changes in public sector policies, we can do even better on the growth front than we have in the past. Government policy changes can both reduce impediments to higher economic growth and encourage activities that promote growth.

Since the early days of economic theory, it has been acknowledged that government should provide certain types of public goods, such as education and infrastructure—roads, ports, and utilities. To these, one could add R & D, where spending to support national defense has often triggered additional research by the private sector.

Still, theory argues that the role of the state in a market economy should be limited, a view supported empirically in this book by Robert Barro. He finds that, in general, higher growth rates are associated with maintenance of property rights and rule of law, fewer market distortions, less nonproductive government spending, and low inflation rates. Growth rates tend to lag during times of political instability, high rates of inflation, or excessive governmental market regulation. Other factors that contribute to growth are investing in human capital in areas such as education and health, improvements in the terms of trade, and reasonable rates of population growth. Going from dictatorship to democracy also has a large impact on a nation's standard of living.

Perhaps the most important function for the government, however, is ensuring macroeconomic stability. Robert Shapiro and Ben Friedman argue for coordination of monetary and fiscal policy in order to offset business-cycle fluctuations. In particular, fiscal policy should avoid large deficits and high real interest rates, a goal that evidence indicates is being attained. Since the early 1980s, the nation's prevailing economic pattern has been one of long expansions with minimal inflationary pressure and relatively shallow recessions.

It is also useful to consider specific policy areas. First, Dale Jorgenson makes the case for replacing the existing federal tax system with one based on consumption, resulting in potentially substantial economic gains. The main reason of course would be a dramatic fall in the cost of capital. There are also a wide variety of other tax-overhaul proposals—such as a national sales tax and various forms of a flat tax—that could contribute to higher growth rates.

If education and infrastructure investments can spur growth, federal regulation can dampen it. In general, regulation slows the growth rate by diverting capital into compliance activities and away from more productive uses. William Niskanen finds that, in many instances, the economic costs of regulation, *i.e.,* losses in GDP, exceed the direct compliance costs. He recommends extensive reform of the regulatory system, including elimination of remaining economic regulation, much of it at the state and local level, and an overhaul of health and environmental regulation. Likewise, Congress needs to rein in the worst excesses of our legal system, which impose billions of dollars of additional costs on businesses while stifling product innovation and inhibiting growth.

Trade is one of the bright spots in governmental policy. Both the president and most congressional leaders understand the importance of boosting exports. Expanded trade raises growth by reducing the trade deficit and improving the performance of companies and workers, which generates additional income, capital investment, increased economies of scale, and higher productivity in key sectors of the economy. While the United States has been at the forefront of efforts to eliminate global trade barriers, we could do more to promote American companies overseas, particularly in Latin America. Congress must learn to resist the temptation to create unilateral economic sanctions that may score political points, but that impose significant costs on firms trying to compete for sales abroad and on their employees whose jobs often depend on these sales.

Finally, an issue that has recently become prominent is reform of national pension systems, including privatization of Social Security. José Piñera, the architect of Chile's successful social security privatization plan, draws on his own experience in analyzing pension reform. Pointing to serious inefficiencies in the American Social Security system and the possibility of a crisis at some future date, Piñera suggests that moving to a system of individual retirement accounts would lead both to improved labor-market incentives and a higher rate of return on personal savings.

CONCLUSION

Advocates of higher growth have reason to be hopeful. In recent months, the Federal Reserve Board has, at least tentatively, embraced the possibilities of higher growth, as pointed out by Felix Rohatyn. But, as was once suggested regarding the Vietnam War, this is no reason to simply declare victory and go home. Instead, we should take the signs that our arguments are gradually being accepted and push for more.

If higher growth is not only good but possible, then how do we make sure it happens? In addition to the policy prescriptions outlined earlier and elaborated upon in some of the book's essays, we must change the way we think about economic and public policy issues. Instead of considering economics as a zero-sum game of permanent winners and losers, we must learn to regard economics as capable of stimulating innovation to create dynamic opportunities for higher productivity and growth.

If there is one insight that comes through loud and clear throughout *The Rising Tide*, it is that the key to America's capacity to grow, both past and future, is the flexibility, innovation, and determination of our people. The new economy opens the door to a renewal of our ingenuity and competitive spirit. All we have to do is walk through it by creatively using our capital, technology, and people in pursuit of greater excellence and growth in the global economy.

1

The Mandate for Higher Growth

Jack Kemp
Felix Rohatyn

The Economic Growth Imperative
Ways to Achieve Higher Growth

The Economic Growth Imperative

JACK KEMP, CODIRECTOR OF
EMPOWER AMERICA; FORMER
SECRETARY OF HOUSING AND URBAN
DEVELOPMENT; MEMBER OF THE
HOUSE OF REPRESENTATIVES,
1981–1989; REPUBLICAN PARTY
CANDIDATE FOR VICE PRESIDENT OF
THE UNITED STATES, 1996

Throughout history, human progress has consisted of a series of accomplishments believed by the experts of the time to be theoretically impossible. As a rule, whenever society allows savants to exert undue power and authority, human advancement proceeds slowly under the tyranny of the status quo. The genius of democratic capitalism, however, is that it gives entrepreneurs the incentives and freedom to prove the experts wrong, and it protects society from this tyranny by placing elected leaders between the experts and the levers of power.

From time to time, however, even elected leaders become captivated by the world view of certain intellectuals and academics, especially economists. Then, progress slows, and expectations for advancement become dampened by the seemingly overwhelming number of theoretical impossibilities facing mankind. When this occurs, the irrepressible optimism of the American people runs head on into the disconsolate pessimism of the experts advising our leaders. What happens? We usually get new leaders. And, if we're lucky, they get new advisers. If they don't, the new leaders are not long in office. In the meantime, the country must endure the tyranny of the status quo.

Since the beginning of the 1990s, many leaders in both American political parties have been captivated by economists and a few prominent business personalities who sincerely believe that economic growth cannot exceed 2.3% a year; that to attempt to achieve more rapid growth would produce inflation; and that our first economic priority should be to balance the budget. America's entrepreneurs and small-business owners know that this conventional economic wisdom has the world turned upside down.

Entrepreneurs on the cutting edge of finance and the high-tech industry, such as Ted Forstmann, T. J. Rodgers, Thom Weisel, and others can explain through personal business experience why this pessimism is unwarranted.[1] Rodgers decries the "frequent outbreaks of naysaying over the years" directed at the semiconductor industry and the U.S. economy.[2] F. Sheridan Garrison of American Freightways Corporation offers a similarly emphatic dismissal of economic pessimism: "When people say the economy is growing well at 3%, they have lower expectations than me. I think it's a shame that people in this country think that's the fastest we can grow. It's a backwards way of running an economy."[3]

These entrepreneurs also will point out that government creates an artificial, policy-induced ceiling on growth by adopting debilitating policies that must be corrected before America's full potential can be realized. Over the past year in the editorial pages of the *Wall Street Journal*, Forstmann repeatedly championed a complete overhaul of the tax system to "get the sluggish economy rolling at a rapid rate."[4]

This article is my attempt to explain why the conventional pessimism about increasing economic growth in America is unfounded, and to sketch out a conservative, free-market agenda to ease the burden imposed on the economy by wrong headed government policies.

Since the end of World War II, the American economy has produced incredible prosperity for most of its citizens despite the fact that throughout this same period, the economy has operated under a growing deadweight burden of ill-advised fiscal, regulatory, and monetary policies. The government has extracted an increasing share of the nation's resources from the private economy to satisfy the insatiable spending appetites of special interests and has increasingly intervened into the free-enterprise system with regulations in a well-intended but self-defeating attempt to fine-tune markets toward a better result.

By 1992, the accumulated weight of antigrowth policies had created a policy-induced, permanent economic slowdown, which will last until policy is changed. Some experts say this economic downshift is inevitable. This is as good as it gets. It's not so bad—get used to it.

I say *baloney.* Here's why.

How Government Retards Growth and Limits Opportunity

When government grows too big, it becomes a drain on the private sector and slows economic growth. A growing body of research indicates that government in the United States is too large relative to the private sector and currently is well above the optimum size that would maximize economic growth.[5] There is also substantial empirical evidence indicating that when government takes more than 20 to 25% of the nation's output, the economy's ability to grow is significantly reduced.[6]

In the United States, all levels of government annually spend about 31% of the gross domestic product (GDP).[7] The federal government alone will spend about 21 percent of GDP in 1997. In order to bring overall government spending more into line with optimal economic performance would require federal spending to fall into the neighborhood of 15% to 16% of GDP.

There is also a growing awareness that the federal tax code is a significant drag on economic performance.[8] The National Commission on Economic Growth and Tax Reform, which I was privileged to chair, found that our current income tax system is economically destructive, impossibly complex, and overly intrusive. High marginal tax rates weaken the link between workers' efforts and reward, depress productivity, and kill jobs. Multiple layers of taxation on work, savings, and investment dry up new capital, retard entrepreneurial activity, and stifle creation of new businesses. Recent empirical analyses of the deadweight burden of the current tax code reveal that a fundamental overhaul of the tax system could raise long-term growth by one full percentage point or more.[9]

Taxing and spending are not the only ways government saps the private sector and slows economic growth. Government also regulates the activities of entrepreneurs, business managers, and workers. One estimate suggests that annual regulatory costs consume as much as 19% of a household's after-tax budget. Regulatory costs for small firms are almost double the costs for large firms ($5,200 per employee for firms with fewer than 500 employees, compared to $2,900 per employee for firms employing more than 500 workers).[10]

Regulations act like hidden taxes. Consumers and workers ultimately pay the tax in the form of higher prices and lower wages. When prices rise to cover regulatory costs, consumer demand falls and output is reduced. Demand for labor falls, and fewer jobs are created.

The empirical record of the 1990s tells the story: Since the end of the 1990–91 recession, the American economy has experienced the slowest economic expansion in more than a century, growing a mere 2.7% a year compared to a 4.4% annual average growth rate during the previous five economic expansions.[11]

THE HISTORICAL PATH OF ECONOMIC PROGRESS IN AMERICA

Since the beginning of this century, the American economy, as measured by inflation-adjusted GDP has grown at a remarkably stable pace (see Figure 1.1).

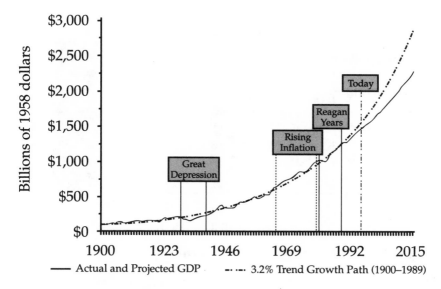

Figure 1.1.   Real GDP vs. 3.2% trend, 1900–2015.

Over this period, even the Great Depression appears as a temporary (12-year) deviation from the upward path traced out by an economy growing at about 3.2% a year. Until now, no economic downturn other than the Great Depression had knocked the economy off this growth path for more than a couple of years.

In 1990, something dramatic happened to the economy, which, seven years later, remains mired on a lower track. Worse yet, many economists contend this break with the past is permanent and that the American economy is now consigned to a lower growth path of about 2.3% a year for the indefinite future.

What does this mean in human terms? It means that the United States will produce less output per capita in the years to come. Remaining on this lower growth path until the turn of the century, we will produce $3,930 (12.5%) less per person (measured in 1992 inflation-adjusted dollars), or $15,720 less per family of four, than if we had remained on the historic growth trend established from 1900 to set since the beginning of the 1990. Twenty years from now, this lower average growth rate means that the economy will produce $10,268 (23%) less for every man, woman, and child in America, or $41,072 less per family of four (see Figure 1.2).

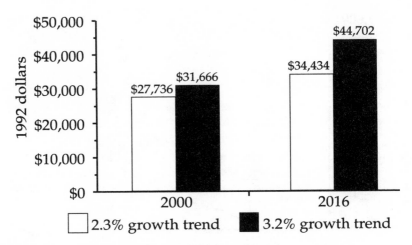

Figure 1.2.   2.3% Growth vs. 3.2% growth.

After the 1990–91 recession, the American economy lost 28% of its growth potential. Astonishing! Such a sudden and dramatic break with past trends cries out for explanation, and the burden of proof is on the pessimists to explain what, other than policy, has changed in America since the late 1980s to send the American economy careening off on this new, lower growth path.[13]

WHAT HAPPENED TO GROWTH?

A conventional rule of thumb frequently used by analysts who actually attempt to measure the economy's growth potential is to collapse the growth accounting equation down to two factors: the predicted rate of increase in the labor force, and the predicted rate of increase in labor productivity (i.e., the increase in output per hour worked). The growth accounting rule of thumb attributes part of the growth in output to more workers in the labor force and the rest to more output per worker.

Within this framework, the first conventional explanation of today's slow economic growth is that population growth has slowed. Since the economy's capacity to grow depends in large part on how fast the labor supply is expanding, a slower population growth could indeed restrict economic growth, everything else being equal. A convenient measure of how fast new workers become available to enter the labor force at any point in time is to examine population growth over the previous 20 years.

How much of today's languid economy can be explained by declining population growth? Not much. The economy grew on average 3.7% a year during the expansion period of 1983–89, while 20 years earlier (1963–69) the population grew an average of 1.2% a year. The average annual economic growth dropped a precipitous 1.4 percentage points (38%) to 2.3% a year during the current expansion period 1991–96. However, over the 20 previous years (1971–1976), the population grew by 1.1% a year on average, only 0.1 percentage points (9%) less than in the 1963–69 period. Therefore, no more than a quarter of the decline in the annual growth rate (0.3 percentage points) could possibly be attributed to a falloff in population growth 20 years previously. A decline in population growth may account for why we would grow at 3.4% a year and not 3.7%, but it cannot account for the remaining 1.1% decline and explain why we appear to be stuck at today's 2.3% annual growth.

Diehard pessimists insist, nevertheless, that even if slowing population growth does not explain today's lethargic economy, the projected decline in population growth inevitably will slow the economy's expansion. Close examination of the data, however, leaves one skeptical of this inevitability.

From 1947 to 1973, annual inflation-adjusted economic growth averaged 4.0%. Robert Barro found that growth in the labor force accounted for no more than a quarter of the economy's expansion during the same period—slightly less than one percentage point. At least three-fourths of the economy's growth was accounted for by the enlargement and improvement of the capital stock and by technological advances.[14] Using these benchmarks, one has to conclude that even if the population had stopped growing altogether, the economy still would have been able to grow by slightly more than 3.0% a year.

Where, then, is the inevitability of a 2.3% growth ceiling? It doesn't exist. Even with annual population growth projected to fall to 0.5% by the middle of the next century, there is no reason to believe, based upon historic precedent, that growth in the capital stock and technological progress cannot be sufficient to sustain annual economic growth between 3% and 3.5% through the middle of the twenty-first century.

The pessimists will counter such wild-eyed optimism with their second conventional explanation of why economic growth has fallen and is destined to remain in the 2.3% neighborhood: trend productivity growth has fallen to 1.0 to 1.5%.[15] If the supply of labor grows at about 1% annually, the growth accounting rule of thumb implies that economic growth would not exceed 2.3%. If productivity growth remains capped at 1.5% and population growth sinks to 0.5% as projected, the "Goldilocks economy" will approach a stuporous 2.0% annual growth rate. In fact, the economic growth rate that is "just right" is the fastest growth rate.

We should not be dismayed. The growth accounting framework describes the past—it does not explain it. And by no stretch of the imagination does the arithmetic of growth accounting predict the future.

With labor force participation rates near all-time highs, it is true that future increases in the labor force are likely to depend mostly on population increases, which are predicted to continue falling over the long run. Therefore, it is true that the economy's ability to grow will depend on our ability to increase output per hour of labor (i.e., on productivity growth). It does not follow, however, that just because we are currently experiencing an apparent slump in productivity growth that we have to face an indefinite period of slow growth. We should also take heart that the productivity slump results from the accumulation of harmful policies that are readily reversible.[16]

We should not become transfixed by the inevitability of the arithmetical constraint of growth accounting. In 1993, Federal Reserve Chairman Alan Greenspan explained why:

CBO [the Congressional Budget Office] estimates that the long-term growth rate is, roughly 2.5% [now down to 2.3%] at an annual rate. I want to emphasize, however, that we should be a little careful about taking numbers of growth as though they are rigid and that we should not endeavor to improve them, because there is considerable amount of gain in productivity that could occur which we will not be aware of except in retrospect. And so we have to be careful not to look at economic policy as being a situation in which there is a fixed level beyond which we are afraid to move.[17]

Chairman Greenspan's admonition leads us to consider the third conventional explanation of why the economy cannot grow faster than approximately 2.5% a year, namely that to do so would be inflationary. Of all the modern economic fallacies, none is so ill-founded and pernicious as the notion that a free economy somehow can spontaneously overheat and head off into an inflationary spiral. Any such idea confuses cause and effect and results from a misunderstanding of inflation.

In the words of Nobel laureate Milton Friedman, inflation is everywhere and always a monetary phenomenon. In other words, inflation is caused by too many dollars chasing too few goods, not too many people working. Inflation results from government printing too much money. Far from being inflationary, a real expansion of the economy soaks up inflation, creating more goods for the same amount of money to pursue.

Under the current policy regime, it is probably true that the only way we can hope to grow much faster than the current 2.3% annual growth ceiling would be for the Fed to artificially stimulate production through surprise monetary inflation. The good news is that today's slow economic growth has nothing to do with the economy's intrinsic ability to produce. The permanent slowdown in production is by policy, not growth. Hence, *this growth ceiling* should not be taken as natural or inevitable. We can raise the ceiling on growth by judicious changes in policy.

INCREASING ECONOMIC GROWTH

Overhaul the Tax Code

The single biggest step we can take to revive economic growth in America is to completely overhaul the tax code to make it fairer, flatter, simpler, and more capital friendly. Numerous plans are under discussion, ranging from House Majority Leader Dick Armey's flat tax, to Ways and Means Committee Chairman Bill Archer's national sales or consumption tax. All these plans have the great virtue of dramatically increasing incentives to work, save, and invest.

Tax reform would increase the economy's capacity to produce. Reductions in marginal tax rates on income from wages and capital would translate directly into lower costs of doing business. In the early 1960s, President Kennedy's tax cuts reduced the marginal cost of expanding output by 4.5%. Twenty years later, President Reagan's tax cuts lowered it by 3.2%. In both cases, the economy responded with a substantial increase in output capacity.

After the Kennedy tax cuts, real GDP growth was more than double the 2.5% average of the 1950s. Likewise, Reagan's tax cuts allowed the economy to grow by 3.9% a year during the 1980s expansion. Not only was this rate of growth noninflationary, it came during a period of highly disinflationary monetary policy by the Federal Reserve Board and falling inflation in the economy. Each of the major tax overhaul plans now on the table has the potential to lower marginal business costs by 10% to 15%—two to three times the magnitude of the effects of the Kennedy and Reagan cuts.[18]

I believe that a number of significant and immediate changes can be made to the tax code will garner bipartisan support. The single most powerful change that can be made this year is cutting the capital-gains tax in half (to zero in enterprise zones) and index it for inflation. Reforming capital-gains taxes in this way would liquefy our capital markets and provide a noninflationary growth tonic to the economy.

Regulatory Reform

The second major undertaking necessary to boost long-run economic growth is a total revamping of how the federal government imposes regulations. Congress has delegated extraordinary rule-making authority to the regulatory agencies, which have frequently abused their responsibility. They have, for example, routinely failed to provide benefit estimates for their major rules.[19] Not only should Congress adopt stringent cost-benefit requirements before regulations are imposed, but the entire regulatory process needs to be overhauled to restore Congress' full legislative role as envisioned by our Constitution.

Congress and the president should enact all major regulations into law before they are permitted to go into effect, and those regulations should expire on a date certain to ensure continuous congressional monitoring and oversight.

In addition to reforming the way the federal government makes rules to implement legislation, we must do something to fix our broken civil justice system. Rather than providing an efficient and effective means of resolving disputes and enforcing contracts, the civil justice system has created a litigation industry that feeds on itself to the detriment of everyone but the lawyers who benefit from it. The abuses of our legal system are a terrible burden on the American economy. When businesses have to pay staggering legal bills, they pass the costs on to consumers or take it out of compensation to employees. In insurance premiums alone, the average American family pays an extra $200 annually to cover the costs of phony claims. By one estimate, lawsuit abuse imposes an effective "litigation tax" of $132 billion per year on our economy.[20]

Reduce the Size of Government

The federal budget deficit is a by-product of an undisciplined Congress and an economy that has grown too slowly. The deficit will disappear only if we revive economic growth and Congress regains fiscal discipline. Unfortunately, an overemphasis on reducing the deficit has confused the issue of what needs to be done to enhance economic growth, and has made it difficult to set long-range goals to bring government and the private sector into more reasonable balance. When "balancing the budget by a certain date" is set as the goal, policy makers give the public the impression that they are intent on "slashing" government benefits. As a result, interest groups become extremely protective of their programs, and Congress and the president have difficulty reforming programs to make them sustainable and effective over the long run.

If immediate steps are taken to cut tax rates and alleviate some of the excessive regulatory burden on the private sector, the economy can be restored quickly to annual growth above 3%. Then it will be possible to reduce the overall size of the government relative to the size of the economy without damaging the benefits of senior citizens and those struggling to get a leg up on the ladder of opportunity. Here's how.

Congress and the president have committed themselves to balancing the budget by the year 2002. If we take bold steps on the tax and regulatory front as I have suggested, the economy could easily grow at least 4.0% a year between now and then. We did it in the 1980s with far less-powerful changes in policy than I have suggested. With the budget balanced and tax and regulatory reforms in place, there is no earthly reason the economy cannot resume its historic growth beyond 2002. By 2006, revenues would be at least as high as they are projected to be under current law with tepid economic growth and, I am convinced, could be even higher. As a share of GDP, spending could be down to 16% without having to slash any federal program for budgetary purposes.[21]

At the same time, as progress is made on bringing the size of government back into balance with the requirements of maximum economic performance, there will be a further "growth dividend," a feedback effect of constraining government's spending appetite. When good policy feeds on itself, positive things start to happen. When Congress has the luxury of distributing relatively smaller pieces of an absolutely larger pie, everyone will benefit.

Ensuring Retirement Security for Young and Old

The 1996 Report of the Social Security Trustees concludes that Social Security is seriously out of balance. Specifically, the trustees report that, based on their intermediate assumptions (which they consider their best estimates), by the year 2012 annual revenues from the FICA payroll tax will not cover the annual costs of the Old-Age and Survivors Insurance and Disability Insurance programs (OASDI). They estimate that between 2012 and 2025, this revenue shortfall will grow to 3.2% of taxable payroll and to 5.5% by 2070. By this time, annual tax revenues are projected to be sufficient to cover only 71% of annual expenditures.[22]

We must act now to ensure that current retirees and those near retirement enjoy the full benefits promised by the current Social Security system. Additionally, we must act to create a new, market-based system of retirement security for our younger generations and tomorrow's generation of workers. Not only will this action guarantee retirement security and freedom for individuals, it will vastly improve the overall economy.

According to recent research by the National Bureau of Economic Research, the current unfunded Social Security system severely distorts the labor supply and the form in which compensation is paid, and it greatly retards capital investment. According to the NBER, every additional dollar of unfunded liability taken on by the current Social Security system reduces private wealth accumulation by about 50 cents. This problem could be resolved by increasing labor-market incentives and higher real return on saving produced by moving to a fully funded, market-based retirement system. The net present value gain would exceed $15 trillion, an amount equivalent to 3% of each future year's GDP.[23]

Empowering Parents for a Stronger America

Finally, we must empower parents and give them the freedom to choose the best way to educate their children. When parents are given the freedom to act in the best educational interests of their children, they will, unencombered by mandates from government, create the world's best educational system. Market-based educational reforms are not only essential to create the best qualified workforce in the world, but also can be instrumental in restoring social tranquility among families of different cultural and religious viewpoints.

Freedom in education would not only raise the quality of education and improve workers' productivity after entering the workforce, it would also produce enormous beneficial effects that could defuse some of our most divisive social tensions. Will children be permitted to pray in school? Will they be required to? Will they receive sex education in the early grades and, if so, what will be the content? Will creationism be taught along with evolution? Will strict codes of dress and behavior be imposed? Will schools have health clinics and, if so, who will run them? Will phonics be taught? Will outcome-based standards be the norm? Trying to answer these sensitive questions with a one-size fits-all educational policy handed down by education experts is destined to fail and to erode the foundations of our democracy. *Trust the people.* Empower mothers and fathers, and let them decide.

DEMOCRATIC CAPITALISM

The end of the millennium has arrived and with it the collapse of totalitarian collectivism in all of its various guises: fascism, socialism, communism, apartheid. Democratic capitalism has survived. Can we confidently assert, however, that it is the ultimate and ideal result of a historical progression that is now coming to an end? I think not.

More likely, we have been on a monumental detour during the twentieth century and simply have returned to where we got off the track when the lamps were extinguished across Europe in 1914. These lamps are being rekindled in places where they have not shone for many years, and they are being lighted in places discovering democratic capitalism for the first time.

Now we have the opportunity to go about the business of deciding what kind of democratic capitalism we will have. We also will be confronted with new challenges. It is, for example, yet to be determined whether democratic capitalism can withstand the forces of nihilism and despair still loose in today's world, forces that would push us into anarchy or toward the despotism of some new theocracy intent on imposing its own version of order on the world.

Whatever challenges may arise, America will always find its greatest strength in the ideas of freedom and equality before the law, concepts that are not only the essence of democratic capitalism, but also its principal virtues. Freedom encourages people to transcend limits, to innovate and explore new possibilities. In this regard, liberty is both the lifeblood of our polity and the spark of our economic growth and progress. Equality instills in people a right to question dogma of all sorts, be it a tyrant's claim to legitimacy or alleged constraints on economic potential postulated by a group of experts.

The policy proposals that I have outlined here are based on the precept that our society is at its best when it empowers individuals and families to make decisions that affect their lives. By eliminating policy-induced barriers to economic growth, reducing the role of government, and allowing people to chart their own courses toward self-improvement and happiness, the United States can utilize the best resources that the American people and democratic capitalism can offer.

NOTES

1. Thom Weisel, Unpublished remarks (at Empower America's Annual Board Retreat, Aspen, Col. July 26–28, 1996).

2. T. J. Rodgers, "The Best is Yet to Come," *San Jose Mercury News*, 28 July 1996.

3. "Smart Move or 'Hogwash'? Debating Dole's Plan," *Wall Street Journal*, 6 August 1996.

4. Theodore J. Forstmann, "Indexing Capital Gains—A Very Big Deal," *Wall Street Journal*, 22 October 1996; Forstmann. "Is Our Tax System Too Broken To Fix?" *Washington Times*, 25 April 1996.

5. See Richard W. Rahn, "The Size of Good Government," *Washington Times*, (9 December 1996), for a good summary of the scholarly research on the relationship between economic performance and the size of government.

6. Robert Barro measured the relationship between government consumption and GDP growth in a large cross section of countries and found that a one standard-deviation increase in the ratio of government consumption spending to GDP, which amounted to 6.5 percentage points in the 1965–75 period covered by the study, was associated with a fall in the growth rate by 0.7 percentage points per year. Between 1965 and 1975, federal government consumption expenditures in the United States went from roughly 10% to 16.1% of GDP. Based upon Barro's findings, one would anticipate that the growth rate would fall about 0.65 percentage points due to the growth of the federal government during this period. See Robert J. Barro and Xavier Sala-I-Martin, *Economic Growth* (New York: McGraw-Hill, 1995), 434.

In a study specifically analyzing the effect on economic growth of the size of the United States federal government, Gallaway and Vedder found a slightly larger effect. Their results placed the growth-maximizing size of the federal government at about 17.6% of GDP and found that between 1965 and 1975, growth slowed by approximately one full percentage point as a consequence of a federal government larger than the optimum. See Lowell Gallaway and Richard Vedder, *The Impact of the Welfare State on the American Economy*. Joint Economic Committee, U.S. Congress (December 1995).

In a ground-breaking study in 1984, Gerald Scully determined that in order to maximize economic growth, the average rate for federal, state, and local taxes combined should be between 21.5% and 22.9% of GDP. Scully found that economic expansion was curtailed by a full 2 percentage points a year between 1949 and 1989 due to higher-than-optimal spending by governments at all levels in the country. See Gerald W. Scully, *What Is the Optimal Size of*

Government in the United States? Policy rept. no. 188 (Washington, D.C., National Center for Policy Analysis, November 1994).

7. According to the National Income and Product Accounts, U.S. Commerce Department and the U.S. Treasury.

8. The National Commission on Economic Growth and Tax Reform, *Unleashing America's Potential: A Pro-Growth, Pro-Family Tax System for the 21st Century* (Washington, D.C., January 1996).

9. Dale Jorgeson, Testimony before the U.S. House of Representatives Committee on Ways and Means (27 March 1996); Laurence J. Kotlikoff, *Economic Impact of Replacing Federal Income Tax with a Sales Tax*, Policy no. 193 (Washington, D.C.: Cato Institute, 15 April 1993); Barry J. Seldon and Roy G. Boyd, *The Economic Effects of A Flat Tax*, Draft policy rept. (Washington D.C.: National Center for Policy Analysis, May 1996).

10. Thomas D. Hopkins, *Regulatory Costs in Profile*, Policy study no. 132 (Washington, D.C.: Center for the Study of American Business, August 1996).

11. Joint Economic Committee, *Liberating America's Economy* (July 1996, 1).

12. Council of Economic Advisers, *1997 Economic Report of the President* (February 1997, 53–54).

13. A simple example will show how profound are the consequences of moving from average growth of 3.2% to 2.3% a year. If a pilot made a navigational error of equal magnitude in charting a flight east from New York to Moscow, the plane would end up somewhere over the middle of the Black Sea.

14. Barro and Sala-I-Martin, *Economic Growth*, 380.

15. Between 1960 and 1990, Robert Barro found that the contribution to economic growth attributable to labor-supply growth increased to almost 1.3 percentage point, and at the same time the contribution from capital and technological progress plummeted to about 1.5%. If one assumes that total productivity growth is capped at 1.5% and that population growth will decline to no more than 0.5% a year, it is evident where the pessimism on the prospects for growth come from. Even annual growth of 2.3% a year appears optimistic if one is convinced that productivity growth must remain within these confines.

16. According to recent research conducted at Chicago Capital, the evidence suggests that the most reliable course of action to improve productivity performance is to lower tax rates across the board. See Robert Genetski, "Taxes and Productivity Performance," *Chicago Capital Report*, 22 October 1996.

17. Joint Economic Committee, *The 1994 Joint Economic Report*, Rept. no. 103–496, 9 May 1994. The JEC report elaborated that Chairman Greenspan's admonition that growth-potential numbers should not be viewed as rigid constraints is extremely important, especially since annual productivity improvement has dipped as low as −1.9% in 1974 and soared as high as 8.5% in 1950. Between 1889 and 1973 productivity increased by an average of 2.4% a year. Labor productivity grew at an average rate of 3% between 1948 and 1973. Since 1973, however, productivity growth has slumped dramatically, averaging 0.8% between 1973 and 1981, and rising to only 1.1% a year between 1981 and 1993.

18. Aldona Robbins and Gary Robbins, "Tax Cuts & Economic Growth," *Investor's Business Daily*, 12 March 1996.

19. The Environmental Protection Agency, for example, provided benefit estimates for only 30% of its planned major rules last year. See Clyde Wayne Crews Jr., *Ten Thousand Commandments* (Competitive Enterprise Institute, September 1996).

20. Bob Dole and Jack Kemp, *Trusting the People* (New York: HarperCollins, 1996), 101.

21. This is not to say that some federal programs should not be slashed or even eliminated. And it is not to say that some programs worth keeping and funding at current levels or even higher should not be radically overhauled. It is to say, however, that programs can be reformed, eliminated, or increased based upon their success and appropriateness independent of a compulsion to balance the budget by an arbitrary date.

22. The Board of Trustees, Federal Old-Age and Survivors Insurance and Disability Insurance Trust Funds, *1996 Annual Report,* Washington, D.C., June 5, 1996.

23. Martin Feldstein, *The Missing Piece in Policy Analysis: Social Security Reform*, National Bureau of Economic Research Working Paper, no. 5413 (Cambridge: Harvard University Press, January 1996).

Ways to Achieve Higher Growth

FELIX ROHATYN, U.S. AMBASSADOR
TO FRANCE, FORMER MANAGING
DIRECTOR FOR LAZARD FRERES &
CO. LLC, AND FORMER CHAIRMAN
OF THE MUNICIPAL ASSISTANCE
CORPORATION

The Dow Jones Industrial Average is at near record levels, the U.S. economy grew 3.9% in the fourth quarter of 1996, and it is far and away the most successful economy in the world today. However, we can and should do better.

A FINANCIAL IRON TRIANGLE

The American economy is now constrained by a financial *iron triangle* from which it is difficult to break out. The first leg of this triangle is the government's commitment to balance the budget in the next five years. Even though there has never been a rational explanation for this commitment, especially concerning its time frame, it has now become part of our political theology. The second leg, an extension of the first, is more restrictive in its effect. It is the acceptance, by both political parties, that our economic growth rate will be between 2% and 2.3% for the next five years. Even though economic projections are notoriously inaccurate over much shorter periods, this particular projection—because it is blessed by the Congressional Budget Office—is becoming both a prediction and a self-limitation. It is doing so by implying that this rate of growth is the limit of what our economy is capable of achieving without inflation. Since this view has the support of the Federal Reserve, the Treasury, and the financial markets, it has become a *de facto* limit on economic growth. The third leg of this triangle is the impact of technology and global competition on incomes and employment. Corporate downsizing combined with ever-increasing differentials in wealth and income among Americans, and the huge rewards to capital resulting from the boom in the securities markets, are creating serious social tensions and political pressures in the country.

Unless we somehow break out of this iron triangle, we could face serious difficulties. The best hope for a breakout is to make a determined effort to achieve a higher rate of economic growth. Only higher growth, as a result of increased investment and greater productivity, can make these processes socially tolerable.

The social and economic problems we face today are varied. They include job insecurity, enormous income differentials, significant pressures on average incomes, urban quality-of-life, and many others. Even though each of these requires different approaches, the single most important requirement in dealing with them is the wealth and revenues generated by a higher rate of economic growth. John Kennedy was right, "a rising tide lifts all boats." Although it may not lift all of them at the same time and at the same rate, without growth we are simply redistributing the same pie. That is a zero-sum game and it is simply not good enough.

Controlling the costs of entitlement programs like Medicare, Medicaid, and Social Security is an integral part of a growth agenda and will help generate the capital needed to provide both private and public investment for the country's needs. Reforming Social Security requires no dramatic changes. Reducing cost-of-living allowances by 1%, as recommended by the federally appointed Boskin Commission, and gradually moving the retirement age to seventy would spur the economy to greater growth. Higher growth, together with entitlement reform, could provide significant tax cuts for the private sector as well as an increased public investment in the country's infrastructure and educational system as we move into the twenty-first century. Increased growth would obviously generate millions of new jobs. The question then is how to achieve it.

While these arguments about tax cuts and entitlement reform will continue with great intensity, they have drawn attention away from an obvious reality: Our economy is clearly able to deliver higher growth without inflation.

THE QUIET GOOD NEWS

Growth in the second quarter of 1996 came in at 4.8% and at 3.9% in the fourth quarter. Growth for the full year is now estimated at 2.6%. The stated rate of inflation is still below 3%.

Many respected economists, including Federal Reserve Chairman Alan Greenspan, believe that the inflation statistics are overstated by more than 1%.[1] That means that real inflation may be closer to 1% while actual growth is higher than reported. At the same time, a recent study by the Brookings Institution suggests that driving the inflation rate down to zero, the nirvana of the bond market, would slow the economy by increasing unemployment by 2%, thereby pushing up, rather than down, the federal budget deficit.

It is also worth noting that, while all this is happening in an environment of near-zero inflation, the overall unemployment rate has been driven down to about 5%. This is despite the recent conventional view that the "natural rate" of unemployment is 6% and that anything below that would unleash wage-push inflation. The fact that real wages were up 1.4% in 1996 should be treated as good news rather than bad. Corporate profits are at an all-time high, which indicates that wage increases are due to higher productivity rather than to increased prices. The fact that working people can increase their take-home pay without causing inflation is very good news indeed.

While one swallow does not make a spring, why is no one paying attention to these facts?

PUTTING INFLATION IN PERSPECTIVE

It is necessary to recognize that a powerful antigrowth bias has been gradually created in this country by the financial markets' theological commitment to the proposition that higher growth inevitably leads to higher inflation. This fear of inflation is somewhat difficult to understand, since the United States, as opposed to Germany, has not experienced a hyperinflationary crisis in the twentieth century. The Great Depression brought deflation rather than inflation, and, except for a brief period after World War II, when wartime price controls were eliminated, even the economic adjustments after the 1950s and the huge deficits of the 1980s did not bring significant inflationary pressures. The double-digit inflation of the late 1970s and early 1980s was largely the result of the Vietnam War and successive oil shocks created by OPEC; the Gulf War should be proof that we would not tolerate a repetition of *those events*. In addition, the proposition that this country cannot do better has become a cottage industry in the financial community and in some parts of academia.

We should not sell this country short. The notion that productivity cannot grow by more than 1% if we put more capital, technology, and education behind every American worker is absurd. So is the notion that the labor force cannot grow by more than 1% if the prospect of good jobs increases as a result of growth. There are millions of people today who are not working and who would jump at the opportunity of a real job with real training.

THE VOICE OF CORPORATE AMERICA

There is some evidence that policy makers at the Federal Reserve are beginning to give more credence to arguments for higher potential noninflationary growth. In July 1997, Greenspan told Congress that there was some evidence that productivity might be higher than official statistics, which failed to capture all of the effects of the revolution in computer technologies. But for the most part, the only active constituency for higher growth has been corporate America and publications such as the *Wall Street Journal* and *Business Week*. The National Association of Manufacturers, and the Business Roundtable and their members are convinced that higher growth is not only possible, but also *necessary* if we are going to deal with our social problems, invest as we should, and balance the budget over time. The experience of company after company indicates that prices and wages are kept down by competition (domestic and foreign) and that productivity improvements resulting from technological applications and downsizing are significantly greater than the statistical evidence shows. These productivity improvements will spread to the service sector, where increases in competition will require them, but where their measurement is highly uncertain.

While inflation cannot be written off as a possible risk, reality seems to favor the opposite view. Powerful deflationary forces are at work all over the globe. The drive to meet the Maastricht requirements for a European currency is a force for budgetary contraction all over common Europe. France and Germany are currently struggling with 13% and 11% unemployment rates, respectively; the overhang of billions of bad debts throughout the Japanese financial system is a lead weight on the country's economy; Italy's inflation rate this year will be about 3%; France's and Germany's will be lower still. The ability to move production all over the world and the entry of over one billion people into the global workforce will keep significant downward pressures on prices and wages in the developed world for the foreseeable future. In a globalized economy, these are not the harbingers of inflationary pressures. On the contrary.

A TAX SYSTEM THAT PROMOTES GROWTH

Higher growth requires a tax system that promotes growth as its main objective, and that encourages higher investment and savings. This is not happening today. The country's current tax system attempts to achieve a level of fairness dictated by distribution tables. This objective, however may not be in the best interests of the country. A better alternative is a tax system with growth as its main objective. It could be a variation of the flat tax, a national sales tax, or another system aimed at taxing consumption, such as proposed by Senators Sam Nunn and Peter Domenici. The power and dominance of global capital markets in today's world would seem to aim in the direction of a consumption tax.

Lowering taxes on capital would unleash powerful capital flows, both domestic and foreign. These, in turn, would lower interest rates significantly and make investment in the United States even more competitive than it is today. At the same time, increased capital would maintain the strength of the dollar and maintain low inflation rates. Achieving higher growth could also include the gradual privatization of Social Security in order to create a massive investment pool with higher returns for beneficiaries and greater investment capabilities for the private and the public sector.

The key to economic success in the next century will be cheap and ample capital, high levels of private investment to increase productivity, high levels of education and advanced technology, and higher levels of public investment in building a national infrastructure that supports the twenty-first century economy.

THREE ARENAS FOR GOVERNMENT ACTION

If growth and opportunity are to be the prime objectives of our society, the government must play an active role in some areas: education, higher levels of infrastructure investment, and the maintenance of a corporate safety net.

Public-school reform, driven by the need for higher standards, is an absolute priority. Even though public schools are a state responsibility, they are a national problem. High educational standards, regardless of today's political conventional wisdom, will ultimately be national in scope. Access to higher education should be made available to any graduating high school senior meeting stringent national test levels and demonstrably in need of financial assistance. The equivalent of the GI Bill, providing national college scholarships to needy students, should be created and federally funded. It should be the primary affirmative action program funded by the federal government.

As part of an economic growth policy, state and local governments should provide higher levels of infrastructure investment. In addition to creating private employment, this would also provide public sector jobs to help meet the work requirements of welfare reform, as well as to provide support to a high capacity modern economy. Financial assistance from the federal government would encourage state and local governments in that endeavor. Higher growth would enable federal, state, and local budgets to take on this responsibility.

A corporate safety net should be provided for dealing with the inevitable dislocations that corporate downsizings and restructurings will continue to create. Business, labor, and government should cooperate to create a system of portable pensions and portable health care to cushion workers' transition from one job to another. Incentives should be provided for business to utilize stock grants for employees laid off as a result of mergers and restructuring. If losing one's job creates wealth for the shareholders, the person losing the job should share in some of that wealth.

Corporate pension funds, to the extent that they are overfunded as a result of the stock market boom, could be part of a system to provide larger severance and retraining payments for laid-off employees.

COMMON GROUND FOR BUSINESS AND LABOR

The benefits to business of such an approach are obvious. Labor, also, can benefit from such new programs. It is impossible to stop the spread of global information, technology, capital, and labor. What is important for working people, union or nonunion, is the creation of more well-paying jobs resulting from high levels of investment and high levels of education; sharing in the financial gains of employers through profit-sharing and stock ownership; reaping the benefits of pension funds vastly enriched by the boom in the financial markets; attaining permanent health care security and levels of education and training to deal with the twenty-first century society. Business and labor, together, should hammer out such an agenda.

Finally, business and labor should find common ground in supporting relentless efforts by our government to open markets for global trade. The creation of NAFTA, GATT, and the WTO are dramatic steps down that road. We should consider the extension of NAFTA to Latin America and an examination of a North Atlantic Free Trade Area. Free trade is not a threat to our economy. It has, and will continue to be, an enormous benefit.

ESTABLISHING A HIGHER GROWTH OBJECTIVE

If we are serious about balancing the budget in a responsible manner, the president and the congressional leadership should establish, as a national objective, that the nation's rate of growth reach a minimum sustainable level of 3% per year by the year 2000 and 3.5% thereafter. They should ask the best minds in the country, from government, business, labor, and academia, to provide a set of options that would lead to such a result. Many of these options would be politically difficult, both for Democrats and Republicans. The only way, however, to abandon long-held notions that may no longer apply to today's world is to discuss them within the framework of a very simple and definite objective—higher growth.

In addition, the president's establishment of higher growth as an objective would have an important psychological impact—the economy is, after all, heavily influenced by psychological factors. If the president set such an ambitious objective, all the elements affecting the economy would be subject to review from a new and different perspective. These elements include fiscal and monetary policy, investments and savings, education and training, and international trade. Most important, they should take place within a framework in which the Democratic Party redefines its concept of fairness and the Republican Party redefines its concept of the role of government. At present, neither concept is appropriate for the revolution that technology, globalization, and the addition of one billion people to the global workforce will bring in the next century.

Setting the United States on a path to higher economic growth will require coordination with our partners in the G–7. Europeans should welcome such an initiative since they need greater growth than we do. Although the process will be slow, it must be put in motion. Ultimately, a rising tide *will* float all boats, and both political parties can help bring this about. If they fail to do so, however, another tide will come along that may sweep all existing parties out and replace them with something that bears only a faint resemblance to our democracy. If this were to happen, arguments about growth or fairness will become totally irrelevant.

NOTES

1. See the report of the Boskin Commission, which estimated the overstatement at 1.5%.

2

America Can Grow Faster

Can We Grow Faster?

JAMES TOBIN, PROFESSOR EMERITUS,
YALE UNIVERSITY; NOBEL LAUREATE
IN ECONOMICS; PAST PRESIDENT OF
THE AMERICAN ECONOMICS
ASSOCIATION

The capacity of the American economy to produce and to grow is commanding unusual attention. Current rates of growth of real (i.e. inflation-corrected) gross domestic product (GDP) are in the range of 2% to 2.3%. They compare unfavorably with the 3.9% spurt from 1982 to 1989 and the 3.5% to 4.0% average rates sustained from 1946 to 1972. "A rising tide lifts all boats" was a favorite aphorism of John Kennedy and Lyndon Johnson. Were the economy to grow 3.5% per year from 1996 to 2050 instead of 2.3%, GDP in 2050 would be $68 trillion instead of $36 trillion. This 86% gain would solve a host of problems, notably Social Security and Medicare, that now look intractable. Such is the magic of compound interest.

That greater national output and faster GDP growth are desirable does not mean they are feasible. It is too much to expect that any government action can raise the GDP growth rate forever, or until 2050, or indeed for more than a few years. Maybe good policy can raise the *level* of GDP for years ahead, but generally not its *growth rate*.

To keep raising GDP year after year, it would be necessary to keep repeating the dose of good policy.

Consider, for example, a commonly asserted cause-to-effect chain resulting from a cut in marginal income-tax rates. People choose to work more; employment and GDP rise. The change in behavior takes a bit of time, maybe a year or two. During this period, growth rates are higher. But once workers' adjustments are complete, the rates of growth of employment and GDP revert to what they were before. Employment and GDP remain at higher levels; but to boost them again, tax rates would have to be cut again.

The same is true of other "pro-growth" medicines, like those involving Federal Reserve interest-rate reductions or cuts in budget deficits. Proposals billed as growth-increasing are more accurately GDP-increasing; the increases in growth rates are transient.

Pro-growth prescriptions stress incentives to produce more. At the same time, they typically augment purchasing power in the hands of households and business firms, thus expanding aggregate demand for goods and services. Frequently actual GDP rises in response. To assess accurately the results of these policies, it is crucially important not to interpret demand-side effects as supply-side successes. Unfortunately confusion of supply and demand, the most fundamental distinction in economics, is all too common in public and political discussion.

DEMAND AND SUPPLY: BUSINESS CYCLES AND SUSTAINABLE GROWTH

In this article, I try to set forth a coherent framework in which levels and growth rates fall into place and supply-side and demand-side are kept straight.

The economy is subject to two supply constraints. One is the level of its capacity to produce goods and services. The other is the rate at which this capacity is growing. The output of the economy in a given year is limited by its available productive resources—labor, capital goods, land and other natural resources—and by their productivity. This constraint determines potential gross domestic product (PGDP). PGDP grows as population and labor force grow, workers improve in skill, capital is accumulated, and scientists, inventors, and innovative entrepreneurs create new products and technologies. These factors change quite gradually. In Figure 2.1, the smooth track is the estimated PGDP (log scale), full employment output from 1952 to 1995. The slope of this track is the PGDP growth rate, shown as 2.3% recently.

The PGDP growth rate can be decomposed into growth of labor input in hours per year and growth of productivity per hour. In the glorious quarter century after World War II, both components were 1.75% to 2.0% per year; now they are 1.0% to 1.25%. The slowdown in labor-force growth is demographic: birth rates are low; and a large number of women are joining the workforce. It is not a matter of political concern, although income-tax cuts are touted as a work incentive. No proposals to subsidize childbearing or open the gates to immigrants are on the table. Instead, the hand-wringing is about the decline in productivity growth since about 1973. It happened in other advanced capitalist democracies, and its causes are mysterious.

Most of the time the economy is not operating at full potential, but with excess unemployment and idle industrial capacity. Actual GDP falls short of PGDP—as shown by the wiggly track in Figure 2.1. The shortfall (indicated by the shaded area), of actual from potential, the GAP, is the business cycle. Occasionally the GAP is negative—the economy has overshot its normal capacity, as in the escalation of the 1966–1969 Vietnam war. Figure 2.2 shows how fluctuations in the GDP GAP and in unemployment are synchronized, with the GAP's amplitude from two to three times that of the unemployment rate, a regularity known to economists as Okun's law.

Business cycles, created by ups and downs in GAPS and unemployment rates, reflect fluctuations in *demand*, that is, in spending on goods and services. When actual GDP falls short of potential, the *supply* constraint is not binding. Aggregate demand is now calling the tune. New demands can be met as

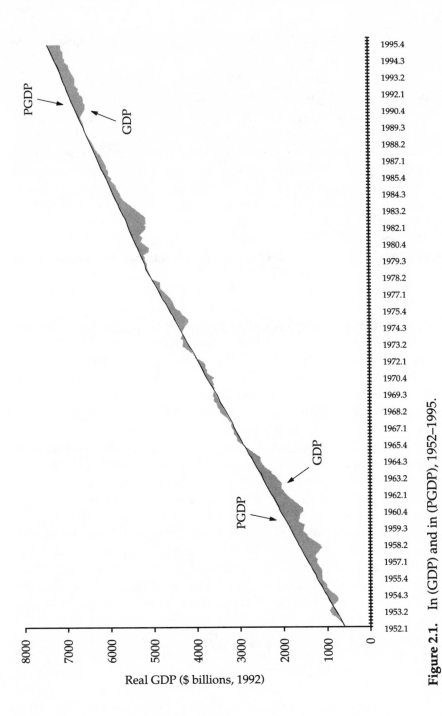

Figure 2.1. ln (GDP) and ln (PGDP), 1952–1995.

30

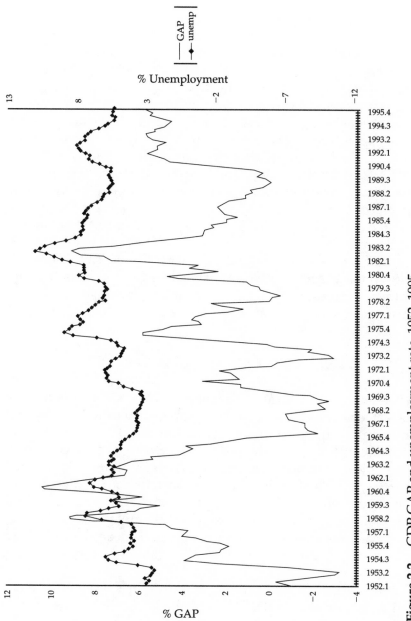

Figure 2.2. GDP GAP and unemployment rate, 1952–1995.

31

employment of labor and utilization of capital are increased. A business-cycle recovery, from 1982 to 1989 or from 1992 to 1996 is a *demand-side* phenomenon, an expansion of *demands* for goods and services and for the workers to produce them. Frequently government policies provide stimuli—in the 1980s tax cuts, defense expenditures, and eased monetary policies. During recoveries, GDP growth rates are high, unsustainably high.

The PGDP growth rate, the 2.0% or 2.25% or 2.5%, is often called *sustainable* growth. It is the growth of GDP at which the unemployment rate and the GAP remain constant. Along the PGDP path, the GAP is not just constant; it is zero. Along a lower parallel path with the same growth rate, the GAP would also be constant, but it would not be zero; it would be, say, 3% or 5%. The economy is not limited to sustainable growth unless it is operating at full capacity. By the same token, it cannot grow at an unsustainable rate once it reaches the PGDP path.

THE NAIRU AS CAPACITY CONSTRAINT

What determines the capacity constraint? For a large and diverse market economy, it cannot be a simple, measurable physical limit. A peacetime free-market economy cannot mobilize the nation into the kind of three-shift, everybody-works command economy that won World War II. The symptoms of a normal economy overheated by excess demand are escalations of price and wage inflation. The unemployment rate is an important barometer of inflation pressure. When unemployment and GAP are low, employers have both means and incentive to bid up wages, and workers have more bargaining power. Product prices rise along with labor costs.

What numerical unemployment rate defines full employment and corresponds to PGDP? What is the lowest inflation-safe unemployment rate, the notorious NAIRU, the nonaccelerating Inflation Rate of Unemployment? The theory is that, at unemployment rates lower than the NAIRU, rates of wage and price inflation rise. Before 1995, the consensus estimate of the NAIRU was 6%. Now that unemployment has been below 6% since August 1994 without evidence of "accelerating" inflation, NAIRU estimates are being revised downward, and PGDP correspondingly revised upward.

Much of the concern and anger evoked by low growth rates is misdirected. In reality the critics are complaining about the NAIRU: the number is too high or the very concept is flawed. If the NAIRU constraint on GDP were relaxed, GDP could grow faster, but only temporarily. For Chairman Alan Greenspan and his colleagues at the Federal Reserve Board, it is the NAIRU—not the 2.0% to 2.5% ceiling on sustainable (PGDP) growth—that stands in the way of monetary stimulus of demand. Were they convinced that the economy had room for noninflationary expansion, they would presumably accommodate or actively stimulate extra demand, which is what they have done the past two years.

The important truth in the NAIRU concept is that GDP cannot be expanded indefinitely by demand stimulus. The practical issue is the location of this constraint. Are we now at or above potential output? Or is there still room for expansion?

The NAIRU is not a precise number so that a further tenth of a point reduction of unemployment suddenly and irretrievably unleashes a torrent of inflation. Rather, it is the midpoint of a zone, within which the lower the unemployment rate, the more widespread and likely are inflationary pressures. And the numerical value of the NAIRU is not an eternal constant. It moves with economic, social, technological, and demographic change. Evidently, it was about 4% in the 1950s and early 1960s, rose to 5% and then to 6% or higher in the 1970s, before drifting down recently.

Neither econometricians nor central bankers know for sure where the NAIRU is at any particular time. Alan Greenspan and his fellow policy makers on the Federal Open Market Committee must balance two risks. On the one hand, they might be keeping unemployment unnecessarily high, depriving the economy of extra output there for the taking. On the other hand, the economy may already be at or below the NAIRU, so that expansionary monetary policy would accelerate prices and necessitate a corrective spell of tighter money and higher interest rates. The policy choice depends both on the Fed's estimates of this trade-off of risks and on its relative value weighting of the two evils, unemployment and inflation.

Consider, for a moment, enough monetary demand stimulus to cut unemployment by half a point over one year, which would raise GDP by 1% ($75 billion). During the year, the growth rate would be a point above the sustainable rate. The addition to the level of GDP would persist year after year, although the GDP growth rate would revert to its sustainable rate.

This policy would be inflation-safe if the NAIRU had fallen to a bit below 5% a possibility suggested by the striking absence of inflationary pressures at unemployment rates as low as 5.3%. Other statistics suggest that labor markets are not as tight as unemployment rates alone might indicate: the increased prevalence among the unemployed of job losers relative to job leavers, and the abnormal scarcity of vacancies indicated by help-wanted advertisements. See Figures 2.3, 2.4a, and 2.4b.

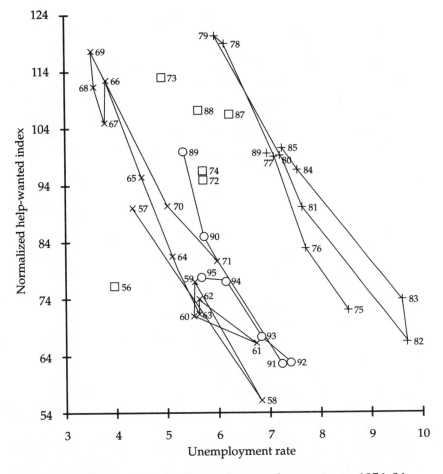

Figure 2.3. Help-wanted index and unemployment rate, 1956–94.

Figure 2.4a. Job leavers/losers ratio and help-wanted index, 1951–1995.

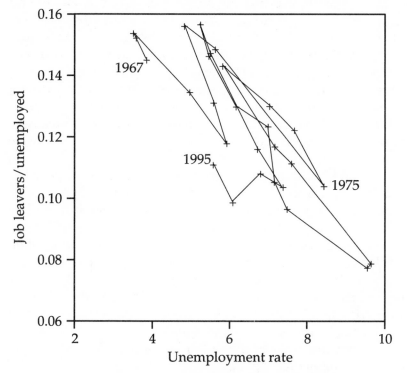

Figure 2.4b. Job leavers vs. unemployment, 1967–1995.

Yet no one can guarantee that the NAIRU is not still close to 6%. If so, the one-year stimulus policy would bring higher inflation and tighter monetary policy.

PRICE STABILITY AS THE FED'S PRIMARY OBJECTIVE

Since 1983, the Fed has pragmatically fine-tuned the macroeconomy, balancing the two objectives of high employment and low inflation. As a result U.S. macroeconomic performance has been by far the best among the G–7 countries.

Nevertheless an increasingly strong movement among financial leaders, central bankers, and conservative economists throughout the world is dedicating monetary policy to "price stability" ahead of all other goals. Inflation hawks want stable zero inflation. The objectives of the Employment Act of 1946, "maximum employment, production, and purchasing power," would be scrapped—a very serious mistake. The cost in jobs and GDP of lowering the inflation trend from its present 3% to 0% would be considerable. Some of the cost would be permanent, not just transitional. The reason is that the relative wage adjustments inevitable in a dynamic economy are easier to make if they do not entail absolute cuts in money wages in declining sectors. Therefore, they can be made with less unemployment when average inflation is moderately positive than when it is zero or negative (Akerlof, Dickens, and Perry 1996).

In any case, zero inflation is an amorphous concept. Alan Greenspan is prominent among the many students of price inflation who believe that official price indexes overstate inflation by anywhere from 0.6 to 2 percentage points a year. Yet there is danger that inflation hawks inside and outside the Fed will weaken its resolve to keep the economy moving even as fast as current estimates of its sustainable rate of growth, and indeed possibly will dilute its determination to avert outright recession. Under a new doctrine labeled opportunistic disinflation leaked from the Fed, patches of softness in the economy would be seen as opportunities to whittle away at the inflation trend, rather than as occasions for expansionary policy.

FISCAL AUSTERITY AS GROWTH POLICY

Monetary policy cannot be expected to lift the long-term sustainable growth rate. The Fed's role is to make sure that any productivity gains occurring spontaneously or as a result of supply-side policies are realized in jobs and output and do not go to waste in recessions and unemployment.

What policies can raise the level of capacity output or its rate of growth or both? Several proposals are prominent in current policy debates: (1) reducing federal budget deficits and balancing the federal budget; (2) cutting taxes, in particular marginal tax rates; and (3) downsizing government, in particular federal nondefense expenditure programs.

Advocates of fiscal austerity see it as positive supply-side policy, on the grounds that it increases the proportion of national output invested in productive future-oriented activities instead of present-oriented consumption. These activities include business acquisitions of plant and equipment, residential construction, and purchases of consumer durables. Some of these government outlays are capital investments. In addition, no less important is the human capital embodied in the education, skill, and health of the population, especially the young. And one component of national wealth is the country's accumulation of claims on foreigners net of their claims on us.

Government deficit spending, it is argued, crowds out private investment by diverting private saving to purchases of government securities. As a result aggregate national saving and investment are diminished and budget balance then augments the supply of saving available to finance productive private investments. Also, interest rates in the capital markets fall to attract the additional private demands that can now be accommodated. As these investments come on line, capacity output (PGDP) is increased by their (marginal) productivity. In the end, workers' productivity and wages increase, because they are equipped with more and better tools.

This is a good story if properly used, but it has a few pitfalls.

First, the payoffs from durable long-term investments will be spread over many future years. Gains to PGDP will scarcely be perceptible within normal political horizons. A balanced budget by 2002 would, by my back-of-an-envelope calculation, raise

PGDP in that year by 1% or 2%. This is the estimated result of reducing the federal debt outstanding in that year by 12% of PGDP and nearly 85% of that amount of private wealth into productive domestic capital and the rest into repayment of foreign debt. Public-debt interest rates would have to fall by 50 to 150 basis points to induce these reallocations. If it is assumed that if a 3-point increase in the percentage share of national saving and investment in PGDP, relative to what would take place otherwise, continues, PGDP will eventually be another 6% or 7% higher. Increases in per-capita consumption would be much smaller, only 1% or 2%, because the gains in PGDP cannot be maintained unless most of them are reinvested.

Second, as an example of a general point I made at the beginning of the article, higher national saving and investment is a recipe for a higher level of PGDP, not for a permanent increase in its growth rate. It is true, that while this new higher level is being approached, the rate of growth will be a bit higher, more so for PGDP than for consumption. But the rate of growth will taper off. This process follows conventional neoclassical growth theory, which takes holds the view that the sustainable growth rate depends on demographic and technological factors independent of saving rates. Younger economists, using endogenous growth theory, seek ways in which growth rates are permanently changed by changes in national saving rates, but these attempts are still too speculative to guide policy.

Third, if the budget is balanced at the expense of public investment programs, the eventual economywide benefits are diminished by the losses of the social returns on these programs. The fervent apostles of budget balance stress that government debt will place burdens on our children and their children, who will be taxed to meet interest charges. Many of these children, however, would lose much more if deficits were attacked by cutbacks in public outlays for education, nutrition, and health. Since the federal government does not distinguish capital and current account budgets, as state governments do, all line items are fodder for the deficit cutters.

Fourth, the potential gains from fiscal austerity will not be realized unless the economy continues to operate at capacity. The immediate impact of cuts in deficit spending is demand-side-contractionary. They reduce spending on goods and services and destroy jobs. If taxes are raised, taxpayers curtail spending. If transfers to the aged, the poor, and the sick are diminished, the beneficiaries cut their spending too. If military procurement and highway- or school-building are slashed, the impacts are direct and obvious. The social gains of austerity require that the resources released by these contractions, or their equivalent, be employed elsewhere, producing the desired new investments. This is the task of monetary policy. It's up to the Fed to engineer the declines in interest rates needed to offset the fiscal contractions. This transition was accomplished smoothly in 1993–94, and little active help from the Fed was needed. This may not always be so, however.

TAX CUTTING AS GROWTH POLICY

Fiscal austerity is the priority of one school of conservative economics. Another school, loyal to the supply-side doctrines of Reaganomics, urges tax cutting as the centerpiece of macroeconomic policy. What are the mechanisms by which cuts in tax rates are supposed to generate additional national output, higher growth of output, and, as by-products, extra tax revenues? The proponents appeal to incentive effects—simple and obvious, the stuff of Econ 101, as University of Chicago economist and Nobel laureate Gary Becker is endlessly reported to have said.

Faced with a lower marginal tax rate, individuals will work more hours per week, more weeks per year, more years per lifetime. They will save more because the government will take less of their interest, dividends, and capital gains. They will invest more in businesses, real estate projects, and education and training because they will be allowed to keep more of the profits, rents, and extra wages. Supply-side effects of this kind are basic economics. No one doubts their existence, but there are other effects too. The question is how important the incentive effects are, and what they add up to in relation to PGDP. The empirical evidence does not justify counting on these changes in human behavior to achieve any noticeable increase in PGDP or its rate of growth.

Consider, for example, a 15% income-tax cut for a married couple with two dependent children with pretax income, all wages, of $35,000. In 1995, the family paid $2,767 in income taxes (zero on the first $16,550 and 15% on the other $18,450), and $2,677 in payroll taxes (excluding the half paid by employers), totaling $5,444 15.6% of pretax income. The couple's marginal tax rate was 22.65%, the sum of a 15% income tax and a 7.65% payroll tax. A reduction of 15%, 2.25 points on the income-tax rate, would lower the family's marginal tax rate to 20.4%, enabling it to keep 79.6 cents of an extra dollar earned, up 2.25 cents (2.91%) from the former after-tax gain of 77.35 cents. These marginal improvements are supposed to be an incentive for family members to seek more work (which proponents assume they will find). Even if they work no more hours, however, and even if their pretax income remains $35,000, the family benefits. A reduction of 2.25 points (15% of 15 points) on the income-tax rate gives the family $415 a year (2.25% of $18,450), a take-home gain of 1.4%.

The example illustrates the point that tax-cut proposals are not purely incentives to change behavior. They give taxpayers more after-tax income even if they do not change behavior. These benefits have "income effects" that counter the incentive effects and may even overcome them. Households might choose to work less, not more. This is the more likely event if, in addition to tax-rate cuts, the legislation offers new tax credits or deductions. This too is taught in Econ 101.

What is the empirical evidence for this view? A Congressional Budget Office study (1996) reviewed empirical analyses of the effects of tax-rate changes on aggregate labor supply in hours. Its conclusion was that a 1% increase in after-tax wage rates would lift labor supply by 0% to 0.3%. The incentive effect—*substitution elasticity* in economists' jargon—lies between 0.2% and 0.4%; the *income elasticity* lies between −0.2% and −0.1%. In the example, the 2.91% increase in take-home wages could be an incentive for an increase in hours of work between 0.58% and 1.16%, while the income effect could take away from 0.14% to 0.28%. Adding $1,000 in tax credits would magnify these income effects by 3.33 times, burying the incentive effects. No supply-side miracles here. And even if positive supply-side effects dominate, they are one-shot increases in labor supply and GDP, not permanent increases in growth rates.

Some tax cuts are designed as investment incentives. As demand stimuli, they have the virtue of expanding PGDP at the same time. This was the purpose of the investment tax credit introduced by the Kennedy administration and turned off and on and off several times since. There is evidence that a good share of the intended response to the ITC was lost in subsidizing ongoing gross investments rather than in incremental ones and in higher prices of capital goods.

On the macroeconomic scene, the supply-side payoffs of capital investments occur gradually over future years, while the demand impacts are felt immediately. If there is no room in the economy, the Fed will raise interest rates and no net increase in aggregate investment will occur. As the Fed knows, investment booms can be just as inflationary as consumption booms. A true progrowth policy, in times of full employment, would offset tax-cut investment incentives by cuts in government consumption spending or by tax deterrents to private consumption.

Incentives for investment are fruitless without saving to match. When labor and other resources are idle, investment spending can put them to work and saving from the new wages and profits will do the job. Consumption will increase along with saving and investment, as long as there is room in the economy for both. At full employment along the PGDP track, however, lower national consumption is a requisite of higher national saving and investment. At full employment, there is no way new investment spending itself can generate the needed saving.

Tax-cut incentives for household saving are popular in Congress. IRAs for a variety of ostensible purposes are multiplying. As growth policy via higher national saving and investment, IRAs are likely to be useless or perverse, for two reasons. One is that taxpayers can usually qualify for tax benefits while consuming no less, or often more; they qualify for IRAs, for example, by using funds they already have, obtain by borrowing, or would save anyway. The other is that the lost tax revenue raises government dissaving, unless Congress offsets it by raising other taxes or cutting expenditures.

A similar problem afflicts proposals for large-scale cuts in capital-gains tax rates. The rationalization is that it provides incentive for investments, especially innovative entrepreneurial ventures. Risk-taking investors themselves might be somewhat ambivalent about the rate cut, because it means that government will absorb a smaller fraction of losses as well as of gains. Nevertheless, this rationalization does not apply to the trillions of unrealized capital gains on assets acquired in the past. Cutting the tax due on their realizations just gives windfalls to their holders, windfalls likely to raise consumption spending. (It's true that tax collections will increase in the short run, as owners who have locked in appreciated assets seize the opportunity to sell them.)

The best way to provide a tax incentive to save rather than consume is to allow a deduction of *net* saving—purchases of capital assets net of borrowing and asset sales—in reckoning taxable income. To minimize windfalls to taxpayers who would be saving anyway, the deduction should be given only for the excess of net saving over a threshold that would rise with income.

The difficulty of targeting tax incentives to particular purposes afflicts many actual and proposed rate cuts, credits and deductions, and many outright subsidies too. For example, though meant for students unable to afford college or other post-high-school education, or to attend private elementary or secondary schools, subventions to everyone who enrolls are mostly windfalls to persons who would attend these schools anyway. There are sharper, more discriminating tools available.

DOWNSIZING GOVERNMENT AS GROWTH POLICY

Budget balancers and tax cutters agree on the ultimate goal of downsizing civilian government. They frequently try to reach the goal by squeezing government between the pincers of tax cuts and budget balance. Their idea is that an economy with small government is more productive than an economy with large government, even if the budget is balanced in both. Both groups rationalize their view by citing the inefficiencies and distortions of higher taxes, a view that is often reinforced by the allegation that government expenditures are inherently wasteful. There are many anecdotes but little evidence to support so sweeping a generalization. European countries with larger civilian governments have had higher growth rates than the United States and have been more successful in other dimensions. A discriminating approach to costs and benefits would give governments credit for supplying public goods, coping with "externalities," and maintaining social safety nets. In the United States today, further cuts in federal discretionary nondefense programs are bound to come mostly from public investments—in education, R & D, public health and safety, medical research, environmental protection, and infrastructure. It is hard to see how such downsizing can increase potential GDP or speed up economic growth.

KEEP DEMAND-SIDE AND SUPPLY-SIDE EFFECTS STRAIGHT

Whatever their supply-side effects, tax cuts are demand-side stimuli unless they are matched by concurrent cuts in government spending. Deficit-increasing tax cuts may be welcome when the economy is operating short of potential; they can help arrest recessions and fuel recoveries. But in times of full employment, with the economy constrained by the NAIRU, the Federal Reserve will oppose additional aggregate demand by raising interest rates. The tax cuts will mainly raise consumption, while the hikes in interest rates will curtail investment. The net result is unfavorable to growth.

Supply-siders invariably count demand-side effects in support of their supply-side proposals. They often cite the increases in GDP and tax revenues that accompanied the Kennedy-Johnson tax cut of 1964. This legislation, proposed as early as 1962, was primarily designed as a demand-side stimulus to keep a cyclical recovery going, reduce unemployment to the 4% then regarded as the NAIRU (though not so named), and close the GDP GAP. Matching cuts in spending were not proposed. Supporters of the tax cut claimed that some productivity by-products would result from incentive effects, which broadened congressional support. The measure had its intended demand-side effects, but there is no evidence that it increased potential GDP. When Vietnam War spending was added to the budget in 1966, the economy was overheated and inflation rose for the rest of the decade.

Worse still, supply-siders are grossly mistaken to claim the 1983–89 recovery as a vindication of Reaganomics and to assert that the same recipe can now lift growth rates again. The 1981 tax cuts and the buildup of defense spending were fiscal demand stimuli unprecedented in peacetime. With unemployment and excess capacity at their highest rates since the Great Depression, the economy could easily meet the new demands upon it. Inflation, which had touched double digits in 1979–80 and fallen to 5% in the subsequent recession, actually continued to abate during the 1983–89 recovery. Interest rates declined too; the Federal Reserve was accommodative. As the 10% GDP GAP of 1982 was closed, actual GDP grew 4.4% per year, about 2 points above the sustainable PGDP rate. It is ridiculous and dangerous to advocate repeating in 1996 the Reaganomic policies of the 1980s. The slack that was in the economy in 1982, when unemployment exceeded 10%, is not there now, when unemployment is only 5.3%.

Nothing at all happened on the supply-side in the 1980s; neither PGDP nor its rate of growth were raised. Reagan's fiscal policy powered the demand-side recovery of the 1980s, but it was not essential. The U.S. economy recovered from its seven previous postwar recessions without anything resembling such drastic policies. The Federal Reserve could have managed a 1980s recovery by itself; absent the bizarre fiscal policies, there was plenty of room for lowering interest rates further. Claims from Laffer curve adherents that expansion of the tax base would overcome the deficits resulting from the tax cuts were emphatically falsified. The economy of the 1980s was tilted toward private consumption and defense, at the expense of investment— the economy was not pro-growth, but anti-growth. The reckless experiment left the federal government with a large debt and a heavy burden of interest payments.

CONCLUSIONS

Although politicians freely promise faster growth, government has no handy set of tools for effecting it. The Federal Reserve can possibly raise GDP somewhat by further exploiting the apparent downward drift in the NAIRU; but the Fed cannot raise the economy's rate of growth for very long. Fiscal austerity, balancing the federal budget, can increase national saving and investment, with modest eventual payoffs in higher GDP and consumption. But public investments of high social productivity should not be sacrificed in the name of budget balance. Supply-side tax cuts are not likely to achieve the gains in output and growth their advocates claim. In practice, these measures often result in less work, less saving, less investment rather than more. Past tax cuts might appear to some to have had positive macroeconomic results, but these were due to demand-side stimuli in periods of economic slack.

The search for a holy grail that will lift permanently the growth rate of productivity seems hopeless. This melancholy conclusion deprives the pro-growth apostles of the miracles of compound interest in calculating the payoffs of their policies in 2050. True supply-side policies are hard work, painstaking and slow, as distinct from free-lunch, supply-side fantasies.

A list of sensible policies, one might say conservative policies, includes basic science, R & D, education and training, public infrastructure, and carefully designed incentives for both private and public sectors to consume less, and save and invest more. If everyone is patient with gains measured in tenths of a percentage point over the coming decades, these policies can pay off. With luck, new technologies may bring dramatic *improvements* in the growth rate. The computer and communications revolutions may well bear fruit in the next century.

Meanwhile, the United States is probably doing better economically than its people think. Our macroeconomic performance is the envy of Europe and Japan. The complaint that Americans are worse off than in the 1950s does not bear close scrutiny. Just compare the inventories of consumer durables *"the typical family"* had then and has now. Statistics of GNP, family incomes, and real wages would look better if the admitted bias toward upward changes in price indexes were corrected. With a stroke of a pen we could have 3.5% growth.

We have yet to figure out how to cope with the developments in demographics and medical science that raise the proportion of the aged in the population and make it possible but costly to keep them alive and healthy. This issue, a compound of good and bad news, raises problems in all advanced capitalist democracies, problems that are not just the fault of spendthrift politicians.

The United States stands out from other democracies in ways that should not be sources of pride: our acute poverty, inequality, and insecurity. Nothing in economic science and economic history says that these are inevitable byproducts of overall prosperity and growth, or that good economic performance is incompatible with progressive taxation, a decent safety net, and a public sector large enough to deal with the host of environmental and social problems that markets by themselves cannot solve.

REFERENCES

George Akerlof, William Dickens, and George Perry 1996. The macroeconomics of low inflation. Washington, D.C.: Brookings Institution. Duplicated.
Congressional Budget Office. 1996. Labor supply and taxes. January.

Bottleneck Inflation and Growth

Joel Popkin, President,
Joel Popkin and Company

Few deny that U.S. economic growth rates are not as robust as they were 20 years ago. The recently introduced, more accurate indexes of U.S. real GDP reveal that the average annual growth rate for the period 1958–87 was a full percentage point above the average growth rate since 1987. The most recent growth data suggest this differential may be narrowing. While the Federal Reserve Board seems more willing to let growth rise somewhat faster than the 2%–2.5% rate it finds comfortable, its willingness to tighten policy is not much below the surface of its public statements.

This willingness is reflected in the relatively high, short-term real interest rate Federal Reserve policy has produced. Long-term interest rates have, on the other hand, been low enough to produce a relatively flat yield curve, signaling that inflation expectations are under control. Such expectations reflect a number of developments. First, retail-level core inflation slowed in the early 1990s and has fluctuated at about 3% for the past few years. Second, prices of semi-manufactured products, excluding food and energy, have been flat to down over the last two years. Finally, manufacturers' prices of finished consumer and producer goods and wages have risen at very low rates that reflect the pressures of international competition. Price trends of finished goods imported into the U.S. have fallen, reflecting those same pressures plus the stronger U.S. dollar.

These developments have caused a growing number of analysts to conclude that the Federal Reserve could provide more stimulus to economic growth without reigniting inflation. This conclusion is reinforced by the sharp reductions in the U.S. budget deficit that, of themselves, restrict growth rates. Tighter fiscal policy often requires the trade-off of easier monetary policy, a trade-off the Federal Reserve has long said it would provide in return for fiscal responsibility.

THE FED'S FAULTY DIAGNOSIS

Such a quid pro quo has yet to occur. When contemplated, it usually has been rejected because of upward spurts in the prices of some raw and semimanufactured goods. The Federal Reserve fears that such increases will be passed through to the prices of finished goods and lead to more generalized inflation.

To examine the likelihood that inflation will spread, it is important to distinguish between the two kinds of inflation that can occur in specific markets. One is *bottleneck* inflation; the other is inflation that can be passed through from one stage of process to another as goods are transformed to final end-user markets.

Bottleneck inflation is a rise in prices in one narrowly defined market (or several markets) that reflect developments unique to that market—developments that typically emerge from a supply-demand imbalance. The resulting price rise signals the need to attract resources to that sector. To result in generalized inflation, such an imbalance must exist in a larger context, such as the manufacturing sector as a whole or the labor market.

A comprehensive measure, developed by Joel Popkin and Company, of the relationship between demand and supply for the U.S. manufacturing sector as a whole and its materials and supplies manufacturing component is found in Figure 2.5. Each measure is a ratio in which demand is represented in the numerator, supply in the denominator. Demand is calculated as the sum of unfilled orders at the beginning of a month and new orders received during the month. Supply is the sum of inventories of finished goods (and one-half of inventories of goods-in-process) at the beginning of a month and the amount of production that could be achieved during the month if output were at full capacity.

This demand-supply ratio is more relevant for predicting inflation than is *capacity utilization*—the ratio of actual output to capacity output—alone. The demand-supply ratio recognizes that new orders can be put on the books for future production, produced when received, or filled from inventories. It distinguishes, for example a situation in which, by operating at 95% of capacity, manufacturers can meet flow demand without a buildup of unfilled orders or depletion of inventories. This is not

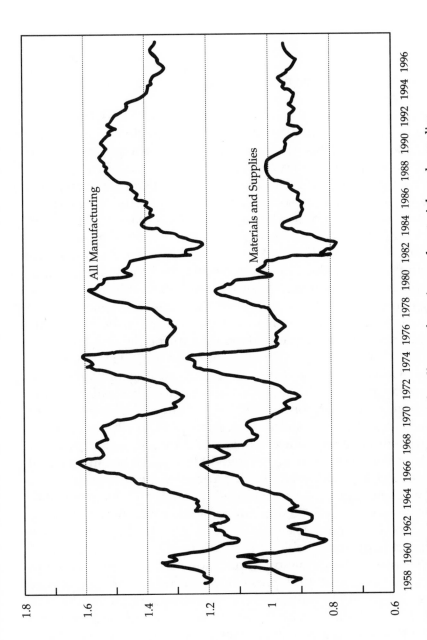

Figure 2.5. Ratio of demand to supply: all manufacturing and materials and supplies.

the same as a circumstance in which excess demand leads to inventory reductions and/or rising backlogs.

Figure 2.5 shows the two demand-supply ratios from 1958, when the data needed to calculate them begin, through mid-1997. Between 1958 and the present, both measures have fluctuated around a relatively trendless level in a cyclical pattern, which has tended to reach a high point at or before cyclical peaks and a low point at or soon after cyclical troughs. Both indexes showed very pronounced peaks on three occasions—the Vietnam War buildup and the two periods of double-digit inflation, in 1973–74 and 1979–80. Both indexes showed steep declines during and after the 1981–82 recession; and the materials-and-supplies index reached its lowest point in December 1982, virtually coinciding with the trough of the recession. Following the recession, the measures rose almost continuously until early 1988. Then the measure for all manufacturing flattened out for a couple of years before declining slightly as the 1992 recession ensued. However, unlike its performance during previous post-recession periods, the index continued to fall steadily before reaching its lowest point since 1982 in late 1995. The index for materials and supplies also reached its peak in 1988. Unlike the total manufacturing index, it began to drop almost immediately and continued to decline until mid-1991, when it began a modest upward drift until early 1995. Currently, both measures are below their historical averages and, while both have risen since the late 1995/early 1996 time frame, neither has shown the steep upward climb that has characterized the cyclical expansions associated with past accelerating inflation.

The rise in the demand-supply index for materials and supplies that began in 1991 presaged the acceleration in prices of these intermediate outputs. In a clearly related move, the producer price index for intermediate materials (excluding foods and fuels) accelerated considerably, reaching an annual rate of 8% in the year ending May 1995. Then, as the demand-supply ratio began to drop in mid-1995, prices decelerated, falling 1% over the 12 months ending in April 1996.

The 1994–95 acceleration in intermediate goods prices caused only a modest ripple in the PPI for finished goods made from these intermediate products and none at all in the CPI for goods, excluding food and fuel.[1] This result was influenced greatly by strong competition in U.S. finished-goods markets from foreign producers. Prices of imported consumer goods have been rising more slowly than producer prices of comparable domestic goods. The lack of pass-through also partly reflects the Fed's move to a restrictive monetary policy in 1994, a move that more than halved the U.S. growth rate in 1995 to below 2%.

Without the Fed's actions, some of the price increases in intermediate materials might have been passed through to finished goods. The pass-through, however, would have been limited considerably by competition from abroad through the behavior of import prices, as noted earlier. Instead, as restrictive monetary policy took hold, the U.S. economy slowed and materials production, as it usually does, slowed even more. Capacity utilization in these upstream industries fell and prices receded. The bottlenecks disappeared—unfortunately, not because their cause was eliminated. Rather, they fell from sight because the rest of the economy *was slowed to a rate consistent with bottlenecks in many primary manufacturing industries.*

RESULT OF THE FED'S UNWARRANTED PRESCRIPTIONS

Is the Fed correct to respond to bottleneck inflation in this way? A bottleneck-induced price rise is like a fever signaling that resources should flow to the sector—presumably capital investment to raise productive capacity. To reduce the fever by taking the pressure off the sore spot is like taking an aspirin to cure a heart ailment.

Rather, the Fed should tolerate sectoral bottlenecks with the expectation that markets will work, in this case through relative price change, to shift resources from excess-supply industries to excess-demand industries. The Fed can be especially tolerant when pressures of foreign competition are keeping final-goods prices under control.

The effect of the Fed's policy to eliminate bottlenecks by reducing demand rather than increasing supply is clear from its own data on capacity. The Fed produces such data as part of its indexes of industrial production. Indexes of capacity growth are shown in Figure 2.6 for both primary and advanced goods, roughly analogous to intermediate and finished manufactured products. For the past 15 years, the data show that primary manufacturing capacity has grown considerably slower—1.3% per year—than advanced goods capacity—3.2% per year. In the most recent 2 years, the gap has remained at more than 2 percentage points, despite the fact that capacity growth quickened in some bottleneck industries. Such capacity growth could not adequately lower the demand-supply ratio without a reduction in demand.

This difference in capacity expansion between primary and advanced manufacturing industries is evidence that Federal Reserve policy is not merely neutral toward noninflationary economic growth potential. Its policy actually is thwarting investments in the U.S. that would permit faster growth without triggering an inflation spiral. Thus, U.S. growth potential seems to be hostage to the rate in industries where capacity grows the slowest. If the Fed did not react quickly to higher prices in bottleneck industries, producers in these industries would be more likely to add capacity at a faster rate. As things stand now, such industries constantly fear that the Fed will render their expansion efforts redundant. Beyond that, Fed policy is indirectly encouraging producers in other countries to expand their productive capacities and, ultimately, to further penetrate U.S. markets.

Bottleneck inflation is the natural and desirable outcome of a market economy. Relative price changes are key to efficient resource allocation. The Fed seems to have difficulty distinguishing between the symptoms of bottleneck inflation and inflation that can become virulent. Perhaps then it should not play doctor or, at least not make house calls on the U.S. economy at the first sign of a sniffle. House calls are expensive.

NOTES

1. These conclusions are based on aggregate indexes similar in scope but not necessarily containing all of the same items with the same weights.

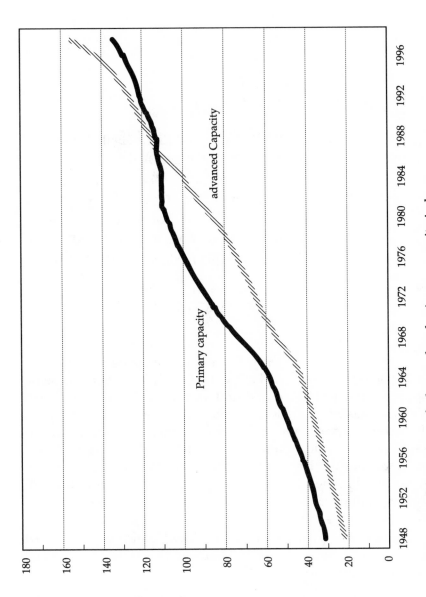

Figure 2.6. Comparison of advanced and primary capacity indexes.

Economic Potential Is Higher Than We Think

LAWRENCE R. KLEIN, BENJAMIN
FRANKLIN PROFESSOR EMERITUS
OF ECONOMICS, UNIVERSITY OF
PENNSYLVANIA; FOUNDER OF
WHARTON ECONOMETRICS
FORECASTING ASSOCIATES; AND 1980
NOBEL LAUREATE IN ECONOMICS

Y. KUMASAKA, CHIEF ECONOMIST,
NLI RESEARCH INSTITUTE

Is the U.S. economy realizing its full potential? We do not think so. We believe that the U.S. economy is being inappropriately restrained and underachieving its potential, a situation that has existed since the end of the recession in early 1991.

In order to appreciate the issues at stake, let's define what is meant by economic potential. Looking at the economy as a whole and not the issues concerned with the *distribution* of income or wealth, there are two key measures for determining economic potential:

1. The potential growth rate of real GDP, which is the highest sustainable rate of growth of total output that does not generate accelerating inflation;

2. The rate of unemployment, at full employment, which is the lowest sustainable rate of unemployment that does not generate wage-cost pressure that would cause the inflation rate to accelerate (this is also known as NAIRU, the nonaccelerating inflation rate of unemployment).

Two important terms used in defining these measures are *sustainable* (growth or unemployment) and *nonaccelerating*. The potential growth rate and the full-employment unemployment rate must be attainable within carefully constructed *error bands,* for periods as long as 5 or 10 years. It is neither meaningful nor helpful to define these terms as values that could be attained for only a few months.

In the appropriately constructed error band, we do not rule out short-run deviations or even discrepancies of longer duration. We do not accept, however, ever-increasing inflation rates, which are acceleration measures of price-index levels, in defining unemployment at full employment. Participants in the present debate frequently overlook this point, and fail to realize that every notch upwards on the inflation scale is not necessarily a step towards ever-increasing inflation rates.

Before the statistics of real GDP were redefined in early 1996, the potential growth rate was commonly thought to be approximately 2.3% per annum. For recent periods, it was felt that the new measurements lowered this rate because, on average, recent observed growth rates of GDP seemed to be about 0.5% below the older measures. We do not know the true rates of growth of real GDP, but those who measure the potential and those who use it for policy purposes felt confident and comfortable with the former 2.3%. We can only infer that they now think that the growth potential is no more than approximately 2%. Either figure looks exceedingly low.

As for the full-employment unemployment rates, we have to consider the changes in the way the household population in 1994 was surveyed, which raised the reported values by about 0.2 percentage points at the time of the rates were introduced. Estimates of the unemployment rate at full employment were often between 6% and 6.5%. Because the reported figures have been well below 6% for so many months without any sign of acceleration of price movements, there has been a recent tendency to put the unemployment rate at full employment in the range of 5.5% to 6%. We feel, however, that this range is much too high.[1]

THE U.S. ENTRY INTO A SUSTAINABLE PHASE OF PRODUCTIVITY IMPROVEMENT

The accepted method for estimating growth potential is to multiply the following three factors:

$$\text{Population} \times \text{Labor Force Participation Rate} \times \text{Labor Productivity}$$

The product provides an estimate of real output, from which the growth rate can be readily calculated. This is all too simplistic, however. The method does not allow for significant secular changes in productivity or for personal taste or lifestyle changes regarding participation in the workforce. Population, which is seemingly predictable within a narrow range of error, has sometimes yielded big surprises, the contribution from immigration being but one.

Have all of the major changes in the participation rate been adequately considered? Probably not. It is not certain, for example, that the trend of female labor-force participation has run its course; there is still evidence of rising female-participation rates through most of 1995. Another way that participation rates might rise is an increase in the minimum age of retirement from 65 years of age.

Finally, this country's recent gains in productivity are not simply manifestations of cyclical recovery, as the proponents of slow growth proclaim. The shift of workers to service-related activities, where productivity is difficult to measure, makes it easy to underestimate productivity gains. The interaction between high-technology capital and service performance has not been adequately taken into account. There are many reasons to believe that productivity gains can continue as a long-run trend.

In April and May 1996, the Bureau of Labor Statistics released data showing that output per worker-hour in the business sector increased steadily, at a slightly increasing rate from 1992 through 1995 (0.2%, 0.7%, and 0.9%) in three successive annual changes. In 1994 and 1995, there were few quarterly decreases. The annual results of change in the nonfarm-business sector were also strong (0.2%, 0.5%, and 1.1%). In manufacturing, the results were even stronger (2.1%, 4.2%, and 3.7%). (Note that the manufacturing figures are different because they are based on the Federal Reserve's industrial production index.)

These results are not conclusive, but they are very promising in supporting the argument that the United States has entered a sustainable phase of productivity improvement, not just a cyclical revival. Productivity gains continued through 1995, even though the overall GDP figures show slightly slower growth in aggregate output, in comparison with 1994 growth figures. This pace did not seem to have slowed in the early part of 1996.

GROWTH ESTIMATION PROBLEMS

One serious problem with the prevailing estimates of economic potential is that the evidence of the 1970s is weighted too heavily. During that decade, productivity declined in the United States and other industrial countries. This was a temporary setback related to adjustment to the new terms-of-trade in energy products. If we treat this period as an aberration, then we find that there is no automatic tendency for price levels to accelerate.

There are two important implications for treating 1970s as a statistical anomaly: (1) the ongoing U.S. recovery in output per hour is part of a long-term sustainable trend; and (2) there are public-policy prescriptions that could reinforce this trend, namely, more spending on the economy's infrastructure.

Statistical studies of infrastructure investment show evidence of significant contributions to overall capital productivity.[2] If capital gets support from the infrastructure—including such items as telecommunications, transportation, health, education, sanitation, water supply, and other activities that make the whole economy function better—then overall capital productivity rises at the margin. Economic policy can be supportive of both these private and public forms of infrastructure.

The full employment rate of unemployment may also be much lower than thought in recent years. At the time when the unemployment rate at full employment was thought to be 6% or more (i.e., before the observed rate had fallen decisively below 6%), an interesting research paper by Geoffrey Tootell was published in the *New England Economic Review*. Tootell found an "estimate of a NAIRU between 5.5 and 5.8%."[3] Now that we have had so much experience with an overall rate near 5.5%, without any indication of inflation, it is reasonable to believe that we could move down another notch, between 5% and 5.5%, without setting off inflation dangers. During the last 24 months, the rate of unemployment went as low as 5.1%.

It is worth pointing out that Tootell's estimates of the NAIRU indicated that the 1970s were different from the 1960s or 1980s, and that disregarding that period's unusual oil-price shocks re-sults in significantly lower estimates of the unemployment rate at full employment.

The U.S. economy has slowed significantly since the period of rapid reconversion and world reconstruction following World War II. It is reasonable to lower the potential growth rate on a gradual basis since those early postwar days, but it is not a con-cept that should be manipulated frequently or by large amounts based on business cycles. The same is true of the unemployment rate at full employment, which should not be adjusted abruptly up or down. This rate started from a base of approximately 3.5% or 4% in the late 1940s. It would have been unthinkable to put it at the wartime rate of approximately 1%, which represented a crisis situation in war economy. The rate at full employment gradually drifted upwards above 4% and then near 5%; but it does not make sense to place it at 6% or more in the 1980s, and then bring it back below 6% in the 1990s. There is no fundamen-tal change to justify such sizable short-run adjustments, up or down. What appears to be at work here is the manipulation of the NAIRU level to serve subjective economic-policy prefer-ences. The observed rate has been below 6% for many months and there are no signs of accelerating inflation.

WHAT ARE REASONABLE GROWTH TARGETS?

It cannot be emphasized enough that potential GDP and unem-ployment at full employment cannot be directly measured. In-stead, they are inferred on the basis of economic theorizing and statistical analysis. As a result, growth targets are subject to sig-nificant error bands. In March 1996, for example, Andre Dramais reported in a UN meeting that economic researchers at the Euro-pean Union constructed an appropriate tolerance interval for the European NAIRU and found that all historical rates fell within the interval.[4] One might conclude that a particular point value of the NAIRU was not very useful. Estimates of a U.S. growth tar-get are subject to a similar margin of error. If there is such great uncertainty about this target, surely we can seek to reach a value in the range of 5% to 5.5%, given that we were well below 6%, the old target that was so confidently held, for a period of 24 months without any sign of seriously accelerating inflation. In fact, those who want to revise the consumer price index say that reported inflation significantly exaggerates the actual value.

If 5% to 5.5% is a reasonable target range for the unemployment rate, what would be a corresponding range for the potential growth rate? We would say that a GDP average growth rate of at least 3%, and possibly as high as 3.5% is reasonable. This rate is based on the new formulas for measuring GDP growth.

Given all the uncertainties of measurement involved in potential growth and unemployment at full employment, and given that inflation fears have been exaggerated for several years, we should take mechanical measures of potential growth with at least a large grain of salt. Indeed, we should test the limits of noninflationary growth at the lowest possible level of unemployment.

The ideas in this paper were developed during the period 1994–1996. It was drafted during 1996, but events have since taken place that reinforce our arguments. Labor force expansion, continuing productivity expansion, dipping of the unemployment rate below 5%, and statistical reports of GDP growth above 3%—all within a benign inflationary environment—support the view that there has been significant underachievement in the economy.

This underachievement represents lost output, but should we simply dismiss this as a case of "letting bygones be bygones." While it is true that the economy is now functioning in the neighborhood of labor-market and production values that correspond more closely to our estimates of potential, we want to emphasize that political disputation about the deficits of federal, state, and local governments has withered in the face of stronger economic performance. The federal government should not have been forced to shut down in the past; decisions about payment of interest on federal debt should not have been taken to the brink of default; and continuing debate about future deficits that will occur when the baby-boomers retire should be discussed in the light of an economic assessment that is more realistic about potential. It does matter a great deal to err on the conservative side.

NOTES

1. Stuart E. Weiner, "New Estimates of the Natural Rate of Unemployment," *Economic Review* (Fourth Quarter 1993); "History Upholds Fed's Rate Moves," *New York Times*, 29 May 1994. See also Keith Bradsher, "3 Central Bank Governors See Inflation As Stable," *New York Times*, 6 June 1994; others in the Fed system and also the Council of Economic Advisors accepted unemployment rates near 6% as natural rates.

2. Lawrence R. Klein and Y. Kumasaka, "The Re-opening of the U.S. Productivity-led-Growth Era," *NLI Research* no. 76 (February 1995): 3–19; D. A. Aschauer, "Is Public Expenditure Productive?" *Journal of Monetary Economics* 23 (1989): 177–200.

3. Geoffrey M.B. Tootell, "Restructuring the NAIRU and the Phillips Curve," *New England Economic Review* (September/October 1994): 31–44.

Damn the NAIRU—and Full Speed Ahead

ROBERT EISNER, WILLIAM R. KENAN
PROFESSOR EMERITUS,
NORTHWESTERN UNIVERSITY; PAST
PRESIDENT OF AMERICAN
ECONOMICS ASSOCIATION

Some economists, like some generals, are always ready to fight past wars. They can also be dedicated slaves to old dogmas. To extend the metaphor, the past war is the fight against inflation; the old dogma is the theory that rapid growth is inflationary. In its most pernicious, current form, the dogma tells us that "too rapid" growth will not only be inflationary but will also bring accelerating inflation, that is, inflation getting greater and greater, until growth is sharply curbed, presumably by a recession.

NAIRU AND THE FEAR OF GROWTH

This dogma stems in turn from the underlying concept of the NAIRU, the nonaccelerating-inflation rate of unemployment. This construct, frequently thought of as the "natural rate" of unemployment, came into economic thought with the December 1967 presidential address to the American Economic Association by the great conservative—or free-market liberal—Nobel laureate to-be, Milton Friedman.[1] Shortly thereafter, and apparently independently, it was presented by E. S. Phelps, a Columbia University economist not known as a Friedman follower.[2]

The basic idea was simple enough, but the conclusion dramatic. It represented a revolutionary repudiation of the still-hardening dogma of the Phillips curve. Named after A.W. Phillips, a native of New Zealand at the London School of Economics, the Phillips curve indicated that lower unemployment was associated with more inflation and higher unemployment with less inflation or even deflation. For more than a decade after the late 1950s, economists seemed to find supporting data for the concept in many countries. The Phillips curve suggested that, as unemployment was reduced, each percentage point of further reduction was associated with a *greater* increase in inflation. There was much discussion of a trade-off, the reduction of unemployment in return for the acceptance of higher inflation. Up to a point the trade-off might seem worthwhile, but conservatives seemed generally willing to accept more unemployment to keep inflation at a minimum, while liberals generally looked for policies to reduce unemployment as long as the cost in added inflation did not seem too great.

But then came Friedman and Phelps, reinforced by the rational-expectations revolution of Robert Lucas, another Nobel laureate to-be, and Thomas Sargent, who told us that we had the Phillips curve all wrong. It showed at best, he argued, only a temporary relationship between inflation and unemployment. There was no way we could use greater inflation to buy permanently lower unemployment. Rather, there was this natural rate of unemployment to which the economy gravitated. Previously, many economists labeled "full employment" as 4% a figure that was the target of the Kennedy years and later embodied in the Humphrey-Hawkins Full Employment and Balanced Growth Act of 1978.

Stimulatory economic policies—whether fiscal or monetary—would indeed temporarily lower unemployment, but precisely because they would temporarily raise inflation above what was expected, leading employers to hire more workers. Because expectations of inflation, however, would quickly catch up to the new actual inflation, the only way to keep unemployment at its lower rate would be to stimulate the economy further, fueling increased inflation. So now the killer conclusion! As long as we kept unemployment below its natural or equilibrium rate we would have not only more inflation but also continually increasing inflation—literally accelerating inflation of 3%, 5%, 10%, 20%, and on up until the economy exploded! The only way to stop the acceleration would be to drive unemployment above its natural rate. Merely getting it get back to that equilibrium would leave inflation at the high rate it had attained.

A frightening diagnosis indeed! It is apparent why, if this theory is accepted, one may not want to risk policies that let the genie of accelerating inflation out of the bottle.

And that brings us right to the heart of current controversy about economic growth. "Too rapid" growth, it is argued, will reduce unemployment. If unemployment is already at the NAIRU, too rapid growth will then begin to put us on that explosive inflation path that is so difficult to reverse.

A considerable number of economists, I am embarrassed to say, accepted the concept of the NAIRU and offered a rationale for policy makers addicted to slow growth. I like to quip that conservative and liberal economists seem to differ only about where they put the rate. Martin Feldstein, of Harvard and president of the prestigious National Bureau of Economic Research, has set the NAIRU at 6% to 7%; Alan Blinder, of Princeton and recently vice chairman of the Federal Reserve Board, has put it at 5.6%.

I don't know if Alan Greenspan has publicly set his figure, but his actions and statements until recently—to the extent they could be divined—suggested that he got very nervous as the rate went below the 6% NAIRU rate estimated by the Congressional Budget Office. Financial markets clearly interpreted Greenspan and the Fed as getting worried when unemployment dropped below this rate. The bond and stock markets dramatically confirmed this when they nose-dived after it was reported on the first Friday in March 1996 that the actual unemployment rate had fallen from 5.8% to 5.5%. Hope was dashed that the Fed might lower interest rates, as had been expected in the face of signs of a slowing economy. As unemployment continued to come down, to 5.1% in August with no evidence of increasing inflation, I am pleased to note that the Fed surprised Wall Street analysts by not raising the Federal Funds rate at its September Open Market Committee meeting.

Events have a way of catching up with even the most stubborn, misconceived theories. The association of the high inflation *and high* unemployment of the energy-shock 1970s gave the coup de grace to the old Phillips curve and prepared the way for acceptance of the forbidding NAIRU.

SECOND THOUGHTS ABOUT THE NAIRU

More recently, however, international statistics have told a story that is fairly perplexing to NAIRU believers. A few decades ago, European unemployment was generally very low, frequently 2 or 3%, and inflation was generally considerably greater than in the United States. But in the last decade we have seen much of Europe with unemployment in double digits: Germany now stands at 11%, France at 12%, Spain at an astonishing 22%. High rates in these countries have persisted for a number of years.

Can the natural rate really have gotten that high? And if not, how can unemployment have remained well above its natural rate for many years without the crashing *dec*eleration of inflation and the fall of prices through the floor that NAIRU theory would predict? As unemployment in the United States has in fact been below 6% for almost two years and remains at only 3% in Japan after a lengthy recession, I am led to ask why God, in creating these natural rates, treats His children so differently.

Some economists have indeed been having second thoughts. One persuasive idea associated with Lawrence Summers and Olivier Blanchard is that of *hysteresis:* if you don't do something about them, higher rates of unemployment become self-perpetuating as employers, the labor force, government institutions and policies—and the NAIRU itself—adjust to them.[3] Studies with Canadian data have challenged the NAIRU concept; and papers in the United States have pointed out that if there is a NAIRU, our estimates of its value are imprecise. Even if there is a NAIRU and if we don't know just where it is, we should not subject the economy to slow growth, let alone the risk of a recession, simply to avoid unemployment falling below its current conjectured value.

There have been other recent fundamental challenges to the concept. Yale's Ray Fair has argued, after sophisticated analysis of data from 29 other countries as well as the United States, that the concept of the NAIRU is "two derivatives off." What he means is that the data show that lower unemployment is associated with higher prices, but not with inflation or rising prices (the first derivative of prices with respect to time), let alone with rising inflation (the second derivative of prices).

NEITHER LOW UNEMPLOYMENT NOR FATTER GROWTH INCREASES INFLATION

The conventional formulations of the NAIRU mask a basic asymmetry.[4] The usual formulations—relating inflation to past inflation, other variables such as measures of changing productivity and food and energy prices (presumably determined in world markets), and current and past unemployment, and fitted to historical data in the United States over the past 40 years—indicate that unemployment is negatively related to changes in inflation. My own conclusion is that unemployment above the NAIRU, estimated to be currently about 6% by a number of researchers (and the CBO, as I have indicated), lowers inflation, and that unemployment below the NAIRU raises inflation. What I have done is separate the data into observations where unemployment is above the NAIRU and where unemployment is below the NAIRU. In doing so, I find that the relation breaks down!

At an elementary level, I find that inflation has been no higher—indeed it has been slightly lower—when unemployment was below the NAIRU. For the 75 quarters that unemployment was above the NAIRU from 1956 through 1995, inflation as measured by the consumer price index averaged 4.32% and, as measured by the GDP implicit price deflator, averaged 4.39%. For the 85 quarters when unemployment was below the NAIRU, the CPI inflation averaged 4.21% and the GDP deflator inflation averaged 4.16%.[5]

Particularly damaging to the NAIRU concept are results pertaining to the basic issue of acceleration of inflation. When these observations are divided into low and high unemployment relative to the NAIRU, the data generally indicate that unemployment above the NAIRU was associated with declining rates of inflation. This is consistent with the considerable evidence that recessions slow inflation; inflation was certainly not a problem during the Great Depression. What is most striking, however, is the lack of evidence that low unemployment, that is, unemployment below the NAIRU, increased the rate of inflation. There is even a suggestion in some of the data that, as unemployment below the

NAIRU got still lower, the rate of inflation declined rather than rose.

There are a number of explanations for this finding that low unemployment does not raise inflation. First, higher employment is associated with greater productivity and lower costs. Second, workers with high take-home pay, which frequently reflects longer hours, are not anxious to rock the boat by pushing for exorbitant wage increases. Third, in a period of high-employment prosperity, firms may think of the longer run and not wish to encourage the entry of potential, cash-rich competitors by offering the even juicier targets of higher prices. But whatever the explanation, the conclusion is clear: low unemployment has not brought accelerating inflation.

After I began reporting my research findings to this effect about two years ago, the record has remarkably confirmed them. The unemployment rate has been below the CBO-estimated NAIRU for every single month beginning in September 1994. Hardly anyone would argue that we have had increasing inflation over this period; there is, rather, considerable evidence that it has declined.

Linking the fear of lower unemployment to the fear of higher growth stems from the calculation that growth in the labor force, plus growth in productivity per worker, is such that a constant rate of unemployment will leave us with growth of output of about 2.2% per year. If output grows more rapidly, the implication is that the proportion of the labor force at work will have increased: the *un*employment rate will be lower. It was to prevent such "overheating" that the Federal Reserve recently raised interest rates six times. The Fed then prides itself on having achieved a "soft landing." From the fourth quarter of 1994 to the fourth quarter of 1995, growth in real GDP was held to 1.3%. But why a landing—hard or soft? Why not keep flying?

Aside from the unemployment connection, there is no direct evidence that faster growth increases inflation. Over the last 36 years (for which revised data are available), simple least-squares regressions suggest that faster growth in real GDP brought *less* inflation. Each percentage point of growth was associated with 0.17 percentage points less inflation. In regressions adjusted for serial correlation, the coefficients were close to zero and not statistically significant, but were still negative; that is, *there was no evidence that faster growth increased inflation.*

THE HIGH COSTS OF HOLDING GROWTH DOWN

The lack of factual support for the fears that faster growth is inflationary makes all the more appalling the costs of policies to hold unemployment up and growth down. Okun's Law, named after the late Arthur Okun, the distinguished Yale and Brookings economist who was the chairman of Lyndon Johnson's Council of Economic Advisors, indicated that each percentage point of unemployment was associated with a loss of 2.5 percentage points of output, as more unemployment was associated with fewer average hours worked and lower productivity. Conservatively cutting that figure to 2 percentage points today, we can conclude that if unemployment were 1 percentage point less today, we would have $150 billion more of annual output. In seven years that would come to well over $1 trillion dollars, enough to finance almost all of our favorite causes.

And for those who care about the budget deficit—whether or not it should be central to our concerns—the CBO estimates that each percentage-point reduction in unemployment would reduce the annual deficit by $90 billion within four years. Getting unemployment to the old full-employment target of 4%—it was around 3% during the Vietnam War—would completely wipe out the deficit, currently projected at under $150 billion, by the new millennium. Increasing the rate of real growth by 1 percentage point would raise nominal GDP by more than $600 billion by the year 2002. With the resulting added tax revenues from higher incomes and reduced outlays for unemployment insurance and welfare, we would then have not merely a "balanced budget," but a substantial surplus—without any of the painful cuts about which Congress and the administration have been wrangling.

Or take Social Security. It is projected that by 2030 the Old Age and Survivors Trust Fund will be exhausted as our population ages. In fact, the ratio of those between 20 and 64 to those 65 and over will have declined from 5 to 1, to 3 to 1; but the total dependency ratio, including young as well as old, will have increased by only 4%. This figure will be dwarfed by the increase in income and output that we would have in 35 years if product per worker grows only at the 1% rate that is at the lower end of past experience. Even after accounting for this increase in the dependency ratio, it would enable us to have 33% more output per *person*. Every retiree, every person of working age, and every child could then have much more, even allowing for greater costs for the elderly, than they have at present. If we were to raise that rate of growth to 2% per working person, income and output per person would be 90% more than now!

FULL SPEED AHEAD

There is of course more to increasing the rate of growth than seeing to it that the Federal Reserve does not follow a deflationary, antigrowth policy. In addition to freeing all of our current potential, we should work to increase it. This means first educating and training all of our population so that they are equipped for full productivity in a rapidly advancing high-technology economy. We must end the functional illiteracy of millions of school dropouts in inner cities and elsewhere. We must provide the public infrastructure and basic research on which private production and progress depend. We must end our obsession with balanced budgets and pursue a policy of optimum public and private investment that promote growth.

Paul Krugman, a versatile Stanford economist, argued in a *New York Times Magazine* article on Federal Reserve policy, provocatively titled "Stay on Their Backs,"[6] that our economy could not grow faster than 2.5%. Policies to encourage—or permit—faster growth would only bring the disastrous inflation that comes from falling below the NAIRU.

This advice could not have been more wrong. The current technological, informational, and communications revolution is spawning all kinds of economies so that we can produce more with less. Only God knows how fast our economy can actually grow, or how low unemployment can get, if we have the purchasing power for all that we can produce.

My advice to the Fed—and to other policy makers—is, "Get off our backs!" Help us do all we can, and full speed ahead!

NOTES

1. Milton Friedman, "The Role of Monetary Policy," *American Economic Review* 58 (March 1968): 1–17.

2. Edmund S. Phelps, "Money-Wage Dynamics and Labor-Market Equilibrium," *Journal of Political Economy* 76, pt. 2 (August 1968): 678–711.

3. O. J. Blanchard and L. H. Summers, "Hysterics and the European Unemployment Problem," *NBER Macroeconomics Annual*, ed. S. Fisher, vol. 1 (Cambridge: MIT Press, n.d.).

4. Robert Eisner, *The Misunderstood Economy: What Counts and How to Count It* (Boston: Harvard Business School Press, 1994). The articles include "Our NAIRU Limit: The Governing Myth of Economic Policy," *The American Prospect* (Spring 1995): 58–63, and reprinted in *Macroeconomics, 1996/1997 Annual Edition* (Sluice Dock, Conn.: Duskin, 1996); "Deficits and Unemployment," *Reclaiming Prosperity: A Blueprint for Progressive Economic Reform* (Economic Policy Institute, n.d.): 27–38; "The Retreat from Full Employment," *Employment, Economic Growth and the Tyranny of the Market*, ed. Philip Arestis (Cheltenham, England: Edward Elgar, n.d.): 106–130. The paper is "A New View of the NAIRU" (presented to the Seventh World Econometric Congress, Tokyo, August 1995); a later version will appear in *Improving the Global Economy: Keynesianism and the Growth in Output and Employment*, eds. P. Davidson and J. Kregel (Cheltenham, England: Edward Elgar, 1997).

5. Eisner, "A New View of the NAIRU."

6. Paul Krugman, "Stay on Their Backs," *New York Times Magazine*, 4 February 1996.

3

Growth Is Coming from Companies

It's Time for a New Productivity Paradigm

J. TRACY O'ROURKE, CHAIRMAN AND CEO, VARIAN ASSOCIATES

In the last few years, there has been a revolution in productivity in American industry. The magnitude of the improvement is not widely recognized and, to some extent, continues to elude the country's policy makers and the news media. As a result, the ability of America's companies and their workers to achieve sustained growth at higher rates than in the last decade is seriously underestimated.

The kinds of companies and industries that have driven America to its current first-place ranking in world productivity are those that strive to improve every aspect of the entire enterprise.

My company, Varian Associates, offers a case in point. An innovation powerhouse for nearly half a century, this technology pioneer entered the 1990s badly in need of a financial and operational turnaround. Simply put, Varian's manufacturing, marketing, and other key disciplines had not kept pace with its ability to create advanced technology. If we had set our sights on becoming merely the lowest-cost producer in our markets, there is little doubt that we would still be a frustrated and floundering organization, rather than one that has enjoyed three consecutive years of record profits.

Instead, we established a goal of becoming the most efficient, effective, and productive company at every level of the enterprise. This sounds like a fairly simple concept, but it makes companies think and do things very differently than those who take a more traditional and much narrower path.

One measure of performance is sales per employee. A decade ago Varian's performance was in the $75,000 to $120,000 range, while today it approaches a quarter-of-a-million dollars and is still climbing.

FAST EVERYTHING

This new enterprise-level frame of reference demands a whole new set of priorities for such key issues as cycle times and information access. Today's policy makers will concede that doing things faster certainly must lead to higher productivity, but they don't yet have standards to measure it. This inability, however, shouldn't be allowed to stand in the way of companies gearing up to establish and meet these new standards.

Today's world demands that industry-leading companies not only must do everything well, they must also be committed to doing it faster. And that applies to every discipline in the company.

Likewise, companies that hope to compete on a global scale will miss the mark if they aren't shooting for an automated information network that will ultimately allow virtually anyone in the organization access to required data anywhere, anytime. Most companies have been working toward such a system and have versions of it available at the local level. Tying it together globally is a tougher challenge, but the time is coming when companies won't be able to compete unless they can overcome that barrier and have immediate access to critical knowledge on a global basis.

"CONCURRENT EVERYTHING"

In driving for continuous productivity improvement in this brave new world, the more successful companies have learned that the time-honored concept of doing everything sequentially no longer works. "Sequential everything" is too slow. "Concurrent everything" is now not only the ideal, but also well along toward becoming the standard.

In the traditional image of the enterprise as a pyramid, economists have approached productivity improvement by beginning at the base and assessing the cost of input and output. In today's world the new productivity paradigm demands that we begin at the top, driving not only toward doing everything faster but also toward doing many tasks simultaneously.

While every organization will need to establish its own set of parameters for charting progress, such measures need not be overly complex. In Varian's case, for example, we chose two principal metrics to track productivity success—sales-per-employee and profits. As noted, both have increased dramatically largely as a result of the actions we took.

OPERATIONAL EXCELLENCE

We organized these company-wide improvement efforts around a program to achieve what we call *Operational Excellence*. Its ultimate goal was straightforward—to make Varian as adept at manufacturing, marketing, and all of the other associated disciplines as it was at world-class technology innovation. The strategy was built around five key initiatives—improved customer focus; an unbending commitment to quality; achieving fast, and highly flexible factories; paring away barriers to fast product-development cycle times; and attaining organizational excellence to make certain we had the best-trained, best-equipped workforce in the markets we serve.

Each of these key initiatives had a wide range of sub-initiatives that were implemented to bring about the necessary changes in how we had been doing business and achieve the desired improvements in productivity. In the beginning, the scope of change seemed massive, but breaking the process down into these smaller pieces made it something our people could deal with everyday. In many cases, the initiatives required employees to approach their jobs in new and sometimes dramatically different ways. Fortunately, their efforts were rewarded with levels of progress and accomplishment they previously would have said were impossible.

A look at each of the key operational excellence initiatives provides illustrations of how the change came about, and the dramatic improvements that resulted from these efforts.

Customer Focus

Because they had pioneered the development of most of the company's key technologies, it was second nature for Varian's founders to work closely with their customers. Over the years, however, collecting and responding to customer input had slipped lower and lower on the company's list of priorities. By the early 1990s, it was not always clear to many of our customers that they represented more to us than orders.

Once we began regularly surveying customer attitudes, requesting feedback, and measuring satisfaction, we learned the error of our ways. The data told us that, while we were respected for our technology, we were also arrogant and very hard to deal with. Erratic performance in on-time delivery and installation times stood out as particular irritants.

To attack the latter problems, we began daily tracking of delivery commitments. Operators and assemblers got more involved with customer performance, and our engineering people directly took part in solving specific customer problems. As a result, nearly everything now ships on time, whereas just a few years ago virtually nothing did. Installation times were cut dramatically through such measures as process mapping and improvement, preplanning customer facilities, greater use of installation-specific parts and tool kits, and improved factory testing.

On a broader scale, we reinvigorated efforts to meet customer needs across the board by forming joint teams, partnering in such critical areas as product design, and enhancing after-sales support. Procedures were implemented to inject the voice of the customer into every area of the company. While we don't always get perfect marks, today's surveys tell us customers know we're trying, and our relationships are greatly improved.

Commitment to Quality

There was never a question of whether we could deliver quality, but what it would cost. The conventional practice of inspecting products at the end of the production line ensured that these costs would be enormous.

Under our operational excellence strategy, this traditional quality-control concept was replaced by the concept of error-prevention through designed-in quality and continuous process improvement. Driving for world-class performance became a way of life in every part of the company. Industry-best performance was benchmarked by every unit and department, with the most successful practices shared across the company. Vendors were brought into the process through what we termed *value-managed relationships* built around close communications and greatly stepped-up certification and training programs. And we began tracking key process-parameters using statistical process-control methodologies.

Expanded use of such techniques as employee-driven quality-improvement teams, automated testing, and a self-inspection program helped us boost first pass yields by 15 to 20 percentage points and more in many units. Employing such tools as Pareto charts, environmental-life tests, and expert systems for problem diagnosis significantly improved results in such areas as mean time between failures.

Waste was attacked everywhere. As the self-inspection effort gained momentum, the need for full-time inspectors disappeared until, today, for all practical purposes, the job title of inspector no longer exists.

How well did these techniques work? Over a four-year period, the cost of quality as measured by 14 elements, including rework and scrap, inventory write-offs, inspection expense, warranty costs, and manufacturing variances, dropped an average of 23% per year.

Flexible, Responsive Factories

Not previously known for their nimbleness, Varian factories took up the challenge of becoming more responsive with missionary zeal. Improved inventory turns, shorter manufacturing cycles, smaller lot sizes, and faster test times were among the goals they targeted for improvement.

Design for manufacturability and just-in-time scheduling and production techniques were implemented at every plant where they made sense. In the past, nearly every manufacturing task was performed internally; now we outsource extensively wherever Varian has no special expertise to add value. Testing was automated and streamlined. Self-directed teams were formed to shorten setup times. Value-managed-relationship programs were employed even more broadly, with a pared-down list of vendors who became highly responsive partners in our manufacturing process.

The benefits of these improvements for employees and customers alike is apparent in the experience of one of our instrument units in converting one of its production lines to a new model. Thanks to extensive cross-training and documentation, the factory is experiencing almost no downtime during the transition. Test times, which often required a month, have been slashed to a matter of hours, with all of the tasks carried out on the production line with automated equipment. By applying the latest self-testing technology, the process can now be accomplished largely without human intervention. If the product passes its first overnight test run, it is put through five days of verification runs and shipped.

As a result of these advances, Varian's overall manufacturing cycle times have fallen by 66%. Inventory turns improved dramatically, climbing by 58%. The cycle time for processing engineering change orders, a traditional bottleneck, has been slashed by 50%. Installation times are continuing to improve at a rate of better than 10% per year.

Fast Product Cycle Times

With its long history of superior technological innovation, Varian, in its pre-1990 days, was noted for wringing the last ounce of performance out of newly developed technology. As a result, new products were launched well behind schedule. The time-to-market concept was too often defined by when the product was ready, rather than when the customer or the market needed it.

Under the Operational Excellence program, that definition changed dramatically. Product lines were pruned to concentrate the company's resources on those technologies and products with the best chances for success. Computer-aided design and other automated tools were employed widely, and a phased product development process was introduced to inject greater discipline and promote *concurrent* rather than sequential design activity.

Concurrent engineering and cross-functional teams were broadly deployed, along with rapid prototyping and other efforts to speed design and development times. Commercially available software and other off-the-shelf tools were adapted instead of developing them from scratch.

As a result, every one of our businesses has gained market share by introducing a continuing stream of new products, each with a shorter overall development time than its predecessor. Although always difficult to measure precisely, we have seen market share improve, in some cases by a considerable amount, for more than 90% of our products. Time-to-market has improved dramatically, by as much as 50% or more in many cases.

Organizational Excellence

In preparing its workforce for the transition to this new and different way of running the business, Varian's investment was substantial for training, equipping, motivating, and rewarding its people. In the midst of a financial turnaround, the training budget was increased fourfold, and training hours per employee increased by nearly 70% annually.

Bureaucracy was attacked and reduced across the company. One such effort, the EASE program (Eliminate All Senseless Effort), slashed the size of the company policy manual by 80%, avoiding an estimated 70,000 hours of what proved to be needless annual compliance activity.

Teaming was encouraged in every unit, and reward programs were created to recognize success. The growing use of self-directed teams and advances in information technology allowed elimination or redeployment of entire layers of extraneous supervisors and managers. Extended use of contract personnel added a new flexibility to many areas of the company.

MEASURES OF SUCCESS

Our key measures—profits and sales per employee—amply demonstrate the overall success Varian's productivity improvement efforts have enjoyed. In 1990, the company had sales per employee of about $130,000. By 1995, it had grown to $223,000, and it rose again in 1996 to $231,000. In 1990, profits per employee had amounted to $1,100. By the end of 1996 that figure soared to $18,000!

While these figures are critically important and essential to tracking our progress, perhaps the most significant measure of all cannot be expressed in numerical terms. This achievement is evident in the fact that the key elements of the Operational Excellence program are no longer seen by our employees as special initiatives. Instead they have established themselves as the parameters by which we now run the business, a sign that tells us that an attitude of continuous improvement is now firmly in place and what the Varian of today is about.

The message in this for American industry and the country's policy makers is that our experience is not unique. No rocket science was required, despite the dramatic results. The Varian example illustrates that, once America's workers are properly focused and motivated, their efforts can and will produce remarkable results.

With that firmly in mind, let's stop selling America's inherent productivity potential short. What we need is a new paradigm to more accurately reflect its truly extraordinary performance.

Growth Is Not a Four-Letter Word

WILLIAM HUDSON, CEO AND
PRESIDENT, AMP INCORPORATED

One of the most remarkable pictures to emerge from the last presidential campaign was that of President Clinton—along with three former presidents (Bush, Carter, and Ford) launching the NAFTA campaign to a select group of business and congressional leaders at the White House. All spoke in support of free trade and the need to generate jobs and promote economic growth. Another remarkable picture was the sight of the three leading candidates for the presidency promising to work hard to increase the rate of economic growth in the United States. Naturally, in an election year we expect our candidates will pledge to help create more jobs. And the candidates promised to do just that. In an election year, we also expect to hear calls for better working conditions and more benefits for working men and women. To no one's surprise, the candidates heartily embraced these issues. But in my experience, it's highly unusual to hear presidential candidates call for higher economic growth, especially when the economy is in pretty good shape, as it is now.

Yet, there they were, candidates for the nation's highest office, actually competing with each other to endorse the principle that America's present well-being and future security is largely linked to free-market economics! I applauded the admission by our political leadership that the basic unit of economic security—a job—is directly related to a healthy business climate. I applauded because the role of successful businesses in providing jobs and a high standard of living has been so frequently misunderstood or overlooked by so many, especially by elected representatives. I applauded because good jobs don't just spring up out of the ground and neither do successful business enterprises.

JOBS ARE NURTURED BY GROWTH

Jobs and healthy businesses alike are nurtured in a climate of sustained economic growth, backed by innovation and a dedication to change, and supported by a political system that encourages and rewards investment, initiative, and risk-taking. This describes the economic climate of the United States. More critical than this, however, is the global economic climate and how our government must likewise encourage and reward investment, initiative, and risk-taking by U.S. companies in this bigger arena.

These days, a great deal of new business investment is occurring in the developing countries of Asia and the Americas. Increasingly, these regions are chalking up much higher annual economic-growth rates than either the United States or Europe. Unfortunately, the public is bombarded with reports in some of our country's most prestigious newspapers, newsmagazines, and news programs that offshore business investment is bad for America, bad for America's workers, and perhaps even un-American. A common thread in these reports is that American business is exporting more than products—it is exporting jobs. Some experts would actually have us believe that there is good growth and bad growth. Growth then, when it occurs outside the United States, is a four-letter word. That's not only unfair journalism, it's plain wrong.

Business leaders have to deal with the world as it is, not as we would like it to be. Twenty-five years ago, economies were fragmented, local, and independent. Markets were protected by government regulation and local custom—in other words, by geography. The concept of a global marketplace existed only in college textbooks. Today, the business world has been completely reshaped by the phenomenon we call globalization. Economies and markets are converging.

In 1970, trade into and out of the U.S. accounted for 10% of its GDP. By 1995, it was 15 percent. Interdependence is no longer an academic buzzword; it is a reality. The reality is that the world economy is steadily overshadowing local economies. Geography no longer shields local business from competition. No one government—not even the U.S.—is strong enough to protect domestic industry from the rest of the world. It simply can't be done. These are facts, but there are a few others.

The reality is that few companies these days can survive by confining their activities to domestic markets, because too much has changed. The days when customers had little or no influence in product quality, characteristics, and costs are gone. Customers are very sophisticated. They know exactly what they want and demand products designed for a particular need. Customers tell suppliers when to deliver a product, how to package it, and even how much it should cost. These are the rules of today's competitive market place.

MANUFACTURERS IGNORE THE RULES AT THEIR PERIL

Why should manufacturers follow these rules? First, there is simply a lot more competition. For most business enterprises, a buyer's market prevails, making it impossible to operate for long without satisfying customers. And they, increasingly, are operating globally. They also know that growth is not a national issue and that their prosperity relies on a prosperous world economy. To win their global business, suppliers such as AMP must play the game by their rules which, fortunately, are few and not very hard to understand.

What else do customers expect of a supplier? Their list of demands is surprisingly short. Customers expect the same things we consumers do: a dollar's worth of value for every dollar spent; top quality at the lowest cost; a convenient place to shop; capable salespeople who stand behind their products; reliable and efficient service.

Consumers expect that products will conform to certain standards, that, for example, Kodak film will fit a Nikon camera, or that a Sony diskette will work in an Apple computer. Customers have similar expectations.

Consumers and customers want on-time delivery as promised. Customers also want consistent global pricing. A soft drink company, for example, wants to pay the same price for bottles in Athens as it does in Atlanta. And with instant global communications, someone is going to give them what they want.

THE WORLD MARKETPLACE IS UNFORGIVING

Another fact of life is that logos do not mean much to global customers. The world marketplace is tough and unforgiving. It does not care how many years a company has been in business or how big it is. It wants to know how reliable it is, how it can adapt quickly to change, and whether it will perform to promised expectations—anywhere, anytime.

All this begs a very simple question: Why would any business want to compete in the world market, given some of the impossibly difficult conditions I've just outlined? There happens to be a equally simple answer to this simple question. AMP and many other companies are investing offshore for one reason: they must. Foreign markets represent a new and challenging group of customers from which will emerge tremendous economic growth.

THE UNITED STATES—A MATURE MARKET

We have to accept the fact that the United States is a mature market, with annual growth rates of between 2% and 3%. Of course, 2% of a $7.1 trillion market represents a lot of business, one that we are not going to neglect. When a manufacturing company like AMP, however, seeks tremendous new growth opportunities, we must look outside this country. Large new telephone systems, for example, are being built in China, India, and Vietnam, and the world's tallest building is in Kuala Lumpur. The world's largest electrification project—which includes the world's biggest dam—is being built in China. If companies want to be part of those projects, they must have a presence in these countries.

Consider AMP, which is the world's leading producer of electrical and electronic interconnection systems. Like most large American firms, we derive a significant percentage of revenue from foreign sales. In 1995, almost 60% of our $5.2 billion revenue came from outside the United States. With plant facilities in 45 nations, the company ships products to more than 100 countries; for example, products built in Brazil are installed in autos in other South American countries, as well as in Europe. Products designed in Europe by Europeans are produced in the United States for American cars. AMP is a global company whose headquarters are in Harrisburg, Pennsylvania.

AMP faces over 1,500 big and small competitors in North America and around the world, who produce products with similar quality and at similar prices. The company is in a tough commodity business with plenty of supply, and with customers having enormous buying leverage. Its customers are global companies—General Electric, Siemens, Ford, Toyota, Motorola, Sony, among others. To succeed and to grow, AMP must do business wherever its customers do business.

Ensuring that the United States shares in global growth requires an enormous desire and resolution to change and keep changing. Sometimes, this requires major transformation, as has been the case at AMP. In step with the emergence of the global marketplace and rising customer pressure, AMP has continually transformed and reshaped itself. For most of its more than fifty years of existence, AMP had been organized along the lines of national boundaries. We had a very long and enviable history of profitable performance and had achieved, we thought, the ideal formula for business success. The company viewed change, even necessary changes, with suspicion. Although AMP was a very good company by traditional standards, could it be a very good company by the standards of the 1990s?

THE ROOF FELL IN

Then, a little more than a decade ago, the global marketplace caught up with us and the roof fell in. Our U.S. customers started to produce in Mexico, and in Singapore, Taiwan, and other low-cost Asian sites. Sourcing shifted to our Asian operations, which adversely affected some of our U.S. plants. Price erosion became an annual event, reversing decades of annual price increases. We had to shut down some plants and effect layoffs, which were distressing necessities because none of us believed AMP could reach prosperity by reducing employment.

When it became clear that these measures were insufficient, we instituted cost-containment programs, quality initiatives, flexible work rules, and changes in our manufacturing processes. In addition we decided to look at our business as if it were a brand-new company. Then we redesigned ourselves to survive in this harsh, new business climate.

We asked ourselves a number of tough questions: What is our vision for the future? How well do we understand our customers' needs? Should we stretch out geographically? How much should we invest in technology that enhances our manufacturing efficiency? What are we doing to stay compatible with our customers' electronic systems? How do we promote change within our organization?

Out of this soul-searching came a clear strategy and concise set of business objectives. The goal we set was to accelerate AMP's growth in order to transform it from a $3 billion company, which took more than 50 years to achieve, to a $10 billion global leader by year 2000.

We also knew that our worldwide growth would come at three levels: local, regional, and international. Over the years, we have evolved a system to work at all levels in an integrated way.

First, AMP operates as a local business. Every one of our employees in China, for example, speaks Mandarin, because most of them are Chinese. Germans manage our German operations. Strategic business decisions for Germany are made in Germany by Germans, which makes AMP incredibly responsive to German customers.

Second, AMP operates as a regional business. Products for the Asia-Pacific region are made in Japan, Taiwan, China, India, Malaysia, Singapore, South Korea, and Australia. Management for the region is multicultural, with strategic business decisions made in Tokyo, Hong Kong, and Singapore.

Third, AMP also operates as a global business. Products flow around the world; markets and customers are managed globally by experienced international managers with a global perspective. Strategic decisions are made by a global strategic-planning committee, which meets periodically in different parts of the world.

THE ROLE OF GOVERNMENT
IN PROMOTING GROWTH

Does the federal government have a role in promoting the growth of American business abroad? Absolutely! American business needs and wants our government at its side. Every business manager I know wants our government to act as if commerce is crucial to our national survival—because it is. There are some problems, however. No other country, for example, deliberately endangers its business community with the imposition of economic sanctions on foreign countries to bring about political change. Instead of these unilateral measures, the government should work through the diplomatic process and through such organizations as the United Nations and the WTO to settle political differences.

Our government should take a more active role in promoting commerce abroad. It disturbs me that a few elected officials seem to have the notion that any program that promotes trade is a form of corporate welfare. Finally, I believe we should try to guard against special-interest groups that advocate the imposition of quick or impossible targets for other countries to meet, especially when these countries have neither the economic capacity nor social development to reach them. In the environmental area, for example, we cannot expect to hold every country to American standards. Even with our top-notch scientists and technology, it took the United States over 30 years to achieve these standards. The best way to improve worldwide environmental conditions (or human rights, for that matter) is to encourage and make it easier for American companies to invest in those countries. Let us showcase America's practices and beliefs, rather than debate them.

The Three Gorges Dam hydroelectric project in China, which I alluded to earlier, is the biggest construction project the Chinese have attempted since the Great Wall. In fact, right now, Three Gorges is the world's largest construction project. A project of this magnitude presents an enormous opportunity for American firms to sell technologically advanced products and services, as well as to lend a hand in nation-building. Unfortunately, U.S. business is at a disadvantage in Three Gorges because some U.S. special-interest groups, which believe this project is environmentally harmful, have placed financial roadblocks in the path of American businesses that might want to participate. The result? China will purchase more earth-moving machinery from Japan than from the United States. More turbines will be bought from Germany, and more electric cable, towers, and transformers will come from Europe than from this country. Three Gorges will basically go forward without us.

IMAGE IS CRUCIAL

Our image around the world is crucial to establishing and maintaining strong business ties with other countries. Despite our problems, a lot of people in the world admire and respect the United States; all things being equal, a lot of them prefer to buy American products. If America looks weak abroad, however, the ability of Americans to win offshore business suffers. To respond to this danger, government must be strong where it needs to be strong. It must look out for Americans and for American interests abroad. Finally, in an era of belt-tightening budgets, we must keep American embassies and other buildings adequately staffed and in good condition.

AMP's SUCCESSFUL GROWTH STRATEGY

AMP has been successful because, rather than reacting to change, it is causing change, which is one hallmark of a growing business. Another is that, when a business grows, opportunities for new jobs and new career paths for employees arise. If a business fails to grow, careers stagnate; and when it hits an economic recession, employees have to be shed. When a growing business hits an economic slowdown, however, it does not let people go. It just modulates hiring. Although there are many measures of business success, one I am particularly proud of is that AMP's U.S. employment is 5% higher today than in its previous peak year of 1984.

We have come full circle to my initial argument: jobs and a healthy business climate are vitally linked. Both are vitally linked to a robust global economy in which U.S. companies are supported, not hindered, in their quest to win against competition. Global growth generates national growth and rewards here at home. Growth is not a four-letter word.

Small Business and Economic Growth

ROSABETH MOSS KANTER, HARVARD
BUSINESS SCHOOL

Small business plays a significant role in
the U.S. economy and is vital to its continuing growth. America's
entrepreneurial spirit fuels high rates of business start-ups compared to other countries, and it is the envy of the world. As secure employment in protected industries declines and the costs
of the welfare state come under scrutiny in Europe, foreign economic development plans cite the U.S. model of job growth
through small business.

Although the data are controversial, it has been argued that
small business is responsible for the lion's share of job creation in
the United States. In 1995, according to Small Business Administration figures, small businesses employed about 53% of the private workforce and accounted for 47% of all sales in the U.S. Industries dominated by small business were responsible for 75%
of the 1.66 million new jobs created in 1995, 62% in 1994, and
71% in 1993.

The job-creation potential of small business makes it an important economic smoothing mechanism. In Massachusetts,
smaller companies, especially in newer technology industries
and in services, drove the recent economic comeback after a precipitous decline in manufacturing jobs caused by large-company
distress and downsizing. In Seattle, business start-ups skyrocket
after every Boeing layoff, especially as engineers find opportunities in the region's burgeoning software and other high-tech industries. Boeing itself created an innovative program to help
laid-off workers buy or start businesses by investing severance
and unemployment benefits. Similarly, one feature of Bank-
Boston's Transition Assistance Package for employees displaced
after a merger enabled them to get loans and technical assistance
if they wanted to start a business (which could create additional
jobs), instead of applying for existing jobs.

The American Dream has long included business ownership, in
addition to home ownership. According to Professor Howard
Stevenson of the Harvard Business School, over a third of Harvard

Business School MBAs, once destined for careers in large corporations and investment banks, will own a business within 5 to 10 years of graduation. Indeed, careers in large organizations no longer seem as alluring to many of the best and brightest. This situation is only partially due to the loss of job security in an era of large-company restructuring and downsizing. It is also caused by the nature of corporate bureaucracies: an emphasis on conformity; a longer wait to assume major leadership responsibilities; fixed salaries with small contingent bonuses, compared to the greater risk but also greater potential rewards of owning equity in a small company.

The most dramatic growth in the small-business sector is in women-owned businesses. For women the allure of a small business is even more striking: a small operation they can run, with all the flexibility they want, and without corporate jobs often perceived as stifling. The National Association of Women Business Owners, using census data, estimates there were nearly 8 million women-owned businesses in the U.S. in 1996, generating nearly $2.3 trillion in sales and employing 18.5 million people. The growth of women-owned firms in the U.S. and Canada outpaced overall business growth by 2:1 during this period. Popular lore often presents women-owned businesses as sole proprietorships for the convenience of mothers who want to work at a home office. But many do not fit this model. Employment in women-owned firms with 100 or more employees expanded six times faster than all firms in the economy in the 1990s and were represented in all industries, with the fastest growth in construction, wholesale trade, transportation, agribusiness, and manufacturing. Women-owned businesses can also be sources of innovation. Women have parleyed their educational credentials in engineering and biology into growth companies such as Lau Technologies or biotech firms. Companies such as Calyx & Corolla, a direct marketer of fresh flowers, have changed industry paradigms.

Because of the self-reliance and job creation involved in small business, its development holds promise for the revival of depressed regions. Economic development groups, such as MACED in Appalachia, that once focused primarily on attracting large-company facilities to a region through tax incentives have increased their emphasis on entrepreneurship. Strategies to turn around impoverished inner cities increasingly include small-business development. The success of South Shore Bank in Chicago or First Community Bank in Boston has demonstrated that there is a profitable market for small-business loans in urban areas. New programs of microlending for the smallest inner-city businesses are modeled after the success of Grameen Bank in Bangladesh, which showed that small-business proprietors clustered in affinity groups could be creditworthy, sometimes more so than larger firms.

Perhaps more important for economic growth than aggregate number of jobs is the role played by small business in innovation. Entrepreneurial companies with new concepts are often responsible for new technologies that ripple throughout the economy, keeping American industry at the forefront of innovation and encouraging the competition that fuels it. High-tech regions such as Silicon Valley or Route 128 in Massachusetts depend on small companies to pursue new technologies—companies sometimes started by large-company dropouts. Some large manufacturers rely on small companies for access to new technologies, investing in startups or creating alliances and joint ventures with them. Pharmaceutical giant Novartis is increasing its position itself in biotechnology not only through internal research and development, but also through equity stakes in small companies. Digital Equipment's alliance with 200-person Dragon Systems, a world leader in voice recognition systems, has resulted in numerous enhanced features in Digital's products.

The fates of large and small companies are becoming intertwined as suppliers and customers work more closely together. Small businesses have played significant roles in the revitalization of large manufacturers, helping America return to its position as the most competitive industrial economy in the world. Large companies have been able to increase quality and reduce costs because they can outsource activities to small companies with greater flexibility and lower administrative expenses. In some cases, large firms have educated their supply base in advanced-management and manufacturing techniques. In other cases, however, small companies have created models of excellence that have served as benchmarks for their large customers. Wainwright Industries, the small-company Baldrige Award Winner in 1994 that supplies parts and services to the auto industry, developed work systems based on employee empowerment and continuous improvement that were much more efficient than those of the corporate giants they serve. Indeed, the greater efficiency of small suppliers and the resultant desire of large (unionized) firms to outsource to small (often nonunionized) companies became the subject of recent labor disputes between the United Auto Workers and General Motors.

In order to serve industrial customers, small businesses are also increasing their global sophistication in order to tap international markets through direct or indirect exports (i.e., supplying components domestically for products destined for international sale). *Small business* used to mean *local business.* Not anymore. *Small* and *local* are not identical, although they are correlated. In 1993 and 1994, I conducted a survey of 2,655 companies in five American regions in collaboration with local chambers of commerce for my book *World Class.*[1] The more international of the participating companies in the survey tended to have much larger revenues and employment, as well as be faster growing, more innovative, and more likely to be involved in networks and alliances. But some large companies were still quite local in inputs, outputs, and outlooks: for example, banks, hospitals, and utilities—the traditional downtown organizations that formed the leadership base of many American cities throughout most of this century. And some small companies were highly cosmopolitan: newer businesses in knowledge-intensive, high-technology industries or local affiliates of large international networks.

Emerging companies in industries of the future—such as software, telecommunications systems, biotechnology, or medical devices—are increasingly "born global." They develop a cosmopolitan mind-set from the inception even before they sell a single product into international markets. They are capable of serving the most demanding customers with the best concepts because they stress global competence and connections. To succeed in a global economy, companies must be "world-ready" whether or not they are yet world-active.

Successful growth companies in new technology fields develop concepts that not only meet world standards, but set them. These companies devise product strategies from the beginning with global elements in mind—market needs, supply sources, international standards, quality processes, technology developments. And they find international partners to extend their reach. Genzyme, for example, a biotechnology leader, has alliances with European, Japanese, and American companies; satisfies U.S. and European regulatory standards; and obtains specialized materials internationally, such as serum from New Zealand, enzyme from Thailand, and tissue from France. Medical research, its managers said, has no borders.

Alliance-building is also evident in several tiny health-technology start-ups still in incubators. One newborn, VideoMed, provides physician consultations to developing countries by satellite. Another, Harvard Design and Mapping (HDM), a small computer-mapping company founded in 1988 by a young woman emigree from Korea, established a representative and joint venture in Japan and development groups in Russia and Canada within four years of its formation. Although small—under $5 million in sales—the company is recognized as an international player because it opened a niche. Like Genzyme, HDM has a multinational, multilingual staff. As a subcontractor to large engineering firms and computer companies, HDM must meet world technology standards.

The success of another firm, Tech Ridge, shows how a small supplier flourished at home by being world-ready.[2] Tech Ridge's large partner, Polaroid, has helped grow the company's local manufacturing through international contracts. Started in 1957 as a machine shop, Tech Ridge specialized in manufacturing identification cameras and components, earning steady profits on sales of close to $10 million a year by 1990. In 1962, founder Leonard Comeau designed a camera useful for instant photo-ID cards for colleges, hospitals, sports clubs, driver's licenses, and the like. His purchase of Polaroid film and camera backs began an important relationship with Polaroid, headquartered nearby. The partnership grew because tiny Tech Ridge was a world leader in its niche, emphasized quality training; got ISO 9000 certification; provided extra service with flexibility—low overhead, fast decisions, willingness to go into weekend shifts if necessary—was reliable and fast, with turnaround for repairs in twenty-four hours compared to weeks for competitors; and partnered with its own suppliers, such as the small firm Screw Machine House that made handles for Tech Ridge. Because of TR's superior ID-camera technology and Polaroid's emphasis on film, Polaroid outsourced some manufacturing to TR.

Polaroid included Tech Ridge in a large contract in Mexico to produce cameras to make government-issued voter-ID cards for Mexico's 1994 voter-registration drive. TR supplied cameras while Polaroid supplied film, a venture that constituted one of the biggest orders in history for both companies. Tech Ridge then used its experience in Mexico, under Polaroid's guidance, to learn about international markets and to further innovate, preparing for a shift in technology. TR began work on a rechargeable battery-powered camera with improved circuits, an innovation for the U.S. market that would also help Tech Ridge compete internationally, especially in developing countries with unreliable and erratic electricity. This third-world-friendly innovation will also add value to U.S. products and give Tech Ridge an edge. For example, when a large bank wanted a battery-operated ID camera, which TR could not yet supply, the bank bought an Italian model for which TR supplied some parts while it worked on its own competitive product. And because of TR's success in Mexico, Kodak asked Tech Ridge to join in a similar venture in the Dominican Republic.

This case is just one example of large company/small company synergies. For world-ready companies, local supply partnerships can open doors to export markets. And when their partners offer them training for world-class competence and international connections, their entrepreneurial and learning-oriented skills enable them to take advantage of new opportunities.

FACTORS HELPING SMALL BUSINESSES START AND THRIVE

If small businesses are vital to America's economic growth, then it is important to understand the factors that help them flourish. Key ingredients include:

- Access to cutting-edge ideas (technology transfer from research centers to commercial enterprises);
- Capital availability;
- Networks to support small business at every stage, from startup through revitalization.

These ingredients of success are especially clear in regional economies, as the following examples will illustrate.

Ideas and Innovation: The Role of Research Centers

Business startups in technology fields often build on leading-edge developments from research universities and technical laboratories. The ideas that emanate from these centers—which are heavily supported by government funding—are the basis for large numbers of new business ventures, indirectly or directly. Three important research universities alone—Massachusetts Institute of Technology (MIT), Stanford, and the University of California—account for half the university license agreements with business in the United States. MIT and Stanford can be considered as the foundation of much of America's post-World War II technology prowess, giving rise to the Route 128 and Silicon Valley high-tech regions.

The economic impact of research at MIT provides an important illustration. MIT has a long history of spawning companies, beginning in the 1880s with engineering consulting firms Stone & Webster and Arthur D. Little. In the 1920s, MIT helped create Raytheon, in the 1940s E G & G and Polaroid, in the 1950s Digital Equipment, in the 1960s Analog Devices. By 1988, MIT's entrepreneurship guru, Edward Roberts, estimated that fully 72% of the new high-technology businesses established in the Boston area since 1975 could trace their origins to an MIT affiliation. A 1989 Chase Manhattan Bank study found 225 companies in Silicon Valley with MIT roots, showing combined revenues of $22 billion. MIT-spawned companies are often world leaders in applying technology to a range of fields. A 1997 BankBoston study showed that MIT graduates have started 4,000 companies, with 1.1 million jobs and $232 billion in 1994 sales worldwide—economic power equal to the 24th largest world economy. Within the United States, companies started by MIT graduates employed 733,000 people—one out of every 170 jobs in America—and 85% of these jobs were in manufacturing, compared to 16% nationally. Over 125,000 of these were in the Boston area.[3]

The role played by research centers can be more active than simply educating people who later decide to start companies.

Between 1986 and 1995, the MIT technology-development team helped create 67 companies and closed several hundred license agreements with existing companies. And over half of MIT inventions are licensed to industry within one year of the issue of a patent. MIT also participates in alliances and consortia, such as its venture with Kopin Corporation, a manufacturer of flat-panel displays, and Philips Electronics North America to commercialize liquid displays for high-definition television and multimedia computer systems, with the U.S. Commerce Department providing half of the $12.4 million funding.

Several states have established their own technology centers to strengthen the link between knowledge developers at universities and knowledge commercializers in business, such as Ohio's Edison program, Pennsylvania's Benjamin Franklin Partnerships, or Massachusetts' Centers of Excellence and now its High Technology Center.

Capital Availability

Ideas and the license to pursue them is not enough without the capital to create the business. The success of high-technology regions has rested heavily on the development of the venture-capital industry. In 1956, American Research and Development, perhaps America's first modern venture-capital fund which started in 1946 with money from Boston insurance companies, backed a young MIT-connected Lincoln Laboratory engineer, Kenneth Olsen, when he founded Digital Equipment to produce the first commercial minicomputer. ARD alumni launched similar firms, starting with Boston Capital in 1963. BankBoston became involved in loans for technology-oriented businesses in the 1960s and was the first bank to offer a specialty in environmental technologies.

When venture capital became a major force in the United States after a 1978 reduction in the capital-gains tax, America's venture-capital pool grew from under $3 billion in 1978 to over $16 billion in 1986, about 12% of which was concentrated in New England.[4] As Silicon Valley grew, the center of venture capital shifted from the East Coast to the West, and venture capitalists began to offer risky start-up funding to young companies that they had avoided previously. Lack of capital is a perennial complaint of small businesses; participants in my five-region survey pointed to this problem and blamed banks for cutting back on small-business loans.

Networks and Collaboration: From Startup to Renewal

An environment for entrepreneurship rests on voluntary social ties, along with the quantity and quality of interactions among people and companies in an industry. These ties and exchanges not only stimulate greater innovation, they also keep people focused on the entire community as an arena for innovation, as new spin-offs emerge from established companies (for example, at least ten software companies were started by people leaving Apollo Computer), as service companies grow to provide specialized support for the industry, and as companies hire each other's people.

The MIT Enterprise Forum, begun in 1978 after a series of informal workshops for MIT alumni, is the model for entrepreneurial networks: a way to make contacts, boost know-how for new ventures, and get practical help in producing business plans. For example, Eric Giler, founder of Brooktrout Technologies, which manufactures voice- and fax-messaging equipment, first discussed his business concept in a start-up clinic at the forum in 1984; 10 years later Brooktrout had about $25 million in revenues. The Enterprise Forum, a revenue-producing venture for MIT's alumni association, has 15 chapters in the United States and 4 international ones in countries with a significant MIT-alumni population, including Israel and Russia.

The independence of entrepreneurs and small businesses is often stressed in popular lore, but the truth is that small businesses gain competitive advantage through collaborative advantage. One study showed that collaborators make more money: technology-intensive new ventures engaging in a variety of cooperative arrangements for product development enjoy higher sales growth.[5]

Small companies derive considerable benefit within their local markets from industrywide and geographically diverse partnerships. These networks can then help propel them into global markets or gain collective strength to recapture a portion of the purchasing dollars giant companies now spend outside the region. To gain the advantages of larger companies' reach over many locations, some smaller companies form cross-company networks, such as the joint-marketing groups organized by Latin American airlines in Miami.

Network membership is a core element of the business concept for many growth companies. For example, the head office of an employee-benefits consulting firm manages a network of independent local-service providers wherever its large national clients have facilities. A specialty construction company works through a network of builders and other groups in skilled trades and crafts to bid together on large contracts. For others, alliances and networks expand markets and distribution. Membership in an international law network provides referrals to a Cleveland law firm and a network of experts to service its clients elsewhere. In Seattle, a group of nine small software companies have formed a cooperative; this maintains each company's independence but offers collective clout.

Small emerging companies benefit most from local networks that provide opportunities for informal exchange of people and ideas, as well as more formal alliances. Over half of the 2,655 companies in my five-region survey engaged in widespread informal local networking; over a quarter occasionally collaborated locally on marketing or special promotions and management education; and over 15% participated with one another on research or worker-skills training. Local business collaboration is associated with collaboration elsewhere. Local joint activities and local networking were slightly more likely to be found in growth industries in new technology areas with international aspirations, and somewhat less likely to be found in older, capital-intensive manufacturing companies serving primarily national markets.

The power of networks for small business is confirmed outside the United States. In Britain, a study showed that entrepreneurs succeeding at product innovation are involved in more professional organizations and have the highest percentage of outsiders in their personal networks. In the successful companies, managers other than the founder also have many contacts, and they travel more.[6] In two Italian industrial districts, network ties among 103 small and midsize firms ensure learning as well as reduced costs through flexible specialization.[7] Competitiveness is network-embedded, a matter of connections across companies. For innovation, an entrepreneur must create, manage, and recombine sets of relationships with external suppliers. The ability to glue together external expertise and capabilities in original and unique ways is a key factor for innovation. Entrepreneurs orchestrate interfirm linkages.

If networks are important to business success, then their absence can cause companies to fall behind, which is a problem my research shows plaguing many inner-city businesses. Minority-owned businesses focusing on urban markets were often isolated from wider access to cutting-edge ideas, capital, and new business opportunities.[8] It is not enough to have a viable business idea; it is also important to have a network of relationships with sophisticated suppliers, customers, venture partners, or colleagues.

Networks and collaboration are equally vital in manufacturing centers with older industries. Regional collaborations can help transfer competence to companies falling behind and from larger firms to smaller ones.

Strong, active chambers of commerce can be catalysts for business networks, establishing an infrastructure for collaboration. The Spartanburg, South Carolina, Chamber of Commerce's programs have directly improved business performance and lured international manufacturing jobs to the region because of a base of trained workers and excellent small-company suppliers. The chamber has a vice president for quality, signifying its activist role in industry. Its Quality in the Workplace program was launched in 1984, very early in the total-quality movement in the United States. It extended the quality principles in use at local companies such as Milliken; when Milliken won the Baldrige Award in 1989, the program became even more widely used, especially in smaller companies without internal quality staff.

Neighboring Greenville's Chamber of Commerce also facilitates collaboration among companies, in order to exchange best-practice ideas, screen employees for jobs, encourage new companies to come to the area, solve each other's problems, and sometimes lend staff. A monthly chamber-sponsored manufacturers' discussion group helps with employee-relations problems and serves as a job-finding network circulating resumes and lists of names. When Sara Lee opened a local plant, Fuji's plant manager helped Sara Lee develop team-management concepts.

A similar kind of collaboration in Massachusetts helped revitalize established companies. The Center for Quality Management in Cambridge was started in 1989 by seven manufacturing companies of varying sizes to develop courses and build links with leading Japanese practitioners. The center arranged a visit to NEC in Japan and developed numerous local university affiliations. Such organizations create a cascade effect that increases the sophistication of small companies supplying larger ones. A 1993 study of 123 manufacturing companies in New England found that 10% already attained certification under ISO 9000, the emerging international quality standard, compared with only 1% companies nationally; 13% planned to register by the end of the same year; and 39% planned to register by the end of 1994. About half the executives said they were doing it to satisfy major customers.[9]

Older manufacturing industries that had lost jobs to cheaper offshore producers are engineering a comeback through intercompany collaboration. For example, the Massachusetts textile industry has discovered niches for survival, including high productivity and fast turnaround time for exporting. Buckley & Mann, a manufacturer of nonwoven fabrics founded in 1856, merged in 1994 with Draper, a textile manufacturer in a neighboring town. The consolidated company now considers itself one of the most innovative small mills in the country. The formerly regional industry has become a network, with hundreds of companies operating like a large family that calls each other frequently for support and information.

THE AGENDA FOR SMALL BUSINESS AND ENTREPRENEURSHIP

This article has argued that small-business vitality is critical to the growth of the American economy—for job creation, economic smoothing and security, revitalization of depressed regions, efficiency in large manufacturing firms, and perhaps most important, innovation. We have also seen that the fates of small and large businesses are intertwined, especially in manufacturing industries.

For small business to continue to thrive, policy makers should pay attention to the entire business system, not just the individual company. They should consider the role of key institutions in every economic region that help businesses start, grow, and renew themselves—research centers, capital sources, business associations, industry councils, supplier-customer partnerships, mediating institutions that help entrepreneurs gain skills and contacts, and informal networks.

Many economic development programs center around reducing costs of doing business, and small-business owners are often the loudest complainers about the burdens of taxes and regulations. Certainly excessive burdens should be removed, especially those that create administrative problems for small business without clear social and economic benefit. But basing economic policy on the cost side of the equation does not guarantee success—and only encourages a "race to the bottom" in which regions compete to give tax breaks to attract and hold companies. The regions that are preeminent in entrepreneurship and innovation do not necessarily have the lowest costs. Instead, they are rich in the engines of innovation and the infrastructure for collaboration that ensure that small businesses will grow and prosper through business excellence.

NOTES

1. Rosabeth Moss Kanter, *World Class: Thriving Locally in the Global Economy* (New York: Simon & Schuster, 1995).

2. Kanter, chapter 4.

3. *MIT: The Impact of Innovation* (Boston: BankBoston, 1997).

4. Kanter, chapter 8.

5. Jeffrey E. McGee and Michael J. Dowling, "Using R&D Cooperative Arrangements to Leverage Managerial Experience," *Journal of Business Venturing*, vol. 9 (January 1994): 33–48.

6. Tone A. Ostgaard and Sue Birley, "Personal Networks and Firm Competitive Strategy," *Journal of Business Venturing*, vol. 9 (July 1994): 281–305.

7. Andrea Lipparini and Maurizio Sobrero, "The Glue and the Pieces: Entrepreneurship and Innovation in Small-Firm Networks," *Journal of Business Venturing*, vol. 9 (March 1994): 125–38.

8. Kanter, chapter 6.

9. *Massachusetts High Tech*, February 17, 1994.

Improving Productivity at the Firm Level

RICHARD M. CYERT, PRESIDENT
EMERITUS, CARNEGIE MELLON
UNIVERSITY

STUART W. ELLIOTT, RESEARCH
FELLOW, CARNEGIE MELLON
UNIVERSITY, AND VISITING
SCHOLAR, RUSSELL SAGE
FOUNDATION

Much of the discussion about growth in the economy is concerned less with growth and more with managing the business cycle. It's easy to confuse these issues because the stages of the business cycle are measured by fluctuations in the economy's overall growth rate. A crucial distinction is that the business-cycle discussion concerns the fluctuations, whereas the growth issue concerns the underlying trend in the economy's capacity to produce. It is indisputably important to minimize the likelihood and severity of a recession over the short run; over the long run, however, there would be far more impact from maximizing the economy's ability to grow. The effects of the business cycle are largely transitory, whereas the effects of true growth are cumulative. Increasing output an extra 1% in a given year by avoiding a recession will affect the output of only *that* year, but increasing output an extra 1% by improving productivity will affect the economy's output for years to come.

When focusing on the business cycle, it is possible to confine attention to the macroeconomic level. Although any economic change must be carried through at the microeconomic level by individual firms and workers, the macro policy drivers of tax policy, budget deficits, and interest rates have proven to be remarkably successful in influencing the business cycle. However, our understanding of the processes underlying growth is less developed, and our ability to influence growth has been less successful. Despite the popularity of supply-side measures, which promise to increase long-run investment and thereby promote growth, they seem to act primarily as traditional demand-side measures that affect the economy by influencing the business cycle rather than the underlying growth rate. Given our lack of understanding about the growth process, it is not sufficient to focus on the macro level; it is necessary to understand the process of change at the micro level to begin to understand what kinds of policies might be successful in promoting growth.

The size of an economy's output depends on the population size, the labor force participation rate, and labor force productivity. Total growth can result from increases in any of these three factors, but the third one is the most important focus for economic policy considerations. On the one hand, changes in population size have little net effect on per-capita income, as long as the scale of investments in both human and nonhuman capital is changed accordingly. On the other hand, substantial change in the labor-force participation rate, such as the enormous increase of labor-force participation by women over the past 50 years, reflects large social forces that cannot be analyzed adequately or influenced effectively from an economic perspective alone. Therefore, an economic discussion of growth must focus primarily on the growth of labor-force productivity.

To begin to understand what kinds of policies might be successful in promoting economic growth, it is necessary to understand the process of change at the micro level.

THE "SEARCH" FOR PRODUCTIVITY GROWTH

One useful way to think about productivity growth at the micro level is to consider a firm's behavior as a *search process*. For over 40 years, search theory has played an important role in the analysis of individual behavior by psychologists and that of firm behavior by economists and managerial theorists. According to the theory, a search process begins with a stimulus for change that defines the goal of the search. Once a search has been initiated and its goal defined, information is assembled about the possible actions that may satisfy the goal. Finally, a decision is made to take one of these possible actions.

Thinking about behavior in terms of search makes it clear how limits on information and attention can strongly influence how decisions are made. In this context, productivity improvements can be viewed as the result of firms trying to do something better; and to find a better way they engage in *search*. Each of the steps of search—the stimulus that defines the goal, the assembling of information, and the final decision for a particular action—affects the nature of the productivity changes that firms make.

Defining the Goal

The initial stimulus that defines a goal plays a strong role in shaping the final solution. In economic theory, a firm's goal is defined as maximizing profit, but in the real world the goal of profit maximization is too abstract to suggest actions the firm should take. Instead, the firm is likely to define its goal in terms that already clarify the way in which the search will be conducted. The goal might be to adopt the latest technology, to close a quality gap with the industry leader, or to cut production costs to a minimum. Each of these is clearly related to the larger goal of maximizing profit, but focuses on a particular arena of action. However, such focus diverts attention from other potential ways to increase profit, so that some very profitable actions may not even be considered. For instance, focusing on adopting new production technology may draw attention away from adopting new managerial technology. When firms increase their use of computers, they may focus on the computer technology itself and fail to realize that the optimal use of computers also requires that management restructure the organization. A recent study found that information technology is more productive when management adopts a decentralized organizational structure and increases investment in worker training.[1] And yet a goal defined in terms of computer technology itself makes it difficult to recognize that such substantial managerial changes are an important aspect of the goal.

Assembling the Information

After defining the goal, the next stage of the search process is to assemble information about potential solutions. Again, the way the goal is defined will bias the firm toward looking for certain kinds of solutions. Even within the range of solutions the firm is considering, however, it is impractical to consider all possible options. The search for information is costly and the value of each additional piece of information is unknown. This restricts the firm to considering a relatively small range of options that are fairly inexpensive to consider.

One way to see the difficulty of the process of assembling information is to measure the time it takes for a new technology to be adopted throughout the economy. A new technology may offer a superior way to satisfy some particular goal, but it can take a long time for this superiority to be recognized and accepted. For example, it took 15 years for computer numerically controlled machine tools to be adopted by only half of their potential users.[2] Although some of this time is spent waiting for existing capital to depreciate before new investments are made, much of it is spent as firms learn about what the new technology can do and how to use it. Firms located in regions with close access to information about a new technology are much more likely to adopt it than firms in regions that do not have such access. This access may occur either because there are a number of other firms in the region that are in the same industry or because there are universities in the region whose graduates have learned about the technology. It is possible that the Internet may allow some kinds of industry-specific information to be diffused more easily in the future, thus increasing productivity by shortening the time that new technology spends in the diffusion bottleneck.

Making a Decision

The final step is making the decision to take a particular action from those that have been assembled as possible ways of satisfying the goal. At this point, it is important to consider the criteria that management uses to make its decision. Of course, the interest rate will influence the level of investment that a firm is willing to make, but this is more important in determining the effect of the investment on the business cycle than its impact on productivity. However, other decision criteria systematically bias firms toward investing in old technology rather than in new technology, a bias that has a detrimental effect on productivity over the long run.

One obstacle to adopting new technology is the tendency of many American firms to use a short horizon in estimating the payback of an investment. Since new technologies frequently require a long period of training before they yield much payback, their short-run performance will not be a good indication of their long-term effectiveness. In contrast, using existing technology requires much less training, so short-run performance can be used as an accurate measure of long-term performance. Although a short payback horizon is acceptable for choosing between different existing technologies, when existing and new technologies are being considered, a short horizon will systematically bias firms in favor of the existing technology.

Another obstacle to adopting new technology is the tendency for American firms to overemphasize the importance of savings from labor costs. On the one hand, the optimal use of new technology often involves changes in organizational structure, changes that themselves can represent an important aspect of the savings. As discussed earlier, the productivity increase brought about by information technology appears to be greater when accompanied by organizational changes that decentralize authority and increase worker skill levels.

Optimal use of new technology often involves increasing quality in addition to, or instead of, cutting labor costs. A recent study found that companies using information technology to improve customer service have substantially higher productivity, but that companies using information technology solely to lower costs do not have higher productivity.[3]

This discussion of the search process leading to productivity improvement at the firm level points out the importance of learning as a determinant of productivity growth. Essentially, the changes that lead to productivity growth are the result of a process of learning, and so the possibilities for promoting growth lie in the possibilities for promoting that process.

IMPROVING PRODUCTIVITY GROWTH IN THE PRIVATE SECTOR

There is much that the private sphere can do to improve productivity growth. The first is that management must develop good search methods so that the firm is aware of new growth opportunities. It is also important that management set goals at the start of the search process that do not bias the firm against certain kinds of solutions, such as changes in management techniques. And it is important that management use decision criteria at the end of the search that do not bias the firm against new technologies that require an initial investment in learning. During the middle stage of the search, when the firm is assembling information about possible solutions, it is important that it has access to the latest research being done in industry and by university researchers. More specifically, it is critical to know when technology will be commercialized so that the firm's plans can take the newest forms of it into account. As noted earlier, firms learn from each other and so they should belong to active industry associations where information on new technology is circulated. An active industry association can play a significant role in making members aware of opportunities to improve technology and productivity.

Management plays a critical role in establishing an organizational environment that is capable of promoting and adapting to change. A flexible work environment can reduce the long period of organizational learning and adjustment when new technologies are introduced. There is evidence that current workforce-related approaches, when used as a total system, can increase productivity. Such an approach includes elements like incentive pay, work teams, employment security, skills training, communication, and other techniques.[4]

IMPROVING PRODUCTIVITY GROWTH THROUGH PUBLIC POLICY

Although there is much that management can do in the private sphere to promote productivity growth, public policy can also play an important role. At the public level, it is important to invest in a highly educated and trained workforce. Such education and training should be focused on basic and advanced skills that are broadly applicable across the economy. Labor-force participants who lack basic skills will always have a difficult time finding jobs and will be a drag on productivity. However, even experienced workers with basic skills can improve their contribution to productivity by learning advanced skills. All members of the workforce must continually upgrade their education level to achieve higher productivity. An educated worker adapts to new situations and particularly new technology more readily. Unlike investments in buildings or machinery, the investment in human capital can be partially achieved by public policy.

In addition to the role the government plays in education and training, it also plays an important role in supporting basic research and development, which provide the foundation for new technologies leading to further productivity growth. For example, much of the basic research underlying America's preeminent position in computer science has been supported by the Department of Defense and the National Science Foundation.

ACHIEVING TRUE GROWTH

True growth involves increases in productivity, and productivity growth at the micro level involves a process of learning and is likely to be influenced by policies that affect that process. Private and public spheres play important roles in fostering growth. Management also has a role by finding effective ways to search for new technologies and by creating a flexible and adaptive organizational environment. Government also has a major role by making appropriate public investments in the broad education and training of the workforce and in basic research and development leading to new technologies. To remain as the world's leading economy, the United States must pursue these various avenues to achieve high rates of growth. The cooperation of all segments of society is essential if we are to enhance the economic welfare of all.

NOTES

1. Unpublished work of Erik Brynjolfsson and Lorin Hitt, MIT Sloan School.

2. Maryellen R. Kelley and Susan Helper, "Firm Size and Capabilities, Regional Agglomeration and the Adoption of a New Technology," MIT IPC

Working Paper, (February 1996). See also Edwin Mansfield, "The Diffusion of Industrial Robots in Japan and the United States," *Research Policy*, 18 (1989): 183–192.

3. Erik Brynjolfsson and Lorin Hitt, "The Productive Keep Producing," *Informationweek*, 18 September 1995.

4. Casey Ichniowski, Kathryn Shaw, and Giovanna Prennushi, "The Effects of Human Resource Management Practices on Productivity: A Study of Steel Finishing Lines," *American Economic Review* (June 1997): 291–318.

Aggregate Productivity and Job Growth

Lessons from Companies

JOHN HALTIWANGER, UNIVERSITY OF MARYLAND; CENTER FOR ECONOMIC STUDIES AT THE BUREAU OF THE CENSUS

 News media reports about downsizing in corporate America and the aggregate statistics on jobs and growth paint a misleading picture of the dynamics of what is actually taking place in manufacturing establishments. Recent research with establishment-level data provides a new perspective, however. A key finding is that output, employment, and investment at the plant level are influenced more by idiosyncratic factors at individual companies than conditions in the overall economy. Seemingly similar businesses within the same industry exhibit substantially different behavior, both over the business cycle and the long run. In the fastest-growing industries, a large fraction of establishments experience substantial declines, while in the slowest-growing industries, a large portion of establishments exhibit dramatic growth. During severe recessions, virtually all industries decline, but each industry has a substantial number of establishments that continue to grow rapidly. Conversely, during robust recoveries, a substantial fraction of establishments contract.

Simply put, the underlying plant-level changes in activity dwarf the aggregate changes for the economy as a whole. Expressed another way, output, employment, and investment growth rates are quite different across establishments within narrowly defined sectors. The associated pace of the reallocation of outputs and inputs is quite high. Such reallocation inherently involves costs such as moving workers from one production site to another. The level of unemployment, as well as the growth rate of real activity, will reflect the efficiency of the economy in carrying out this reallocation.

ESTABLISHMENT-LEVEL EVIDENCE

This discussion is based on recent research using the Longitudinal Research Database (LRD) housed at the Center for Economic Studies at the U.S. Bureau of the Census. The LRD contains detailed data on individual U.S. manufacturing companies for the period 1963–1993. The data are from the Annual Survey of Manufacturers (ASM) and the Census of Manufacturers (CM). For further discussion of the properties of the LRD, see Davis, Haltiwanger, and Schuh (1996).

Aggregate Net-Employment Growth Rates Are Misleading

There is much more evidence of high job turnover at the firm level. Most of these job changes are permanent: when employment declines, jobs are abolished; when employment increases, jobs are more stable. The implication is that job changes depend much more on conditions at individual firms and factories and less on overall economic conditions. In other words, trends in manufacturing are more complex and heterogenous than previously believed.

First, let us look at the decomposition of net-employment growth into gross job creation and destruction. Gross job creation is defined as the sum of employment gains at all expanding establishments, and gross job destruction is defined as the sum of employment losses at all contracting establishments. Net-employment growth is simply the difference between the rate of gross job creation and gross job destruction. Examination of gross job-creation and job-destruction rates yield several striking patterns.

1. *Job-creation and job-destruction rates are remarkably large.* On average, one in ten jobs is created and one in ten destroyed every year in U.S. manufacturing. The gross job changes are larger than the net-employment changes observed from aggregate statistics. The implied rate of job reallocation is about 20%, which means that, about one in five jobs are reallocated across establishments every year.

2. *Most of the job creation and destruction observed over 12-month intervals reflects permanent changes.* On average, more than half of all jobs created and nearly three-fourths of all jobs destroyed in any year remain created or destroyed two years later. Even during recessions, such permanence is high—in fact, in recessions a greater proportion of job destruction is permanent while only a slightly lesser proportion of job creation is permanent. This contrasts with the common perception that most job loss in recessions is temporary.

3. *Job creation and destruction are concentrated at establishments that experience large employment changes.* About two-thirds of all jobs created or destroyed are at establishments that expand or contract by at least 25% in one year. About one-quarter of job destruction takes place at establishments that shut down completely. In contrast, total manufacturing net employment rarely changes by as much as 5% per year.

4. *Job-destruction rates exhibit greater cyclical variation than job-creation rates.* In particular, recessions are characterized by a sharp increase in job destruction accompanied by a relatively mild slowdown in job creation. This striking asymmetry is impossible to detect in the aggregate data. Further, and most important, this result is one indicator that the establishment-level heterogeneity doesn't simply "cancel out" at the aggregate level.

5. *Idiosyncratic factors dominate the determination of job creation and destruction.* Easily observable factors such as industry, region, employer size and age, capital and energy intensity, wage level, and exposure to foreign competition account for very little of the differences in job growth across establishments. Put differently, most of the job reallocation observed reflects the reallocation of employment opportunities across establishments in the same narrowly defined sector.

The magnitude and pervasiveness of job creation and destruction fit imperfectly with common conceptions about structural adjustment in the economy. To be sure, it is widely understood that market economies reallocate resources in response to the emergence of new products and production techniques. However, the common perception is that these factors are reflected in differences in growth rates between sectors. That is, sectors facing favorable changes in cost and demand conditions expand, while sectors facing unfavorable changes contract. While these between-sector employment shifts are often important, the results show rather strikingly that they are dwarfed by the magnitude of the within-sector employment shifts across establishments. The tremendous heterogeneity among seemingly similar businesses underscores the complexity of economic growth. In the next section, the implications of this heterogeneity is considered for productivity dynamics.

Implications of Reallocation for Productivity Growth

One useful way to characterize the role of reallocation in productivity growth is to examine the connection between the role of downsizing and changes in productivity. During the 1980s, manufacturing industries, on average, experienced rising labor productivity and falling employment. This led to the conventional wisdom that rising labor productivity in manufacturing had been driven by the pervasive downsizing during this period. Examination of the establishment-level data, however, shows that establishments that increased employment as well as labor productivity contributed almost as much to overall labor-productivity growth as establishments that increased labor productivity at the expense of employment. In addition, more productive entering establishments displaced less productive exiting establishments, a phenomenon that contributed approximately 30% to the increase in labor-productivity growth over the 1980s.

It is useful to classify establishments into four groups:

1. Successful upsizers, which grew and raised productivity;

2. Unsuccessful upsizers, which grew but did not raise productivity;

3. Successful downsizers, which shed labor and restored productivity growth;

4. Unsuccessful downsizers, which shed labor but did not raise productivity.

Establishments in mature industries (e.g., steel) were more likely to follow the conventional wisdom, namely, a disproportionate number of them fell into the successful downsizer group. Establishments in the Sunbelt and New England are disproportionately represented in the successful upsizer group. The smallest establishments are disproportionately represented in the group that increased employment and decreased labor productivity. Strikingly, the largest establishments are disproportionately represented in the group that increased both employment and labor productivity.

In spite of the striking differences across sectors, most of the variance of labor productivity growth is accounted for by idiosyncratic factors. For example, four-digit industry differences account for only 13% of the variance of establishment-level productivity-growth rates.

Not only is job reallocation important for changes in labor productivity, reallocation of resources and technology is important for total-factor productivity. Specifically, the reallocation of output to establishments with rising productivity, and away from less productive exiting establishments, accounts for about half of the growth in total-factor productivity in manufacturing over the 1980s. In addition, the contribution of reallocation to productivity growth varies over time, suggesting that understanding fluctuations in aggregate productivity growth requires tracking reallocation.

THE ROLE OF THE ECONOMY

An understanding of productivity and job growth requires an analysis of establishment-level data. Simply examining industry-level data on jobs and productivity misses most of the crucial information and yields a very misleading picture of the micro level. Aggregate productivity and job growth can only be understood by examining the complex patterns and interactions among those establishments that are expanding and lowering both employment and productivity. In short, the research mentioned earlier suggests that the success of the economy in terms of aggregate job and productivity growth depends in large part on the ability of the economy to continuously reallocate jobs, capital, and output to the most successful establishments.

REFERENCES

Baily, M., E. Bartelsman, and J. Haltiwanger. "Downsizing and Productivity Growth: Myth or Reality." *Small Business Economics,* (August 1996):259–278.
Davis, S., J. Haltiwanger, and S. Schuh. *Job Creation and Destruction,* Cambridge: MIT Press, 1996.
Haltiwanger, J. "Measuring and Analyzing Aggregate Fluctuations: The Importance of Building from Microeconomic Evidence." *Proceedings of the Annual Policy Conference of the St. Louis Federal Reserve* (1997).

NOTES

The views expressed here are those of the author and do not necessarily reflect the opinions of the Bureau of the Census. The paper draws heavily from the results and discussion in Baily, Bartelsman, and Haltiwanger (1996), Davis, Haltiwanger, and Schuh (1996), and Haltiwanger (1996). See these for discussion of the methodology and data underlying the results reported here as well as references to the extensive related literature.

4

People Are Key

The Power of Employees

ROBERT A. LUTZ, VICE CHAIRMAN, CHRYSLER CORPORATION

Employee empowerment may not be the only management practice needed to forge and sustain a modern, successful company, but it is an essential one. Competitive efficiencies and a strong return to shareholders depend on constantly improving the productivity of capital, materials, and, most important, people. People productivity is also the engine of rising living standards, and empowered employees are the fuel.

Chrysler used to develop new products with the traditional method of separate and sequential operations. The design office would throw a new design "over the wall" to the engineering office, which often had to throw the design back because it was not feasible or was not compatible with engineering standards. The engineering office would try to work within the confines of the design and would, in turn, throw its rework of the design over the wall to the procurement-and-supply office. Procurement and supply would let the specifications out to multiple competing suppliers and would usually accept the lowest bid. The whole package was then tossed over another wall to manufacturing, which had to try to figure out how to make the vehicle. At the end of the whole process were the sales and marketing people, who were told to go sell the thing. The results were long development times, huge costs, and, often, uninspired products. The products were uninspired because so were the people creating them. Nobody really had any ownership of the final result.

Then in the late 1980s, we began to rearrange the company into crossfunctional "platform teams." Chrysler has one platform team for each major type of vehicle: small cars, large cars, minivans, light trucks and jeeps vehicles. The major principle is to organize people around the *flows of information* rather than around functions. So, instead of separate departments working independently, we now have one team made up of designers, engineers, procurement specialists, and manufacturing people all working on the same vehicle simultaneously from concept to launch. All of the blending of resources and decisions about trade-offs are made at the team level. Senior management defines the *what* of the concept (the constraints, the budget, etc.), while the teams determine *how* to accomplish the goals. The results are development times that have been cut almost in half, much lower costs, much improved quality, and leading-edge products that have helped to boost our market share significantly.

It's not surprising that organizing the company around platform teams has had a major effect on employee morale. Employees are more enthusiastic than they used to be; they engage in more broad-gauged thinking and come up with more productive ideas than in the past. They are no longer compartmentalized and told to work on just one small part of the vehicle; they share responsibility for the whole product. And the company, its shareholders, the communities in which we operate, our suppliers, and, last but not least, our customers are the beneficiaries.

We have also expanded the principle of empowerment to our suppliers. The SCORE program (Supplier COst REduction Effort) is our initiative to reduce the costs of making cars and trucks by eliciting ideas from suppliers and agreeing to share any reduced costs with them. After suppliers learned that we were true to our word, they quickly provided a number of ideas. As a result, cumulative reduced costs amounted to more than $2.5 billion at the end of 1996. The SCORE program is also an integral part of what we call Chrysler's Extended Enterprise, concept with suppliers—described recently in an article in the *Harvard Business Review* as an "American keiretsu." This program treats all suppliers as true *partners*, since we know that our fortunes and theirs rise and fall together. This empowerment is already leading to further reductions of cost and a flood of new ideas.

But empowerment by itself won't ensure success. A company must also have the kinds of employees and suppliers that are comfortable accepting broader responsibilities, and who have the discipline and training to capitalize on them. And the company needs executives with the confidence to truly trust its employees and suppliers. Everybody involved in the enterprise must also be able to combine the kind of right-brained thinking associated with creativity, innovation, and intuition with the left-brained traits of discipline and problem-solving skills. They have to be empowered to make decisions based on both calculation and intuition, and they must be allowed to make some mistakes because mistakes are essential to learning.

Empowered, "full-brained" employees drive up productivity; and the longer that happens, the better the results. We now have a "thinking organization" in which success has become repeatable. Our vital statistics as a company have improved with every new vehicle introduced in the last five years.

Furthermore, our ongoing success does not depend on one or two outstanding individuals working their wills on the company. Instead, it depends on thousands of competent, sensible, and empowered employees, transcending leadership by communicating among themselves, working together in teams, and continually improving the processes.

Having said all that, there is a natural proclivity of individuals and organizations to take any good thing too far, which is a risk that can come with empowerment. Too much of one kind of thinking or another leads to imbalance. You can't quantify everything or depend solely on creativity without the balance of common sense. Too much focus on what the customer wants, for example, can lead to products that satisfy what the customer used to want or currently wants, but fail to satisfy those desires at the time the product actually reaches the market.

Too much teamwork can lead to lack of accountability group-think. The fashion nowadays is to acclaim teamwork almost like motherhood and apple pie. But teamwork taken too far can hinder creativity. Sometimes it's considered politically correct to say that all good ideas must be the products of collective thinking rather than individual thought. In fact, some truly new and different ideas that can be squashed by groupthink require an intellectual defiance on the part of the thinker in order to survive.

Too much emphasis on counting the beans can lead to neglect of the bean patch. The goal of business is not to make money, but rather to make great products out of which the money will flow.

Similarly, too much emphasis on strategy and detailed planning can lead to failure if they don't allow the flexibility needed to adapt to unanticipated changes, which will almost inevitably take place because, for example, interest rates go up, or a key supplier's plant burns down, or the competition turns out to be smarter than you thought.

As we look around the world, we see more and more companies casting aside their old cultures and incorporating whole-brained thinking to become continually more efficient. They are abandoning their old "command-and-control" systems, which have proved too inflexible and too lethargic to keep pace with today's fiercely competitive global economy. As they have undergone such transformations, they have found—as we have at Chrysler—that they are gaining competitive advantages from working together in teams and from empowering employees.

But, in the end, there is no silver bullet, except maybe a corporate mind open to new ideas and disciplined by common sense.

The Economic Power of Ideas

ROBERT J. SHAPIRO, VICE PRESIDENT,
PROGRESSIVE POLICY INSTITUTE

Let us begin by acknowledging that a democratic government's proper role in the economy is determined not by a consensus among its economists, but by the votes of a majority of its citizens. Should there be any doubt, compare the inflation preferences and roles for central banking in Germany, Italy, and the United States, or the range of approaches in advanced nations to regulating access to health care. What economists bring to public-policy debates are not answers, but historical perspective and informed suggestions about how different policies might affect future outcomes.

By historical standards, the American economy in recent decades has grown at a significantly slower rate than it used to. Since the early 1970s, the economy has expanded by barely 2.3% to 3% a year after inflation, compared to 3.5% to 4% annual real growth in the 1950s and 1960s, and 3.7% average annual real growth from 1870 to 1969.[1] Because strong growth is a condition for broad upward mobility, the last two decades also have been a period of very modest income progress for most Americans. Typical 20- or 30-year olds who entered the workforce in 1950 roughly doubled their real income by the time they reached age 40 or 50 in 1970. By contrast, most working people increased their real incomes by only 10 to 15% from 1970 to 1990, with only the most affluent one-fifth of Americans continuing to make strong income gains over that period.

Can the U.S. economy grow faster in the future? Yes it can, but not as a result of any policy change. Faster growth can come only from people in private businesses developing new ideas and skills to create new value.

WHAT MAKES THE ECONOMY GROW?

One reason for slow growth may be that the economic policy debate has been dominated by faulty assumptions about what drives growth. For more than a generation, the reigning assumption of most economic policy has been that the key to faster growth is increased national saving channeled into increased business fixed investment. These views have a long pedigree. Since economists first noticed that the triumph of industrialism coincided with a sustained investment boom in plant and equipment, many have assumed that these investments held the key to growth. And for the many decades when international capital flows were small and not much noticed, it seemed reasonable to assume that the U.S. could invest no more than it saved.

Neither view can be fully sustained today. U.S. investment depends much less than it used to on how much we save, because our capital markets operate in a global system that makes the whole world's savings available to firms willing to pay the price to borrow it. Furthermore, how much our businesses invest depends on their prospects for earning returns that exceed the cost of long-term borrowing. Business investment depends primarily not on domestic savings, but on sound macroeconomic policies that maintain low interest rates and on how productive our firms and workers are.

Yet our policies have chased the illusion that the best way to restore strong growth is to cut taxes on personal saving and business capital. By 1983, roughly 80% of all personal saving received some form of tax preference.[2] From 1970 to 1990, corporate tax revenues as a share of GDP fell by half, from 3.2% to 1.6%.[3] And from 1977 to 1990, the federal tax burden on the top 10% of Americans who own most corporate stock declined by more than 8%.[4] Including both corporate and individual taxes, the effective tax burden on capital income is now roughly 16%, or less than two-thirds of the tax burden on labor income.[5]

By virtually any measure, these strategies have failed. Since 1980, the personal saving rate has fallen from roughly 6% of GDP to 4%. Nor has business investment been much more responsive to tax incentives: after replacing worn-out plant and equipment, U.S. companies took on additional capital investments at a lower rate than before despite the tax inducements. Finally, the economy's underlying growth rate has failed to rise.

These results do not surprise economists familiar with a generation of econometric analysis of growth. Nobel laureate Robert

Solow analyzed America's economic record from 1909 to 1949 to measure the relative role of various factors.[6] He found that apart from the growth of the workforce, the expanding stock of business plant and equipment accounted for about 12% of the growth of that period. The other seven-eighths of growth could be traced to technological progress and improvements in the skills and use of workers.

Edward Denison reached generally similar conclusions analyzing the postwar years of strong growth from 1948 to 1973.[7] He found that economic innovation accounted for 37% of the nation's 3.8% average annual growth in GDP. U.S. worker's rising education and work experience accounted for 29% of the growth, while 15% was traced to increases in business plant and equipment. In addition, greater economies of scale in corporations and shifts of labor and capital to more efficient uses each accounted for about 10% of growth.

The heart of growth, in short, lies not in how much new plant and equipment the economy adds, or even how many new workers, but in the *knowledge embodied in both*. The chief reason is that everything in economic life *except* knowledge is subject to the law of diminishing returns. For example, a farmer with an acre of land cannot produce 100 times as much with 100 tractors as he or she could with 1. Similarly, the first employee a company hires will be assigned the task that generates the most profit; after that, each new hire will be put to uses that produce increasingly *lower* returns, because the more profitable uses have already been taken. This is one reason why in Germany and Japan, with saving and investment rates far higher than ours, business capital is one-third less productive than here.[8]

WHY IDEAS MATTER SO MUCH

New knowledge has unique economic qualities, as Paul Romer, one of the country's leading thinkers about innovation, has noted.[9] Unlike a piece of equipment or a worker, an idea can be used by any number of businesses at the same time. Once the cost of developing an innovation has been incurred, it can be used again and again at no additional cost. Finally, knowledge builds on itself, so that one innovation reduces the cost of the next—as the invention of the combustion engine paved the way for the automobile.

The role of economic innovation or knowledge extends to all aspects of economic activity. Technological progress, properly conceived, includes not only the development of new products, materials, and production methods, but also new ways of working, financing, marketing and distributing goods and services, and better ways of organizing the workplace and managing a business.

If this is so, why don't public-policy economists focus more on innovation and less on business fixed investment? The reason lies in the classical view of how markets work. Here's the puzzle: If well-oiled markets ensure that all capital and labor are already used efficiently, why would any firm incur the additional cost of coming up with a new idea, especially when the return is uncertain? The answer of traditional economics is that innovation occurs when someone has a bright idea and applies it, *not* because he or she has a rational economic incentive to come up with it. In technical terms, innovation is seen as *exogenous* to the economy, and therefore economic policy cannot affect the pace of economic innovation.

This answer sacrifices common sense to a narrow theory of markets, and in the process leaves economic policy with few ways of increasing the underlying growth rate *except* subsidies for business investment. But thousands of firms see what theory cannot: being first has its own rewards, because it creates a pocket of monopoly that raises an innovator's potential returns by holding back normal competitive pressures.

As a general rule, if a company tries to sell its product for more than it costs to produce it, plus a normal rate of profit, competitors will undercut it with lower prices. But when, for example, a software maker develops a powerful new program, market competition cannot force it to sell each copy at its marginal cost of production, so long as the innovation can perform useful tasks better than any other product. For a time, no one can compete with the new product, and the price that the company charges can include a monopoly profit that enables it to recover the costs of development and more.

So long as the monopoly holds, an innovating company can capture most of the new value produced by its new idea. And copyright and patent laws prevent a rival from simply appropriating the idea, duplicating the product, and selling it at a lower price that does not include the cost of development. Competitors, however, can study the innovation and learn from it—and, unlike a piece of equipment or a worker, the new idea can be used by more than one firm at the same time. In time, competition will usually drive an innovator's rivals to either produce a product that does what the innovator's did in a different way, or learn enough to go beyond it. The power of innovation to drive growth lies mainly in the additional value created by these competitive forces and spillovers.

People can be imbued with the economic power of ideas, as well as of objects and activities; and in the calculus of growth, the skills and education of the workforce come close behind innovation. In fact, our growing income inequalities largely follow from our patterns of investment in education. Most of the top 15% to 20% of Americans whose incomes have grown at healthy rates over the last 25 years—principally professionals and managers—are products of a higher-education system that is arguably the world's finest. In addition, once on the job, professionals and managers receive an estimated 70% of all training expenditures by private businesses. On top of that, the jobs they perform tend to enhance their knowledge and skills on a consistent basis because their positions require them to continuously evaluate new information and solve new problems. Based on their daily activities, they usually will know more at the end of the year than at the beginning, and so become more productive and efficient—and more highly paid.

By contrast, the real incomes of most other American workers have risen much more slowly. Most of them have been educated in our elementary and secondary public schools, which are often subjects of national despair. On the job, most office and factory workers receive little or no additional training after their orientation; and their work rarely exposes them to new information or demands new thinking. And by not gaining new knowledge or skills, many working people see their economic capacities slowly depreciate, leaving them relatively less productive and efficient—and less well paid.

Since better-trained workers are usually more productive, why do firms invest less in training than economic logic seems to demand? The principal reason is that workers have the freedom to get jobs with competitors. For example, if McDonald's trains a burger flipper to use a computer to monitor inventory, the worker's new skills may enable him or her to get a better position with a competitor, who then would reap the benefits of McDonald's training investment. This market failure especially affects less skilled workers. Large corporations spend liberally to ensure that their executives or in-house lawyers are up-to-date on management techniques and legal developments, because improving their decisions produces returns from all the workers they direct.

The result is that workers at the top generally receive the education and training they need to prosper, while many working people on the lower rungs receive less than they or the economy could profitably use. In the end, growth is less than it could be and inequality is greater than it need be.

WHAT GOVERNMENT CAN DO ABOUT GROWTH

There is no magic elixir in tax policy that will restore strong growth. Rather, faster growth can come only from people in private businesses developing new ideas and enhancing their skills. The government's proper role lies mainly in fostering conditions that are favorable to these private efforts.

The government can, for instance, help foster innovation by maintaining a favorable financial environment. Fiscal and monetary policy should maintain the expectation, reflected in the financial markets, that the era of big deficits and accelerating inflation is truly over, so long-term interest rates can remain relatively low. Rising interest rates discourage all investment; but they have a particularly adverse effect on R & D, because they reduce the net value of its future returns while increasing current returns on less risky investments. In this respect, faster growth will require long-term reforms in the government's largest and fastest-growing programs, namely Social Security and Medicare.

Government also can encourage innovation by strengthening the competitive forces that help drive it. For example, to the degree consistent with its social purpose, incentive-based environmental regulation can replace current command-and-control approaches. Further, today's spending programs that subsidize particular industries should be phased out. By artificially raising the rate of return for politically favored sectors and companies, these subsidies discourage innovation by reducing their need to create new ways of competing. Tax simplification can provide similar benefits. While some of the complications in the corporate tax reflect the economy's real complexities, many others testify to the ability of some industries to win special tax treatment. Like their counterparts in the budget, tax subsidies act as barriers to innovation because they reward companies for using their capital and labor in the same ways they have in the past.

Tax policy can also encourage businesses to increase their workers' incentives to create new ideas. For example, most large corporations today have bonus systems that reward executives and professionals for superior performance with stock or stock options. There is a well-established rule in tax policy that says when a company provides a tax-favored form of compensation, such as health care coverage or pension contributions, it cannot discriminate by excluding any significant group of employees. By applying the nondiscrimination rule to these bonus systems, we can encourage companies to provide every employee with a genuine incentive to come up with new ways of improving the firm's performance.

The additional training that many executives and professionals receive is also a tax-free form of compensation. If we apply the nondiscrimination rule here as well, firms would be encouraged to give all full-time workers opportunities to improve themselves. Workers who accept additional training, however, should have an obligation to the company that provides it to remain with the company for a reasonable period—much as stockbrokers and lawyers who receive extensive training must sign employment contracts to remain where they are for a specific period of time.

The government can also support innovation by pressing the case for open global markets and open trade. The traditional case for free trade stresses efficiency: every nation gains when everyone can buy the products they need at the lowest prices, regardless of who produced them. Just as important, open trade and open markets allow U.S. firms and workers to learn from, borrow, and improve on the ideas and advances of firms throughout the world, in effect placing the world's human capital at our disposal. In addition, open trade encourages investment in R & D because a larger potential market enables firms to spread the costs of developing new products over a larger base of potential sales.

Finally, spending and tax reforms should be used not only to reduce the deficit and lower tax rates, but also to support public investment in those areas that are crucial to growth and where private markets tend to underinvest. Government has an essential role to play in supporting basic research at the frontiers of science through spending and tax incentives. The government also must ensure that a lack of family resources does not preclude any student from attending college. Fiscal discipline is not an end in itself but a means for higher growth, and efforts to roll back public investment in these areas defeat this purpose.

For an advanced economy like the United States, the decisive factors for growth are not how much business invests in plant and equipment or how much government spends, but the capacity to expand our knowledge and imaginations in every aspect of economic life. Encouraging American workers and firms to do so is the proper role of national growth policy.

NOTES

1. Bureau of the Census, *Historical Statistics of the United States, Colonial Times to 1970,* part 1, (Washington, D.C., 1975), table F, 10–16; *Economic Report of the President,* (Washington, D.C., February 1996).

2. C. Eugene Steuerle, *Taxes, Loans and Inflation: How the Nation's Wealth becomes Misallocated,* (Washington, D.C.: Brookings Institution, 1985).

3. Calculations from *Economic Report of the President* (Washington, D.C., February 1996), tables B–1 and B–76.

4. House Committee on Ways and Means, *Tax Progressivity and Income Distribution,* 101st Cong., 2d sess., 26 March 1990, table I, 12.

5. Jane G. Gravelle, *The Economic Effects of Taxing Capital Income* (Cambridge: MIT Press, 1994); Steurele.

6. Robert Solow, "Growth Theory and After," *The American Economic Review* (June 1988): 307–317.

7. Edward F. Denison, *Trends in American Economic Growth, 1929–1982* (Washington, D.C., Brookings Institution, 1984).

8. *Capital Productivity* (Washington D.C.: McKinsey Global Institute, June 1996).

9. Paul M. Romer, "Endogenous Technological Change," *Journal of Political Economy* 98, no. 5, pt. 2 (1990): S71–S102.

Investing in Education and Training for Higher Growth

ANTHONY P. CARNEVALE, VICE
PRESIDENT FOR PUBLIC LEADERSHIP
AT THE EDUCATIONAL TESTING
SERVICE; FORMER VICE PRESIDENT
FOR THE COMMITTEE ON ECONOMIC
DEVELOPMENT; CHIEF ECONOMIST
AND VICE PRESIDENT FOR THE
AMERICAN SOCIETY FOR TRAINING
AND DEVELOPMENT

DONNA M. DESROCHERS, SENIOR
ECONOMIST, OFFICE OF PUBLIC
LEADERSHIP AT THE EDUCATIONAL
TESTING SERVICE

RICHARD A. FRY, SENIOR
ECONOMIST, OFFICE OF PUBLIC
LEADERSHIP AT THE EDUCATIONAL
TESTING SERVICE

As the American economy enters the new millennium, it faces three interrelated challenges:

1. The double whammy of relatively slow income growth and even slower growth in take-home pay;

2. The growing income disparity among Americans;

3. The insecurity that accompanies adaptation to a new global economic reality.

It is common knowledge that education and training investments are a key element in responding to these challenges. Millions of Americans have responded to the increasing economic value of learning by obtaining education and training beyond high school. Education and training markets are working but structural barriers to their efficiency and equity remain. In spite of agreement about on the economic value of education and training investments, there have been few, if any, dramatic public policy changes that have appreciably enhanced the impact of education and training on productivity, growth, income inequality, or the adaptive capabilities of individuals and families.

In this section we'll explore the United States' apparent inability to from a consensus in principle on the importance of education and training to concerted public action that matches resources to obvious needs.

TESTING THE PREMISES THAT UNDERLIE THE EDUCATION AND TRAINING CONSENSUS

Does Education and Training Increase Growth and Productivity?

Economic growth depends on our nation's ability to work smarter, not harder. Growth derives from two sources: growth of output per hour worked (productivity) and growth in hours worked. Since the end of World War II, the rate of growth in hours worked has increased steadily because of increases in the size of the labor force. As a result, most of the decrease in the growth rate since 1973 can be attributed to slower growth in productivity, rather than fewer hours worked. In order to solve our growth problems, we will have to achieve higher productivity.

Historically, about 27% productivity growth has relied on increased educational attainment[1] (Denison 1985). Without increased education—principally, improvements in high-school graduation rates—our economy would have grown even more slowly after productivity growth collapsed in the early 1970s. In the future, the contributions of education and training to productivity and overall growth should become even more important, as retiring baby boomers reduce the total number of hours worked and more of our economic growth relies on investments.

A number of other targeted studies tend to confirm the economy-wide data on the economic importance of education and training in improving productivity growth. One typical analysis states that increasing the education level of workers by one year increases productivity by 8.5% in manufacturing industries and 12.7% in nonmanufacturing industries (Black and Lynch 1996). Other studies find that formal employer-provided training increases productivity anywhere from 10% to 16% (Bartel 1989; Bishop 1994).

Do Education and Training Cause Income Differences?

Since the early 1970s, the gap between economic winners and losers in the global economy has widened because economic and technological change has increasingly demanded higher levels of education. It was not always so. The value of a college degree compared to a high-school degree actually declined in the 1970s, before it began to grow again in 1983. By the early 1990s, the earnings differences between high-school and college graduates had nearly doubled, from 49% in 1979 to 89% in 1993 (*Economic Report of the President* 1996). Each additional year of schooling after high school is estimated to be worth about 5% to 15% in additional earnings (*Economic Report of the President* 1996).

The economic benefits of education continue into the workplace. Those with more education and better skills are more likely to participate in high-performance workplaces in which they can further develop their skills and get more training on the job (Levine 1996; Krueger 1993). Workers who receive employer-based training earn 10% to 15% more than those who have similar education but do not receive on-the-job training. Workers with access to computer-based technology earn 15% to 25% more than similar workers who do not use a computer on the job (Mishel and Bernstein 1994; Krueger 1993).

Can Education and Training Reduce Income Inequality?

If unequal access to education and training creates earning differences, conversely, a more equal opportunity to learn can reduce such inequality. The evidence here is robust. The increased returns from education and training create parallel incentives for individuals to go to school and learn on the job in order to achieve wage gains. Americans have responded to the increased value of higher skill levels by educating and training themselves more. The proportion of college-age individuals attending college increased by one-third between 1980 and 1994, from 26% to 35%. Accordingly, the number of associates, bachelor's, and doctoral degrees awarded increased by 28%, 35%, and 29%, respectively, despite a 15% decrease in the college-age population (*Economic Report of the President* 1996).

It does not necessarily follow that the growing number of young people pursuing a college education will by itself reverse the growing wage premium associated with college education. Two observations cast doubt on the notion that a crash in the market for highly educated and trained individuals is imminent. First, although college attendance has grown, incompletion rates remain high, so that the proportion of 25- to 29-year olds actually attaining a bachelor's degree has risen only modestly. Second, the current college-age population is made up of baby-bust cohorts—so-called because they represent 50% fewer people than the baby boomers—so that there has not been, and will not be, an increase in the number of new B.A.s relative to the number of jobs.

Market forces will help move job supply and demand together among the advantaged, but providing the economically disadvantaged with more equal opportunity to learn will require an increasingly active response. As differences in earnings become even more dependent on learning opportunities, we will need to ensure more equal educational opportunities. Rising educational costs are a barrier to entry for students from low-income families. For instance, a 10% increase in costs reduces enrollments by about 2% among low-income students (*Economic Report of the President* 1996).

The experiences students receive in their K–12 education influence their later social mobility. Accumulating evidence suggests that improvements in the quantity and quality of the schooling received by disadvantaged individuals can narrow labor-market disparities. Money spent on education has more effect on labor-market outcomes than on schooling outcomes. For instance, a 10% increase in school expenditures produces no discernable difference in school performance, but a 10% increase in K–12 spending processes a 1% to 2% increase in annual earnings for students later in their lives (Card and Krueger 1992).

Can Education and Training Help Adults Adapt to New Learning Requirements on the Job?

As our economy changes, so do job requirements. Since the end of World War II, the overall proportion of manufacturing jobs fell from 35% to 16% of total employment (*Economic Report of the President* 1996). In general, the economy is producing high-skill, high-wage jobs in every industry, but continues to lose jobs, especially in manufacturing, that once paid well and required only high-school degrees.

Almost half of the new jobs created between 1983 and 1994 and projected through 2005 were in managerial and professional occupations; most of these were in service industries (Kutscher 1995). This situation raises the ante on skill requirements for anyone seeking employment, and a substantial number of Americans do not have the skills they need. Forty percent of all 17-year olds do not have the necessary math skills and more than 60% do not have the necessary reading skills to work in a production job paying $33,000 per year at a modern auto plant (Murnane and Levy 1996).

Skills are particularly important in this age of decreased employment security. More skill is not only necessary to get a job, but to keep one as well. Modern high-performance work systems require highly skilled employees who can think and act independently and in groups. As a result, employees need better basic, occupational, and problem-solving skills, as well as continuous skill upgrading. Employees in high-performance systems need to be more highly skilled in order to utilize widely distributed and flexible technology and to take on new responsibilities in flexible organizational systems (Carnevale 1991; Levine 1996).

Does Knowledge Result in Higher Wages or Are Employers Just Buying Degrees?

Economists agree that education and training on and off the job lead to higher earnings, but there is less agreement on why education and training produce higher earnings returns. Surely, some portion of the payoff to education and training is the result of both the real value of skill and the use of credentials for choosing among prospective employees. By one estimate, signaling accounts for as much as a third of the growth in the male college-wage premium and all of the increase in the growth of the female college-wage premium (Murnane and Levy 1996).

There is growing agreement, however, that earning differences attributed to education and training are actually a result of what people learned rather than the amount of time in school and the degrees they earned. After controlling for the effects of native ability and family background, studies show that more than 75% of what they learned in school remains with people of similar abilities and family background (*Economic Report of the President* 1996). Even among identical twins, those with more education tend to earn more (Ashenfelter and Krueger 1994); and, while there may not be agreement on the ultimate effect a college diploma has on future wages, there is little doubt that even a college learning experience without receiving a degree significantly increases earnings. A recent estimate suggests that a degree per se amounts to 50% of the total value of a college education (Jaeger and Page 1996).

MOVING BEYOND CONSENSUS

In spite of the consensus on the economic value of education and training, public investments in education have not increased dramatically. Per full-time equivalent student, real public spending on higher education increased from $6,690 per student in 1979–80 to $6,831 per student in 1992–93. Public investments in training, however, have actually declined since the late 1970s. Although private employer spending on formal training increased from $40 billion to $63 billion (in 1991 dollars) between 1983 and 1991, the proportion of employees receiving company training to qualify for their job and to improve their on-the-job skills is still relatively low, about 12% and 16%, respectively (Carnevale and Desrochers 1997; BLS 1992).

Barriers to Action

The lack of apparent action on education-and-training policy results from many factors. First, the consensus on a public investment strategy is oversold. Reaching common ground on any issue is always difficult in public discourse, and education and training provide common ground almost automatically. It is much easier to agree on the need for education and training than on any other policy options for addressing growth and equity, such as fiscal and monetary policy, industrial policy, affirmative action, or public-service jobs for the unemployed.

Second, the education-and-training consensus is trumped by an even broader consensus on our overall economic strategy. Arguably, the American government's consensus on deficit reduction and deregulation precludes substantial increases in public investments for education and training or substantial changes involving such issues as training mandates or skill standards. One typical analysis suggests that increasing overall federal spending on education and training from the current level of roughly $30 billion to as much as $120 billion would add about 0.1% to overall growth; but it would reduce savings available for private investments, including human capital investments, and would not generate sufficient revenue to pay for the new programs (Schultze 1997). Instead, we rely principally on the pull of increased earnings to encourage individual adaptation through private education-and-training investments, rather than the push of dramatically expanded public investments.

Third, the consensus on education and training does not translate into action because they are simply too expensive. Talk is cheap; education and training are not. For example, one estimate suggests that, given the current levels of efficiency in our education-and-training systems, it would cost as much as $1.6 trillion to reduce our growing income inequality to the more acceptable levels of 1979 (Heckman 1994). In order to meet on-the-job skill requirements, employers will have to spend an additional $15 billion between 1991 and 2005. In addition, they would have to spend another $65 billion to extend training from the current 27%[2] of all workers to 50%. Most agree that extending the school year from 180 to 220 days and reducing class sizes from 25 to 15 would make a difference in schooling outcomes, but the annual cost would be $150 billion (*New Republic* 1996). Our public job-training programs currently serve about 9% of dislocated workers and 1.5% of poor adults. By one estimate, an increase in annual earnings of $5,000 would be necessary to lift a welfare recipient out of poverty; a human capital investment of

$50,000 per welfare recipient would be needed to realize this gain (Heckman 1996).

Fourth, employer investments in training are inherently complex and incremental; and only the largest firms can afford to train. Not only is the structure of employer investments always changing, but also employers are constantly confronted with trade-offs between investments in education, and formal and informal training on the job. These trade-offs include the strategic value of hiring more-educated employees versus training less-educated hires; the value of formal training versus informal training embedded in work processes or technology-based job aid; and the trade-off between making or buying education and training. Therefore, employer education-and-training programs have not increased suddenly and dramatically because by themselves they rarely result in clear competitive advantages. Work-based training is valuable only when it is bundled with changes in work processes and technology. As a result, employer investments are always incremental and irregular. Only large employers have enough trainees to realize economies of scale in work-based training. In a school classroom, only the teacher gets paid; in a workplace training class, everybody is being paid. While large employers can afford high wages and benefits along with training, mid-sized and small employers who train lose their workers to other employers who pay higher wages and provide better benefits but who do not train.

Fifth, recent education-and-training proposals have not taken hold because they do not fit the decentralized structure of American education or the flexible structure of American labor markets. Since the early 1980s, education-and-training advocates have been enamored with reforms drawn from the heavily centralized education-and-training systems of European nations, especially Germany. Over the past decade, we have debated European-style reforms, including employer-training mandates, school-to-work apprenticeships, nationally regulated education, and skill standards, as well as national, regional, state, and local labor-market boards. These reform proposals presume highly centralized and tripartite governance systems with responsibility shared by business, labor, and government, which is an idea outside the American experience.

Americans also resist reforms that imply class distinctions in learning and opportunity. Our educational system has avoided the tracking of students into separate academic and occupational channels. European and Asian cultures, on the other hand, are more comfortable with such a dual system.

Sixth, the economic recovery that began in the second quarter of 1991 and the reemergence of America's global economic preeminence threw cold water on the urgency for education-and-training reform. It is commonly assumed that this reemergence was due, in part, to the inherent flexibility of our labor market. As a result, our recent economic success has dampened enthusiasm for reforms that might have actually reduced our flexibility and ability to adapt. If anything, the continuing American resurgence suggests to many, including many Europeans, the need for further deregulation, rather than increased regulation, in labor markets.

An Information Strategy

The key to eliminating the current impasse in our education-and-training dialogue is the use of information that allows us to assess how we are doing, to understand what works, and, ultimately, to match learning outcomes and economic opportunity. Better information on education outcomes, training outcomes, and current labor markets will reinforce and increase the efficiency of market incentives to invest in education and training that are already in place. These incentives preserve and even encourage flexibility in American labor markets, as well as individual responsibility and adaptation to economic change.

There is not enough new money, so we will have to use our current resources more effectively by encouraging more informed choices on the part of providers and consumers. Informed choices also increase access to more effective education and training, while preserving the current flexible structure of our education-and-training institutions. We want programs driven by informed choices from the bottom up, rather than creating a top-down bureaucratic mechanism to support lifelong learning. Such a system parallels recent private reforms among high-performance employers who use outcome measures and other information to integrate complex, even global, networks. These outcome-driven networks preserve the autonomy of individuals and institutions, but use performance-based information to encourage overall efficiency and consistent quality. For instance, adherents of the recent revamping in the health care industry have used information on costs and created outcome standards to drive reform among a bewildering and constantly changing array of health care providers.

Using information about the real impact of education and training to improve accountability is perhaps the only way we can afford the education and training we need. If we could get more bang for the $720 billion bucks we spend each year on education and training, we could increase the effectiveness of individual education-and-training decisions without massive in spending increases. For example, a 10% improvement in the effectiveness of the current $720 billion we spend each year on education and training would give us the equivalent of a $72 billion increase in funding. The easiest way to find this savings is by unleashing market forces that support efficient programs and efforts and reduce those that fail.

More effective education and training resulting from more informed choices by educators, trainers, individuals, and employers would increase the supply of skilled labor, thereby driving down college earnings premiums and income differences more quickly and effectively than by simply increasing the proportion of Americans with college degrees. Better information on learning outcomes and job opportunities would result in better matches between individuals and available jobs, reducing costly inefficiencies in labor-market transition. For instance, only between 4% and 26% of sectoral job changes from 1966 to 1980 can be attributed to sectoral shifts (Jovanovic and Moffit 1990). So, three-quarters or more of sectoral job changes would seem to be caused by job mismatches.

K–12 education

Efforts to measure outcomes in elementary and secondary education must be maintained in spite of pressures to abandon the effort. Over time, states and districts adapt their curricula to whichever standardized test they use (Carnevale and Kimmel 1997). As a result, the majority of students in most American school districts are above average—like the children in the mythical community of Lake Wobegon (Cannell 1988; Shepard and Dougherty 1991). State and local performance does not hold up on the few occasions when it is subjected to national or international standards. There are no nationwide standards that can be tracked to school districts, schools, or individual students. International comparisons are primitive.

Our ability to measure educational progress in elementary and secondary schools has stalled in the face of political difficulties. Comparative data create discomfort because they raise unfavorable racial, ethnic, and gender issues that point toward and, when used to govern access to schools and jobs, reinforce more profound inequalities in our society. Our assessments are the best measures of individual excellence, but they also measure our collective social failure to provide an equal opportunity to learn. When such data are released, elected officials and educators fear the hostility of an increasingly unforgiving public. Conservatives who have an understandable fear of big brother have also been adroit in blocking the creation of such measures.

Unless we begin to measure differences in performance, we cannot learn from them. In an environment where there is no obvious relationship between marginal differences in resources and outcomes, we need actionable information to get at the more profound differences in learning and teaching processes. For instance, New York spends $7,770 per pupil; Utah spends $2,967 per pupil, but 72% of Utah's students are judged proficient on the *National Assessment of Educational Progress* (NAEP) compared to 62% in New York (NAEP 1994). The Czech Republic spends a third as much per pupil as we do and has a worldwide ranking of 6th in math and 2nd in science, while the United States ranks 28th in math and 17th in science (NCES 1996).

Postsecondary education
There is ample evidence that markets work in higher education. Even as overall enrollments continue to increase, one-third of higher-education institutions lose enrollments every year as students vote with their feet. In addition, a substituted share of the public funding follows the students. In addition, community colleges, public and private four-year schools, proprietary schools, and virtual universities provide a diverse institutional basis for competition.

Better information could make postsecondary markets work better. Higher education is long overdue for measures that would demonstrate effectiveness in performing its economic mission. The current higher-education accrediting system is based on inputs, such as the number of books in the library, not outcomes. With the cost of higher education rising faster than nearly any sector in our economy, taxpayers and parents have the right to information such as those courses and schools that actually train students in ways that pay off and those school curricula that produce students best able to compete for and succeed in jobs. All colleges and universities should build on the experience of a growing number of public institutions that are collecting and publishing comparable data on costs, inputs, and outcomes (Education Commission of the States 1994).

Public training

Most in need of reform is training for disadvantaged and dislocated workers. This second-chance system is highly fragmented and poorly administered because it lacks measures on the effectiveness of education and training and information that links training to job prospects. Ironically, the most cost-effective services delivered in the public job-training system are not education and training, but job-search-assistance services that provide clients with information matching their skills with available jobs.

Current reforms that create one-stop career centers that provide information-based services such as counseling, job-search assistance, and education-and-training referrals based on full disclosure performance by education-and-training providers are the first steps in the right direction. Common definitions and standards for commonly provided services are an important next step to encourage performance comparisons across jurisdictions.

Private training

Large employers train effectively whenever they need to, but midsize and small employers cannot afford to train. Tax subsidies to encourage training among small employers could have a great number of positive results for relatively little money. A tax credit patterned after R & D tax credits would be most appropriate because R & D and employer-based training have similar risk profiles. Such a credit would encourage stronger links between employer and education-and-training providers, and promote complementarity and greater efficiency in the use of training dollars.

Labor market information

An important part of any robust information system is information that answers the question: Education and training for what? The government already has access to a significant amount of important job data. For instance, each quarter, private employers in the United States report wages, hours worked, and other information for all existing and new jobs. The government uses this information principally to verify eligibility for unemployment insurance and to locate people (e.g., parents who try to skip child-support payments). It would not be difficult to use these data to predict available jobs. Four times a year, wage records tell us where the jobs are. Once we know that, it is not hard to predict where the jobs will be.

Wage records also can be used to evaluate education-and-training programs. For example, think of the savings that could be captured if these records were searched to determine which training programs resulted in real wage increases and sustained employment and which had no effect. Trainers and educators— and consumers—would know the relative labor-market value of the training offered, as well as the training institutions. Providers that had poor records would get less business, while successful schools with very good records would attract consumers and grow. The information could also be used to improve the match between job training and available jobs.

Our ultimate objective should be to create a high-performance education-and-training system that allows for a decentralized education-and-training structure that would preserve the autonomy of individuals and institutions while using information to guarantee consistent quality and overall efficiency. Such a system would be relatively objective about where learning occurred, so long as providers were accountable to individuals, governments, business, and other final consumers. Usable information would preserve and enhance the flexibility of education-and-training markets, gradually eliminating existing institutional and technological barriers to lifelong learning.

REFERENCES

Ashenfelter, Orley, and Alan Krueger. 1994. Estimates of the economic return to schooling from a new sample of twins. *American Economic Review*, vol. 84, no. 5.

Bartel, Ann P. 1989. *Formal employee training programs and their impact on labor productivity: Evidence from a human resource survey.* Washington, D.C.: National Bureau of Economic Research, working paper no. 3026.

Bishop, John H. 1994. The impact of previous training on productivity and Wages. In *Training and the private sector: International comparisons.* Edited by Lisa Lynch. Chicago: University of Chicago Press.

Black, Sandra E., and Lisa M. Lynch. 1996. Human capital investments and productivity. AEA Papers and Proceedings, vol. 86, no. 2 (May).

Bureau of Labor Statistics, U.S. Department of Labor. 1992. *How workers get their training: A 1991 update.* Washington, D.C.: U.S. Government Printing Office.

Cannell, J.J. 1988. Nationally normed elementary achievement testing in America's public schools: How all fifty states are above average. *Educational Measurement: Issues and Practices*, vol. 7, no. 2 (summer).

Card, D., and A. Krueger. 1992. School quality and black/white relative earnings: A direct assessment. *Quarterly Journal of Economics*, vol. 107 (February).

Carnevale, Anthony P., and Donna M. Desrochers. 1997. *The high road, the low road and the muddy middle path,* forthcoming.

Carnevale, Anthony P., and Ernest Kimmel. 1997. A *national test: Balancing policy and technical issues.* Princeton, N.J.: Educational Testing Service.

Carnevale, Anthony P. 1991. *America and the new economy.* San Francisco: Jossey-Bass Inc.

Denison, Edward F. 1985. *Trends in American economic growth.* Washington, D.C.: Brookings Institution.

Economic Report of the President. 1996. Washington, D.C.: Government Printing Office.

Education Commission of the States. 1994. *Charting higher education accountability: A sourcebook on state-level performance indicators.* N.P.

Heckman, James J. 1994. Is job training oversold? *The Public Interest* (Spring).

Heckman, James J. 1996. What should our human capital investment policy be? *Jobs and Capital.* Santa Monica, Cal.: Milken Institute for Job and Capital Formation.

Jaeger, David A., and Marianne Page. 1996. Degrees matter: New evidence on sheepskin effects in the returns to education. *Review of Economics and Statistics* (November).

Jovanovic, Bryan, and Robert Moffitt. 1990. An estimate of a sectoral model of labor mobility. *Journal of Political Economy*, vol. 8, no. 4.

Krueger, Alan. 1993. How computers have changed the wage structure: Evidence from microdata, 1984–89. *Quarterly Journal of Economics* (February).

Kutscher, Ronald. 1995. Summary of BLS projections to 2005. *Monthly Labor Review.* (November).

Levine, David. 1996. *Reinventing the workplace: How business and employees can both win.* Washington, D.C.: Brookings Institution.

Mishel, Lawrence, and Jared Bernstein. 1994. *The state of working America, 1994–95.* Armonk, N.Y.: M.E. Sharpe.

Murnane, Richard J., and Frank Levy. 1996. *Teaching the new basic skills.* New York, N.Y.: The Free Press.

National Assessment of Educational Progress, 1994.

National Center for Education Statistics, U.S. Department of Education. 1996. Pursuing excellence: Study of U.S. eighth-grade mathematics and science teaching, learning, curriculum, and achievement in international context. NCES. Washington, D.C.: U.S. Government Printing Office. 97–198.

New Republic. 1996. 9 September.

Schultze, Charles L. 1997. Is faster growth the cure for budget deficits? In *Setting national priorities: Budget choices for the next century.* Edited by Robert Reischauer. Washington, D.C.: Brookings Institution.

Shepard, L.A., and K.C. Dougherty. 1991. Effects of high-stakes testing on instruction. Paper presented at Annual Meeting of American Educational Reading Association.

NOTES

1. From 1929 to 1982, education contributed 14% to the growth in total output. However, from 1973 to 1982, education's contribution to total output increased to 30% of the growth in total output, again demonstrating that education played a strong role in softening the impact of the post-1973 economic growth slowdown.

2. This estimate includes workers who received formal qualifying training or skill-improvement training provided by their employer and may be biased upward if some workers received both types of training.

Increasing Hours Worked through More Efficient Labor Markets

AUDREY FREEDMAN, PRESIDENT OF
AUDREY FREEDMAN ASSOCIATES

Today's economy is operating smoothly at low unemployment rates—in fact, at what some would call full employment—with no inflation. The expansion of the past three years has helped reduce the federal budget deficit at a moderate, steady pace. People could say that this is as good as it gets and we ought to leave well enough alone because any attempt to use resources more intensively would set off accelerating inflation. In fact, that's about what the Council of Economic Advisors, the Federal Reserve Board, and many mainstream economists *are* saying.

Long-term growth can only flow from a combination of two elements: increases in productivity (output per hour worked), and/or increased aggregate work hours. Our productivity record, has averaged only slightly over 1% since 1973.[1] This article focuses on the possibility of increasing aggregate hours worked in the economy, which, like increased productivity, can boost economic growth.

LIMITED POTENTIAL FOR INCREASING TOTAL WORK HOURS

Total work-hour projections are based mainly on population increase, the proportion of workers (or participation rate), and average hours worked per person, per year. The most powerful influence is *population growth,* which right now is extremely slow at slightly more than 1% annually. In fact, because of low domestic birthrates, between 35% and 40% of that growth is due to immigration attracted by U.S. labor-market opportunities. It's clear that workforce growth will be noticeably curtailed if current anti-immigration rhetoric leads to tighter borders.[2]

Raising the number of total workers faster than population growth would require profound changes in labor-force participation rates. Such cultural changes do occur very gradually over many decades, but no sign of such a participation surge is on the horizon. If anything, all appearances are that it will remain rather static. U.S. labor-force participation rates are already the highest in the developed world, at 63% to 64%. The biggest boost to participation rates has already taken place, as women's working lives were greatly extended throughout adulthood in the 1970s and 1980s. Only modest further gains among women seem likely, while male participation rates continue to decline moderately, especially among middle-aged and older men. In addition, the U.S. will not have a spurt in young people entering the labor force, as the baby boomers did during the 1970s. The population bulge of the next two decades will be among middle-aged and older cohorts—where participation rates are characteristically lower.

Total hours of contribution to GDP per worker could be increased by extending workweeks and work years. However, it is important to face facts honestly: proposals to increase U.S. growth that rely on this work-hour expansion would imply radical changes that look very much like a return to the nineteenth century. A drive to increase work hours would mean major extensions of the "normal" workday to ten hours and the "normal" workweek to six days. Eliminating traditional holidays and vacations could lengthen the work year of people on regular payrolls. Employing young people while they are still in school or cutting years of schooling by reducing the proportions of college entrants would also add to total work hours, but it would also reduce the quality of workers available. Deferring retirement of the elderly until the age of infirmity may be a trend already upon us, but it probably will not completely eliminate the last two *decades* of life when few people work very much. Such drastic moves, however, do not seem to merit practical consideration.

On the other hand, companies have diversified employees' working arrangements on an as-needed, or contingent, basis. The growth of unconventional schedules tends to raise total work hours in the population; the more varieties of paid opportunities there are, the more hours will be worked by individuals. This expansion of the forms of productive employment will continue to augment aggregate work hours in the U.S. economy, as well as extend work opportunity to those who otherwise might not participate at all. It's clear that a trend toward flexible employment may ultimately produce some of the cultural changes mentioned earlier.

CONTINGENT, FLEXIBLE PRACTICES TEND TO INCREASE TOTAL WORK HOURS

Varieties of contingent work have proliferated to the point where the term *typical career* carries almost no meaning. Combinations of self-employment, duration-of-project engagements, contract work, and temporary assignments coexist with traditional payroll jobs. Self-employment, particularly of technical, professional, and managerial people, is increasing because of new opportunities to fit paid work together with other responsibilities. Contingent work practices also encourage participation of both younger and older people according to their individual availability. Flexible work situations are more popular than the media and political commentators seem to recognize: to an increasing extent, lifetime security with one employer is considered both stultifying and potentially risky.

Opportunities to work on a part-year or part-time basis can raise participation rates by attracting more women and students into the workforce. Such arrangements may also be opportunities to retain older people who otherwise would leave the workforce entirely. On the other hand, partial schedules make it possible for an individual to work *more* total hours than the traditional full-time week. With such flexibility, individuals can augment income and workhours by piecing together two or more jobs. It is also possible to work "regularly" on a project, or on a contract or temporary basis, going from one assignment to another with little or no free time between.

Perhaps the most subtle aspect of contingent work practices, from a worker's point of view, is that the loss of a job is more easily overcome when so many ways of being reemployed are available.

Availability goes in both directions: all kinds and varieties of work opportunities are available to fit individual schedules and needs, and a willing population is available because our culture stresses both industriousness and responsiveness to change. In fact, we have created a governmental system in which there is very little economic incentive for idleness, either in the form of unemployment payments or welfare.

LABOR-MARKET FUNCTIONING

Under these circumstances of increased flexibility, it is most important that the labor market itself operate with full vigor so as to achieve the highest utilization of potential hours. Put simply, the hours between jobs must be kept to a minimum. Even minor incremental improvements in the labor-market matching of openings with individuals would create greater economic growth. There are two reasons for this. First, individual capabilities should be fully exploited in every job match because anything less represents underemployment of available knowledge and skill resources. Second, the optimum match should be accomplished with the shortest amount of downtime because unused hours constitute wasted potential output for the entire country.

Since speedy job posting and job matching have greater economic value today than in a slower-moving economy, labor-market intermediaries have new profit opportunities. New kinds of employment service firms and entire industries have been growing faster than government data systems can define and measure them. In the process, the trend toward using such outside specialists has reduced reliance of companies on their in-house personnel departments.

Profit-Making Intermediaries

The clients of labor-market intermediaries are employers who pay for the service of assembling an appropriate workforce. The temporary-help industry has been the fastest-growing, with a volume of about two million jobs monthly and an annual flow of individuals of at least five times that number. These firms may also provide training and testing for client companies because such service upgrades the quality of their job-ready employees.

The temporary-help industry provides workers in all of the major occupational sectors, with the greatest present growth in technical, professional, and managerial fields. A more basic pay-roll function is being provided by employee-leasing firms and other staff suppliers who act as coemployers with their client companies.

By extension, most of the industries classified as business services are actually providing a type of flexible staffing to client companies on a bulk contract basis. For example, accounting companies provide audit services; speciality marketing companies provide staff for a major campaign; data-processing firms take on entire functions through service contracts. These firms may provide their services on a client's premises with staff for a period of time or they may operate off-site in their own facilities. The extensive mixing and blending among these businesses is so great that former distinctions are rapidly losing their meaning in today's business world.

The most recent arrival in labor-market intermediaries is the Internet. This and other electronic communication systems are offering job posting, and will shortly be used for matching and interviewing, perhaps for testing and evaluation, and credential checking.

Nonprofit and Public Sector Intermediaries

Universities, community colleges, and trade schools provide some labor-market connections for their graduates and students because employers tend to initiate contacts and recruitment with such schools. Schools have increased the variety of their assistance by offering cooperative work-study programs and internships, and by permitting faculty and junior faculty to engage in other types of employment in the nonacademic world. Compared with private industry labor-market operations, however, the academic response has been only modestly innovative.

The states and federal government operate what once was known as the Employment Service and is now called the Job Service in most areas. Fundamental reform, however, has not been evident here. While work patterns have expanded in volume and variety, such public labor-market intermediaries have hardly fulfilled even the basic requirements of their mission.

The problem is that they mistake the unemployed as their client—when the employer with labor needs should be their true customer. These services have developed a social-work outlook by authorizing income support for the unemployed. As a result of changing political winds, they have been charged with filling vocational training slots, distributing government subsidies, monitoring minimum wage and affirmative action compliance, qualifying immigration certification, and other public policies. And, through it all, they have continued to think of themselves as the bureaucratic providers of the "work-test," which entitles an unemployed client to collect unemployment insurance. If there is one governmental reform in the U.S. labor market that could enhance growth, it would lie in the reorganization of the state and federal Job Services to serve the needs of private employers who need workers.

UNUSED HOURS OF AVAILABLE LABOR

According to the U.S. Bureau of Labor Statistics (BLS), our economy used about 252 billion hours of labor in 1995 to produce a record GDP, but about 20 billion hours of labor were available and *not* used. Although the economy operated at nearly 93% of workforce capacity, it could have operated at a higher level. Theoretically, a total of 271 billion productive hours could have been achieved.[3]

The level of hours of labor fluctuates, of course, with the business cycle. Even though exactly comparable data does not exist, some rough comparisons can be made to previous years. During the 1982–83 recession, only 86.8% of labor-force capacity was in use. In 1968 and 1969, an economic resurgence pushed labor-force capacity utilization at above 95%.[4] (Note, though, that 30 years ago the proportion of adults who were working was lower because women's participation rates had not yet begun their long climb.)

How exactly do we waste 20 billion hours of potential contributions to economic growth? Mostly, these were hours spent searching for work. In 1995, the BLS calculated that 13 billion work hours were lost by people who were available for full-time work, and another 1.5 billion hours by people searching for part-time jobs. Another 1.5 billion hours were lost by people who were employed, but whose full schedules had been cut back by their employer.[5] Add another 3.3 billion hours lost by people who usually work part-time, but whose schedules had been also cut. Finally, those who wanted to work but had become discouraged and stopped actively searching, account for 414 million lost hours. Even leaving out the last group, our wasted aggregate hours of work in a year amount to 19.6 billion.

We should acknowledge that the U.S. labor market absorbs workers easily. If this were not so, we would have much less immigration, both legal and illegal. Also, in recent decades there has been a relaxation of such barriers to employment as licensing hurdles, hiring halls, closed shops, and overt discrimination.

Nevertheless, hundreds of millions of hours lost in a full-employment economy suggest another and more urgent way of regarding unemployment. That is, even with "only" 7.5 million unemployed out of a labor force of 133 million, there would be greater economic growth if labor markets operated more efficiently.

Our first priority should be to make job matchups faster and more effective. Every available hour should be used. This goal is even more important if we are going to try to require welfare recipients to work, if we are going to try to raise the proportion of adults supporting themselves through paid jobs.

WASTING OPPORTUNITIES

Washington should take advantage of a stable economy by moving quickly to improve both federal and state job-placement activities. We have squandered three-and-a-half years of economic recovery by not reforming the public Job Service. The present administration dreamed away two years; *then* it approached a hostile Congress and asked for legislation. Worse, it focused on the wrong issue by requesting legislation to simplify subsidized training programs. The administration never changed the way it guides and operates the federal and state Job Service.

FIX THE JOB SERVICE, NOW

Today, three years into a recovery that has produced extraordinarily low unemployment and low inflation, we are searching for a few more inches of economic growth. They are not available in rapid population expansion, higher participation rates, or vast cultural shifts in working lives. However, a slight improvement in aggregate hours worked could be engineered by public agencies if they were to focus on their true clientele—private enterprises that create job opportunities and need workers.

Some radical administrative reform will have to come. Job Service civil servants must be deprived of the role they think they have now: dispensing income support such as unemployment insurance and training subsidies, gatekeeping, and "coordinating" training courses. Public service staffs must be firmly redirected towards serving private businesses. Job Service personnel should be rewarded according to their measured effectiveness with their business clients, with new performance-based compensation such as bonuses. First-level Job Service employees must become familiar with the realities of rough-and-tumble competitive pressure. They should be motivated to increase their ability to help private enterprises grow and to take pride in closer contact with business owners and line managers. Any job that is open and available for more than a few days should be considered a blot on the performance of the local Job Service—period.

These measures need to pervade the entire federal and state Job Service. Private employment and staffing industries, such as temporary services, view open jobs as business opportunities. Not only are they eager to fill them quickly with satisfactory workers, but they actually make a profit on the deal. Of course, no one expects to hold a public employment service to a profit standard. Nevertheless, as a matter of public policy—and as a path to greater economic growth—the public Job Service must become effective in reducing the nearly 20 billion hours of GDP that are wasted in fruitless job search. This is the only practical and manageable way to use our labor resources more effectively.

NOTES

1. Audrey Freedman. "Productivity Needs of the United States," Report no. 934 (New York: The Conference Board, 1989), 1–2.

2. "Summary," *The Jerome Levy Economics Institute of Bard College*, vol. 5, no. 3 (Summer 1996), 16. See also Fullerton, Howard N. Jr., "The 2005 Labor Force," *Monthly Labor Review*, (November 1995): 36.

3. All data regarding work hours usage and capacity were provided by the U.S. Bureau of Labor Statistics to the author of this chapter.

4. Ibid.

5. Ibid.

5

The Role of Technology

Michael J.
Boskin

Frank R.
Lichtenberg

Technology's Powerful Contribution to
Growth

Technology Investment Is Driving
Economic Growth

Technology's Powerful Contribution to Growth

MICHAEL J. BOSKIN, T. M.
FRIEDMAN PROFESSOR OF
ECONOMICS AND HOOVER
INSTITUTION SENIOR FELLOW,
STANFORD UNIVERSITY

The role of technology in economic growth is one of the most important and widely debated in economics, government, and society. Since the days of the classical economists and the industrial revolution, technology has alternately been viewed as a savior of the human race from stagnant living standards, or a force generating immense social disruption, societal hardship, and worker dislocation. While technological advances do require and accelerate other social and economic change, and some temporary dislocation does result, technological improvements have been and will continue to be an enormous positive force for improving the human condition.

THE IMPORTANCE OF TECHNOLOGICAL CHANGE

In this section, I present my own perspective on the contribution of technological progress to economic growth, exploring several conjectures on the role of technology, especially its impact on labor, and drawing two major conclusions:

- First, on balance, technological change has been capital-augmenting. The nature of technological change, at least in the post-World War II period in the rich industrialized countries, has been biased toward enhancing capital rather than toward replacing labor.
- Second, as a consequence technology and capital formation have been complementary—their combined impacts on economic growth have been more than the sum of their parts. Capital-rich economies have been able to benefit more from technological progress than those that have lower rates of capital formation.

I am not suggesting that there are no important impacts and dislocations on labor; only that on balance, the effect has not been to displace labor, but to provide it with more, newer, and better complementary factors of production so as to become more productive.

My conclusion on the importance of technological change might lead some to suggest that government takes a far more active role in "promoting" technology. I believe that this view is badly mistaken. The primary role of government should be to set general economic conditions—both microeconomic and macroeconomic—within which private incentives are distorted as little as possible. There is, however, a role for government to play in financing (but not necessarily producing) the types of R & D that meet two strenuously applied criteria:

1. That the outcome of the R & D is generically such that it is impossible or extremely unlikely that an individual firm or group of firms could appropriate the bulk of the benefits;

2. That any such government financing produce societal benefits that are very likely to exceed the costs.

I cannot emphasize enough from analytical, empirical, and practical experience that because every industry and group will want the government to subsidize or finance its R & D, these criteria must be rigorously enforced. This is difficult in a political system even with highly qualified civil servants. However, society would be underinvesting in R & D if the government did not finance activities meeting these criteria.

THE EVIDENCE OF HISTORY

History is replete with examples, even epochs, of faster economic growth being generated by new technology, from railroads to jet planes. Many discussions of the evolution and growth of modern economies focus on new products, from pharmaceuticals to fax machines. There is much talk about the incredible rate of current technological progress, especially in information technology. People routinely claim that the rate of technological progress and the pace of dislocation is at an all-time high. Certainly, the information age is generating economic growth and opportunities of historic importance. (And, I might add, it is systematically undercounted in the statistics of all countries.) Perhaps the early part of the nineteenth century, however, was even more dramatic. People who had been unable to communicate other than by mail that took months or years could communicate almost instantly via the telegraph. The everyday concepts of time and distance, which could be reckoned only by how far a sailboat or a horse could travel in a day, were transformed completely by the steam engine and the railroad. That epoch carried with it various dislocations as well as enhanced opportunities, but, on balance, it greatly improved the human condition.

THE LARGE RESIDUAL OF TECHNOLOGICAL CHANGE

Enhanced capital, labor, and technological progress are the three principal sources of the economic growth of nations. Since the rate of growth of labor is generally constrained by the rate of growth of population, in industrialized countries population growth is generally quite modest even with international migration. Indeed, while most rich industrialized countries are dealing with a baby boom and the increased life expectancy of the elderly, little notice has been paid to the dramatic decline in birth rates. Fertility rates are well below replacement, which is a trend that, if not, implies the population ultimately will start to decline. Previously, declining population has been caused only by famine, disease, or war.

Consequently, a number of distinguished economists have found that in rich industrialized countries, the rate of growth of capital (tangible and human) and technical progress has accounted for the bulk of economic growth. (See, for example, Abramovitz 1956, Denison 1962, Griliches and Jorgenson 1966, Kuznets 1971, Jorgenson, Gollop, and Fraumeni 1987, and Solow 1957).

Economists have taken a variety of approaches in trying to understand the sources of economic growth: econometric models, growth-accounting exercises based on some simple accounting identities, etc. Simply and heuristically, technological progress has been identified with the residual, namely, the amount of output growth that cannot be explained by the growth of input. Compare real GDP at two points in time and ask how much of the increase can be explained by more capital and more labor. In the several ways economists go about answering that question, they all wind up concluding that for many decades in the rich industrialized countries, labor growth accounts for only a very small part of economic growth; capital formation for a sizable part (perhaps a quarter to a third); and there is a large residual left over for technological progress—ranging up to one-half of economic growth.

Table 5.1 presents these basic data for the so-called G–7 countries. The first column, real GDP growth rates for the period from the 1950s through 1994, reflects a far more rapid growth rate prior to 1973 than since then. Column 5 shows the percentage point deterioration in economic growth rates since 1973.

Table 5.1 Postwar Average Annual Rates of Growth (percent per annum)

Country	1 Real GDP	2 Utilized capital	3 Human capital stock	4 Total labor hours	5 Post–1973 real GDP growth slowdown
U.S	2.9	3.1	2.1	1.3	1.1
Canada	3.7	5.5	3.0	2.0	1.8
Japan	6.3	8.2	2.1	0.6	5.7
W. Germany	3.3	4.9	1.5	−0.5	2.4
France	3.4	5.1	2.0	−0.2	3.2
U.K.	2.4	3.9	1.2	−0.1	0.8
Italy	3.2	3.2	1.8	−0.4	3.2

Source: Author's computations; dates are for 1958–1994, except U.S., 1950–1994, and Italy, 1960–1994.

Columns 2, 3, and 4 show the corresponding growth rates of capital, human capital (as proxied by schooling completed), and labor hours. Since the responsiveness, or elasticity, of output (real GDP) to capital-input growth is thought to be in the one-quarter to one-third range, and since labor input is growing more slowly than output (as is human capital), or even declining in the European countries, it is clear that something else must explain a large part of the growth of output.

Likewise, there are perhaps many culprits in the explanation of the growth slowdown in these countries in the last quarter century compared to the previous quarter century (see column 5 in Table 5.1). A slower pace of capital formation and of technological progress are at the top of my list, what caused these slowdowns is a deeper question involving market conditions, and tax, budget, monetary, regulatory, and litigation policy, among many other issues.

THE IMPORTANCE OF HUMAN CAPITAL

Economists have increasingly focused on the importance of human capital—the knowledge and skills of the workforce—in

economic growth. One question is "Does human capital complement raw labor, tangible capital, or both?" Is the increased
knowledge, skills, and education of the workforce similar to
having more manual laborers, or do these elements interact
more with complex capital equipment? Several studies suggest
that human capital is more a complement for tangible capital
than for raw labor (see, for example, Griliches 1988). This idea
perhaps also explains the widening earnings disparity between
more and less educated workers in virtually all countries in the
last two decades. That is, the increased earnings premium reflects higher returns to human capital, generated by technological progress, capital formation, and shifts in demand toward
products that require greater human-capital input relative to
raw labor.

The big shift in the composition of output towards goods and
services that have a higher knowledge content—and that require
more knowledge-intensive workers to produce—has been un-
derreported. This is not just true in high-tech industries like
computer hardware and software and biotechnology, but even in
traditional goods and service sectors such as the automobile industry. A much larger fraction of the value added to a 1997
model car is derived from the application of human capital—
knowledge and skills—relative to raw labor, than was the case,
say, for a 1977 model. From the sophisticated electronics to the
aerodynamic design, to the lighter-weight materials necessary to
improve fuel economy, there has been a fundamental shift in the
share of output that derives from knowledge and skills. This has
led to an increase in the demand for highly skilled labor and is a
main source of the increase in the earnings premium for better
educated workers.

AMERICA'S TECHNOLOGICAL LEADERSHIP IS INCREASING IN MANY AREAS

Media pundits, politicians, and even some economists took the
slower improvement in living standards in the last quarter century relative to the previous quarter century as a sign of serious
fundamental decay or decline in the American economy. The
economy certainly is capable of doing better than it has in recent

decades, but the notion that it has been in a long decline is simply wrong. These experts have clamored for expanded government spending programs, protectionist trade policies, and government subsidies for special commercial technologies.

While the fortunes of particular industries have ebbed and flowed, America is not deindustrializing. Manufacturing's share of total economic output has been roughly constant for the last 30 years, and America today accounts for as large a share of industrial output of the developed OECD countries as it did in 1970. In addition, America is not losing its technological edge. Rather, the country has maintained or enhanced its tech edge in areas such as microprocessors, advanced telecommunications, software, biotechnology, aerospace, chemicals, and pharmaceuticals.

THE IMPORTANCE OF TECHNOLOGY IN THE NEW GROWTH THEORY

Theories and studies of the relationship of technology and economic growth abound. In recent years, endogenous growth theory has postulated several mechanisms by which technology, human capital, and the formation of ideas form a "virtuous" circle and feedback to growth rates (see, for example, Romer 1990 and Barro 1991). This theory contrasts with classical economic growth theory in which the rate of technical change is exogenously given, unaffected by economic incentives and activity. The economy converges toward a steady state in which it grows at the sum of the rates of technical progress and labor-force growth; therefore living standards grow at the rate of technological progress. Policies that raise the rate of saving and investment can temporarily raise the growth rate until a new higher level of output per worker is reached, but the economy will return to a long-run and steady growth path, with output per worker expanding at the rate of technical progress.

While the so-called new growth theory has come under a variety of attacks, there are a variety of reasons one might find this approach at least partly appealing. Two related models popular in economics in the early 1960s are the embodiment hypothesis and learning by doing (see Boskin 1985). The former suggests that new technology must be embodied in new capital, or at least that the process is substantially less costly than retrofitting old capital; hence high rates of investment will lead to higher rates of technical change or its rate of diffusion. Learning by doing implies that higher rates of investment lead to new products and new processes, which, again in a virtual circle, leads to higher rates of growth.

Much empirical research documents the correlation between the rate of growth and the rate of investment, particularly in equipment (DeLong and Summers 1991). Alternatively, if technical change is capital augmenting, one of the main puzzles the endogenous growth theory seeks to solve—the very slow pace of convergence of standards of living among economies—is explained by the fact that countries with more capital will benefit more from technology and vice versa, thereby making it harder for poorer countries to catch up. In general, one would expect that the returns to saving and investment be high in capital-poor countries and that high rates of saving and investment will lead to more rapid growth rates, taking account of these high rates of return until they start to diminish toward those in the richer countries, which should lead to some convergence among economies. This is the implication of the simple neoclassical growth model, although several plausible elaborations of it can ultimately reduce or eliminate this implication. My own research (Boskin and Lau 1994) finds that at least for the rich industrialized countries, technical change and capital formation are complementary, in other words, technical change has been capital augmenting and capital saving. This growth model explains the slow pace of convergence of living standards, on the one hand, and contradicts the notion that on balance, technological progress has displaced labor, on the other.

CAPITAL AND TECHNOLOGY

In the rich industrialized countries, capital and technology have complemented each other during the postwar era. In contrast to the popular conception that technology automatically displaces labor, it has, in fact, made capital more productive, creating new and often better jobs.

The economic system in the United States, with flexible dynamic markets, a very efficient capital market, a tradition of entrepreneurship, new firms forming and small firms growing, has been the best microeconomic environment in the world for generating and disseminating new technology and its economic and social benefits. This is a quite different environment than in most other industrialized economies. Indeed, Japan and Europe will have to undergo radical transformation of their economies if they are to prosper in the technologically driven information age. A stable macroeconomic environment with low inflation and the lowest possible tax rates are also vital for continued strong technology driven growth. It must also be complemented by market-based policies that reform education and job training to enhance human capital; reduce and make more flexible federal, state, and local regulation; expand open rules-based trade; and reduce unnecessary litigation. This is a powerful recipe for reinforcing the natural competitive forces of American technological innovation and entrepreneurship and the best prescription for maximizing long-term economic growth.

REFERENCES

Abramovitz, M. 1956. Resource and output trends in the United States since 1870. *American Economic Review* 46:5–23.

Barro, R. 1991. Convergence. *Journal of Political Economy* (April):223–51.

Boskin, M. J. 1985. Macroeconomics, technology and economic policy. In *Technology and Economic Policy.* Edited by R. Landau and N. Rosenberg. Washington, D.C.: National Academy Press.

Boskin, M. J., and L. Lau. 1992. Capital, technology and economic growth. In *Technology and the Wealth of Nations.* Edited by N. Rosenberg, R. Landau, and D. Mowery. Stanford, Cal.: Stanford University Press.

DeLong, J., and L. Summers. 1991. Equipment investment and economic growth. *Quarterly Journal of Economics* (May): 445–502.

Denison, E. F. 1962. The sources of economic growth in the United States and the alternatives before us. New York: *Committee on Economic Development.* Supplementary Paper no. 13.

Griliches, Z. 1988. Capital-skill complementarity. *Technology, education, and productivity: Early papers with notes to subsequent literature.* New York: Blackwell.

Griliches, Z., and D. W. Jorgenson. 1966. Sources of measured productivity change: Capital input. *American Economic Review* 56:50–61.

Jorgenson, D. W., F. M. Gollop, and B. M. Fraumeni. 1987. *Productivity and U.S. economic growth.* Cambridge, Mass.: Harvard University Press.

Kuznets, S. S. 1971. *Economic growth of nations*. Cambridge, Mass.: Harvard University Press.

Romer, P. 1990. Endogenous technological change. *Journal of Political Economy* (October):71–102.

Solow, R. M. 1957. Technical change and the aggregate production function. *Review of Economics and Statistics* 39:312–20.

Technology Investment Is Driving Economic Growth

FRANK R. LICHTENBERG, COURTNEY
C. BROWN PROFESSOR, GRADUATE
SCHOOL OF BUSINESS, COLUMBIA
UNIVERSITY; RESEARCH ASSOCIATE
OF THE NATIONAL BUREAU OF
ECONOMIC RESEARCH

T wo centuries ago, the primary determinants of a nation's wealth were the land, labor, and physical capital (structures and equipment) it possessed. These classical factors of production were emphasized by Adam Smith, David Ricardo, and their contemporaries. Around the middle of the twentieth century, however, analysts of U.S. economic growth such as Moses Abramowitz and Robert Solow discovered that most of the growth in per-capita output could not be explained by growth in physical capital per person. Only 10% of the twofold increase in per-capita GDP during 1909–1949 was attributable to greater amounts of capital. Evidently, the classical theory of production and national income was incomplete.

In the last 40 years or so, economists have recognized and established that long-run economic growth depends on the rate of investment in *intangible,* as well as tangible capital, and on the rate of technological progress. One important form of intangible capital is human capital—skills and knowledge embodied in the labor force—which is the result of previous investment in formal schooling, on-the-job training, and other activities. Another increasingly important form of intangible capital is research capital (or intellectual property)—the portfolio of products and processes (some of which are patented) that have resulted from previous investments in R & D. In recent years, some of the most important issues in international trade and antitrust policy have been concerned with the protection of intellectual property.

This section examines the impact of two key forms of technology investment on U.S. economic growth: R & D and information technology.

R & D Investment and Productivity Growth

The theory of production that properly accounts for research capital implies that the rate of economic growth is directly related to the level of R & D intensity—the share of output devoted to R & D investment. There is a great deal of literature on the contribution of R & D to economic growth. The majority of these studies have found there to be a strong, positive, statistically significant relationship between *privately financed* R & D investment and subsequent productivity growth.[1] For example, Griliches and Lichtenberg (1984) estimate that the rate of return to investment in R & D during the period 1969–76 was 34%. The estimate of Lichtenberg and Siegel (1991), in a study of over 5,000 manufacturing firms during the period 1972–85 was remarkably similar: 35%.

The econometric evidence suggests that the rate of return to R & D investment, hence its contribution to economic growth, is quite high—much higher in fact than the return to ordinary investment. This is not really surprising, for several reasons. First, R & D investment is known to be much *riskier* than ordinary investment. A small percentage of R & D projects yield extraordinarily important and valuable discoveries (the transistor, Zantac, etc.) but most yield nothing of economic value.[2] Risk-averse investors therefore demand a much higher average rate of return to R & D investment.

A second reason for the high social returns to R & D is that there are often knowledge spillovers from the R & D performer to other firms in the industry or elsewhere. Suppose that a firm invests $100 in R & D this year and discovers a new manufacturing process that reduces its annual costs by $20 in all future years. The other three firms in the industry learn half of the discovery; their annual production costs each fall by $10. The *private* rate of return to the innovator is 20%, but the *social* rate of return (including the benefits realized by the imitators) is 50%. R & D's contribution to national output growth is enhanced because the knowledge yielded by R & D can be used by other firms.[3]

The evidence indicates that changes in privately financed R & D intensity have an important impact on per-capita output growth.

Table 5.2. Nondefense R & D Expenditures As a Percentage of GDP, Major Industrialized Countries, 1972 and 1991

Country	1972	1991
Japan	1.9	3.0
Germany	2.1	2.7
France	1.5	1.9
United Kingdom	1.5	1.7
Italy	0.8	1.3
Canada	1.2	1.4

Source: Science & Engineering Indicators—1993, Appendix Table 4–36.

It is estimated that the private R & D intensity of U.S. manufacturing has increased steadily and markedly since the late 1950s, when the National Science Foundation began its industrial R & D survey.

From 1957–58 to 1991–93, company-funded R & D as a percent of sales of R & D-performing manufacturing companies more than *doubled,* from 1.55% to 3.20%. As Table 5.2 indicates, the U.S. experience was not unique: nondefense R & D expenditures as a percentage of GDP increased in all of the major industrialized countries from 1972 to 1991. Japan's R & D intensity increased especially rapidly.

Because the rate of return to R & D investment is so high, the increase in private R & D intensity is estimated to have increased the annual rate of productivity growth by just over half a percentage point between the late 1950s and the early 1990s.

Some evidence suggests that the returns to R & D have actually risen in recent years. Lichtenberg and Siegel's estimates, for example, implied that the rate of return was twice as high during the period 1981–85 as it was during the period 1973–76: 51% versus 25%. Our estimate of the R & D-induced acceleration in economic growth is therefore conservative.

INFORMATION TECHNOLOGY AND PRODUCTIVITY

In any era, there is usually a handful of technologies that play a far-reaching role in fostering change in a wide range of sectors, resulting in sustained and pervasive productivity gains (Bresnahan and Trajtenberg 1995). The steam engine during the first industrial revolution, electricity in the early part of this century, and information technology (microelectronics) in the past two decades are widely thought to have played such a role. Some authors refer to them as general purpose technologies (GPTs). GPTs are used as inputs by a wide range of sectors of the economy because they perform some generic function (such as continuous rotary motion for the steam engine or binary logic for microelectronics) that has virtually universal applicability throughout the economy.

GPTs may serve as engines of growth: as better ones become available, they foster complementary advances. The increase in demand for the GPT induces further technical progress, which prompts a new round of advances downstream, a process that is repeated again and again. As the use of the GPT spreads throughout the economy, its effects become significant at the aggregate level, thereby impacting overall growth.

During the last two decades, information technology has diffused rapidly throughout the U.S. economy. Average computer investment per employee by large corporations increased from $67 in 1977 to $279 in 1987—and the price of computers was falling rapidly during that period. The number of computer specialists employed in industry increased more than fivefold from 1976 to 1986. Between 1984 and 1993, the probability of using a computer at work almost doubled, from 25% to 46%.

Some early studies failed to find any effect of information technology investment on productivity. Since casual observation suggested that computers enhance efficiency, this lack of statistical evidence came to be referred to as the productivity paradox. But more recent studies at the aggregate, firm, and organizational levels have demonstrated a strong positive impact of computers on productivity; the failure of early studies to detect this was apparently due to methodological and data limitations.

Lau and Tokutsu (1992) investigated the impact of computers at the macro level. They found that computer technology has made a very significant contribution to the growth of aggregate real output in the U.S. economy during the past three decades. In fact, approximately 50% of the growth in aggregate real output during this period can be attributed to the growth in computer capital. Moreover, they argue that they "may have underestimated the contribution of . . . computer technology to the growth in aggregate real output" and that "technical progress affects the economy primarily through the reduction of the price in computer capital." Industry-level evidence considered by Siegel and Griliches (1992) is consistent with this; they found a strong positive correlation between productivity growth and investment in computers across industries.

However, it is the recent organizational-level evidence about the relationship between information-technology investment and productivity that is perhaps the most compelling. Lichtenberg (1995) analyzed data for several hundred companies during the period 1988–92; his results indicated that the rate of return to investment in computer capital is significantly higher (by a factor of three or more) than the rate of return to investment in other equipment or structures. He also found that information-systems employment made a larger contribution to output growth in the period 1976–86 than other employment, due in part to the very rapid growth (16% per year) of jobs in this sector.

Lichtenberg and Lehr (1996) found that the impact of computers on productivity in the public sector is similar to the impact in the private sector. They found that federal government agencies exhibiting the highest rates of productivity growth during the period 1987–92 tended to be those with the highest growth in computer assets per employee.

The finding that information-systems capital and labor earn excess returns suggests that small changes in information-systems spending result in large changes in output and productivity. A model developed in a recent paper by Kremer (1993) suggested a mechanism that could possibly underly this. He hypothesized that the expected output of the firm depends on the *product* of the skill, or quality, levels of all of the workers in the firm, not on the *average* skill level. Worker skill level is defined as the probability of not making a mistake (such as producing defective space shuttle O-rings) that destroys output (makes the shuttle explode). He argues that "production consists of many tasks, all of which must be successfully completed for the product to have full value," so that expected output depends on the *joint* probability that no worker makes a mistake. Kremer showed that this model "provides a mechanism through which small differences in worker skill create large differences in productivity and wages." If information systems have the effect of raising the firm's average skill level—i.e., reducing the probability that workers make mistakes—Kremer's model implies that their impact on productivity would be large.

Because economists believe that an employee's wage is positively correlated with his or her productivity, estimates of the relationship between computer use and wage rates may provide indirect evidence about the productivity impact of computers. Using data from the Current Population Survey and the High School and Beyond Survey, Krueger (1993) found that "workers who use computers on their job earn 10 to 15 percent higher wages." Berman, Bound, and Griliches (1993) also found strong positive correlations between skill upgrading and increased investment in computers within industries.

TECHNOLOGY PLAYS AN IMPORTANT ROLE

Between the late 1950s and the early 1990s, company-funded R & D as a percent of sales of R & D-performing U.S. manufacturing companies more than doubled. Because the rate of return to R & D investment is so high, this increase in private R & D intensity is estimated to have increased the annual rate of productivity growth by just over half a percentage point during this period. In addition, during the last two decades, information technology has diffused rapidly throughout the U.S. economy. Recent studies have demonstrated the strong positive impact of computers on productivity at the aggregate, industry, and organizational levels, and in both the private and the public sectors.

Like the general purpose technologies of previous eras—the steam engine during the first industrial revolution, electricity in the early part of this century—information technology appears to be playing a far-reaching role in fostering technical change in a wide range of user sectors, thereby bringing about sustained and pervasive productivity gains. The U.S. economy straddles a line between the present and the future much as it did early in this century. The computer, and its technological progeny, will soon change our economic prospects for the better as much as these earlier industrial revolutions.

REFERENCES

Bresnahan, Timothy, and Manuel Trajtenberg. 1995. General purpose technologies: engines of growth? *Journal of Econometrics* 65:1 (January): 83–108.

Griliches, Zvi, and Frank Lichtenberg. 1984. R & D and productivity at the industry level: Is there still a relationship? In *R & D, Patents, and Productivity.* Edited by Zvi Griliches. Chicago: Univ. of Chicago Press.

Kremer, Michael. 1993. The O-ring theory of economic development. *Quarterly Journal of Economics* 108 (August): 551–76.

Kreuger, A. 1993. How computers have changed the wage structure: Evidence from microdata: 1984–1989. *Quarterly Journal of Economics* 108:1 (February):33–60.

Lau, L., and I. Tokutsu. 1992. The impact of computer technology on the aggregate productivity of the United States: An indirect approach. Unpublished paper. Stanford University Department of Economics. August.

Lichtenberg, Frank. 1995. The output contributions of computer equipment and personnel: A firm-level analysis. *Economics of Innovation and New Technology* 3, 201–17.

Lichtenberg, Frank, and William Lehr. 1996. Computer use and productivity growth in federal government agencies, 1987 to 1992, *National Bureau of Economic Research Working Paper, no. 5616* (June).

Lichtenberg, Frank, and Donald Siegel. 1991. The impact of R & D investment on productivity: New evidence using linked R & D-LRD data. *Economic Inquiry* 29 (April): 203–28.

Siegel, Donald, and Zvi Griliches. 1992. Purchased services, outsourcing, computers, and productivity in manufacturing. In *Output Measurement in the Service Sectors.* Edited by Zvi Griliches. Chicago: University of Chicago Press.

NOTES

1. Productivity growth seems to be essentially unaffected by government-funded R & D, a substantial portion of which is devoted to national defense and health care. Problems of measuring output in these sectors may be partly responsible for the apparent lack of correlation.

2. Even most *patented* innovations turn out to have little economic value—and many innovations are not even patented. Investing in R & D bears some resemblance to buying a lottery ticket.

3. The fact that a firm can benefit from another firm's R & D expenditure is, of course, a mixed blessing, since it gives rise to the "free rider" (underinvestment) problem: each firm refrains from performing R & D, hoping to appropriate the returns to other firms' investments. Various government policies, including enforcement of patents, R & D tax credits, and direct government support of R & D may be used to correct this market failure.

6

Global Competition Drives Growth

Jeffrey D. Sachs

Marina Whitman

Globalization Is the Driving Force for
Growth in the United States
Trade and Growth: Restoring the Virtuous
Circle

Globalization Is the Driving Force for Growth in the United States

JEFFREY D. SACHS, GALEN L. STONE
PROFESSOR OF INTERNATIONAL
TRADE, HARVARD UNIVERSITY;
DIRECTOR OF THE HARVARD
INSTITUTE FOR INTERNATIONAL
DEVELOPMENT

The driving force of future economic growth must be the dramatic globalization of economic activity that is currently underway. The special characteristics of the U.S. economy will allow it to take particular advantage of globalization. Of all of the world's advanced economies, the United States is the best placed to respond effectively to globalization because it is, by far, the most innovative and flexible. On the one hand, the United States is in the strongest position to provide innovative goods and services to a vastly expanded world market, as is plainly evident in areas ranging from information technology to biotechnology to financial services. On the other hand, the U.S. is the most able of the leading economies to retrench in areas of the economy (such as labor-intensive manufactures) that are squeezed by greater foreign competition. In fact, much of the industrial downsizing caused by low-wage competition from developing countries has already taken place in the United States, but still lies ahead for Western Europe and Japan.

There are, of course, significant risks to long-term growth, as well. The clearest risk lies in fiscal policy. Compared with Europe the U.S. relies largely on moderate rates of taxation and a public-sector deficit that is kept under control. If middle-class entitlement programs, especially health care and Social Security, continue to impose an enormous intergenerational transfer of wealth from future generations to today's elderly and their successors, the baby-boomers, the bright U.S. growth prospects could be overwhelmed by a future fiscal crisis, which is now at hand in parts of Western Europe, where social programs are even more generous and therefore funded at the expense of economic growth.

GLOBALIZATION AND U.S. ECONOMIC GROWTH

One of today's economic ironies is the growing political challenge to globalization, even though the dramatic expansion of world markets offers one of the best hopes for faster growth in numerous countries, including the United States. Patrick Buchanan's nativism and xenophobia in the 1996 presidential primary elections struck a chord among some segments of the U.S. population, even though it was a relatively small part of the electorate. To many citizens in the U.S. and Europe, globalization seems to bring little more than the closure of textile and footwear firms caused by low-wage competition from abroad. A much greater force, the dynamic growth in world markets and the expanded opportunities for U.S. sales of technologically advanced goods and services, is only dimly perceived by many.

To gauge the powerful positive forces that accompany globalization, it is good to start with a clear appreciation of the phenomenon itself. For the first time in history, virtually all of the world's nations have adopted market-based economic policies and open trading systems, thereby linking more than five billion people in global markets for goods, services, capital, and technology. The formation of this global marketplace has been dramatic, indeed revolutionary. More than three billion people have been brought into the global market system in the last 15 years alone, as dozens of countries in Asia, Latin America, Africa, Central Europe, and the former Soviet Union have abandoned nonmarket systems. The results include a stunning growth of world trade; a burgeoning of capital flows to emerging markets; and a rapidly evolving international division of labor, with production and technology being relocated around the globe. The full ramifications of these dramatic changes are only now coming into focus.

THE FIRST GOLDEN AGE OF CAPITALISM

In some ways, the 1990s are the second time in world history that a world market system has prevailed. Between 1870 and 1914, a world marketplace also took shape, although unlike today, it was a system built by European imperial powers and ruthlessly imposed upon colonial dependencies in Africa and Asia. The globalization of 100 years ago, nonetheless, can teach us a lot about the economic effects of expanding international markets; and the news is mostly good for economic growth. Economic historians consider the previous globalization as a Golden Age of Capitalism because worldwide economic growth expanded dramatically as major regions—Latin America, Africa, and Asia—were pulled into a trading network with industrialized Europe. While worldwide per-capita economic growth is roughly estimated as 0.6% per year between 1820 and 1870, it is judged to have increased to 1.3% per year during the period 1870–1913, according to data prepared for the Organization for Economic Cooperation and Development.[1]

The nature of economic growth during this Golden Age is also notable. As today, globalization was supported not merely by policy changes—such as Britain's move to free trade and the spread of currency convertibility via the gold and silver standards—but also by a dramatic improvement in transportation and communications. The Internet of 1896 was the international telegraphic system, which linked much of the globe, and especially most of the British Empire, through nearly instantaneous electronic messages. Such advances as modern steamships, the opening of the Suez Canal, the spread of railways across every continent, discoveries in canning and refrigeration contributed to the dramatic increase in international trade. As in recent years, international trade significantly outpaced economic growth. We can safely say that the increased scale of world markets, and the increased division of labor supported by the global markets, fueled the technological advances and the rapid pace of capital accumulation that underpinned the acceleration of world growth.

The Golden Age, of course, came to a dramatic and horrific end. In 1914, Europe plunged into 30 years of unmitigated disaster, including two wars, the Great Depression, and the Bolshevik revolution. By the end of World War II, the world trading system had been destroyed. Currencies were inconvertible; trade was blocked by quotas, licenses, and astronomical tariffs; and faith in capitalism in much of the world had vanishes. Upon gaining independence from colonial rule, most Third World countries adopted some form of statist economic system. It has taken 50 years to reconstruct a global market system, first by the return of Europe and Japan to open trade in the late 1950s and early 1960s; then by the incorporation of East Asian tigers into the world trading system in the 1960s and 1970s; and finally by the return of most of Latin America, Africa, South Asia, and the former communist economies to market systems in the 1980s and 1990s. This gradual process, filled with twists, turns, and sometimes-painful reversals, has positioned the world to benefit from another Golden Age of Global Capitalism—if we are smart enough to avail ourselves of the chance.

THE SECOND GOLDEN AGE

The next Golden Age, assuming the world system is consolidated, will be characterized by several qualities. First, markets will extend over nearly the entire world population. Only a few renegade countries—North Korea, Iran, Cuba—and a handful of countries stuck in civil strife are not now part of the world system. Virtually all of the rest are part of the emerging global market and are scrambling to increase competitiveness and attract internationally mobile capital. Second, the widening scope of markets will favor increased innovation, since the returns to research and development will be reaped in a far larger international marketplace. Third, special bonuses will exist for advances in communications and transportation, whether in digitized information or in improved systems for intermodal transportation. Fourth, there will be increased pressure to harmonize national standards in information and telecommunications systems, as data transmission increasingly underpins the global division of labor. Fifth, international capital flows as a proportion of global saving are likely to increase as the systems governing capital mobility become more transparent and harmonized. Sixth, the new global division of labor will force major changes in the location of production, not only in manufacturing (as has been occurring for two decades), but also increasingly in services as well.

In all these areas, the United States is ahead of its competitors in Europe and Asia. U.S. producers are far in the lead in the development and use of the new information technologies and biotechnologies; indeed, U.S. industry effectively sets the global standards in these and related fields. The enormous flexibility of the U.S. economy allows it to adjust rapidly to the changing international division of labor. The country is ahead of Europe in shifting from low-skill, labor-intensive manufacturing, into new high-tech industries and services, including finance, entertainment, and global communications. The much discussed downsizing of American industry is, of course, a reflection of this process. While continued job turmoil remains ahead, the U.S. is much farther along in the process of restructuring than are the European and Japanese economies. Germany, for example, still has some 30% of its workforce in industry, much of it in standardized technologies; it is therefore prone to shift abroad. The United States, meanwhile, has just 15% of the labor force in manufactures.

The 1996 *Global Competitiveness Report*, prepared jointly by the World Economic Forum and the Harvard Institute for International Development, makes clear that moderate government, flexible labor markets, and a technological edge has put the U.S.

in a superb position to avail itself of global trends. It ranked 4th out of 49 countries in competitiveness (edged out by 3 small, very open economies, Singapore, Hong Kong, and New Zealand), far ahead of Japan (13th), Germany (22nd), and France (23rd).[2]

Early signs of a pickup in global growth are appearing. According to calculations of the International Monetary Fund, developing countries averaged 4.5% annual growth during the period 1978–87; but since the early 1990s, growth has increased to around 6% per year, a remarkable achievement affecting perhaps half of the world's population.[3] Developed country growth has not picked up, and in fact has declined slightly from the 1980s, mainly because of poor performance in Europe and Japan, as both regions struggle with financial and fiscal problems. We have to conclude once again, that the U.S. is in the best position to take advantage of the economic boom in much of the developing world.

POTENTIAL OBSTACLES TO FUTURE U.S. GROWTH

There are potential external and internal obstacles to future U.S. growth. A reversal of globalization, for example through a sharp rise in protectionism in advanced countries, would of course undermine long-term growth prospects. Such a protectionist backlash is more likely in Europe than in the United States, given the adjustment difficulties in the less flexible European economies. Even so, the best estimates see the continued openness of the European economies, since major European enterprises are increasingly global in their strategies and will be a critical counterweight to populist and reactionary calls for protection.

The major internal obstacle is the possible U.S. failure to grapple with the long-term implications of entitlement spending. With a shrinking federal budget deficit as a percent of GDP in the past three years, pressures for long-term fiscal reform appear to have abated. All forecasts, however, point to a sharp deterioration in the fiscal balance in the early years of the next century, as entitlement spending rises sharply in tandem with an increase in an aging population. Only a deep reform of entitlement programs, including a shift from pay-as-you-go financing to an individualized and funded Social Security system (as Chile has brilliantly accomplished), is likely to avert serious longer-term difficulties. These difficulties would include a surge in budget deficits, a fall in national saving rates, and the need to hike up tax rates markedly—all of which would tend to throw the U.S. economy off a high-growth trajectory.

There is an overriding moral from the First Golden Age of Capitalism a century ago. Just when capitalism was triumphant and the world order was widely thought to be secure, it came crashing down through a lack of vision and deep flaws in the international system. If we want to secure the promise of globalization in our own time—and thereby reap the benefits of faster global growth through open markets—we will have to nurture the emerging global system and to underpin it with prudent domestic policies and sound international leadership.

NOTES

1. Angus Maddison, *Monitoring the World Economy: 1820–1992*, OECD Development Centre Studies (Paris: Organisation for Economic Cooperation and Development, 1995).

2. World Economic Forum, *Global Competitiveness Report 1996* (Geneva, World Economic Forum, 1996).

3. Table A5, "Developing Countries: Real GDP (Annual percentage change)" in *World Economic Outlook*, (Washington, D.C., International Monetary Fund, October 1996).

Trade and Growth

Restoring the Virtuous Circle

MARINA WHITMAN, PROFESSOR OF
BUSINESS ADMINISTRATION AND
PUBLIC POLICY, UNIVERSITY OF
MICHIGAN; FORMER CHIEF
ECONOMIST AND GROUP VICE
PRESIDENT, GENERAL MOTORS

By most conventional measures—unemployment, inflation, job creation, global competitiveness—the American economy is robust. However, the slow growth of that economy and its concomitants—the fact that many Americans have seen little or no growth or even a decline in their inflation-adjusted incomes and continue to feel a heightened sense of economic insecurity—continue to fuel unease and discontent. And, as is so often the case, international trade or, to use the broader and trendier term, globalization, is a natural scapegoat.

Actual experience, however, tells quite a different story. Not only does healthy growth tend to dissipate pressures for trade protection, but also openness to trade and foreign investment can be a major contributor to economic growth. The potential for such a virtuous circle exists; the challenge to American policy makers is to make it a reality.

The trade-bashing views of Pat Buchanan and Ross Perot may be extreme, but talking tough on trade is popular with Americans across the political spectrum. Both candidates in the 1996 presidential elections backpedaled substantially from their earlier support for trade liberalization; the bipartisan vision of Presidents Bush and Clinton of expanding NAFTA into a hemispheric trade alliance has been put on indefinite hold. And, having pressed hard to bring the fledgling World Trade Organization into being, the United States periodically threatens to undermine its authority by acts of "aggressive unilateralism."

The sharp growth slowdown that most industrialized nations have experienced since 1973 has had somewhat different impacts in different countries. It has manifested itself mainly in the form of high and persistent unemployment and little or no private-sector job creation in most continental European nations; while in the United States and, to a lesser extent, other English-speaking nations, it has taken the form of wage stagnation and increased inequality in earnings and income. Although the effects differ in important details, however, most of the leading industrialized nations are experiencing a combination of persistent slow growth and increased economic nationalism.

The longer this combination of slow long-run growth and pressures for inward-looking trade policies persist, the more it will result in continued frustration and missed opportunities. My intent is to spell out how open trade and faster growth can reinforce and promote each other and what steps might help bring such a virtuous circle into being.

THE IMPACT OF TRADE ON GROWTH

The increased importance of trade and foreign direct investment in the U.S. economy is often blamed for the stagnation of real earnings since 1973 and for the loss of "good" jobs, by which is generally meant well-paid production-worker jobs in manufacturing. In fact, however, most of the slowdown in real compensation as generally measured is attributable to the slowdown in the growth of labor productivity over the same period; and the two trends are virtually identical when both are measured using the same price index. Here, too, the real growth rate of the economy (which is primarily a function of increases in labor productivity) is front and center.

There is also evidence that expanded trade, rather than destroying "good" jobs, actually creates them. One recent study found that, holding other characteristics constant, U.S. exporting plants paid higher wages, particularly to production workers, and experienced faster growth of both wages and employment than did nonexporters over the period 1976–87. In addition, a slightly earlier study found, that exporting industries tend to be associated with high wage premiums and import-competing industries with low ones (the two major exceptions are autos and steel), reinforcing the positive relationship between trade and wages.[1]

A recent examination by the McKinsey Global Institute regarding productivity differences in manufacturing industries in Germany and Japan, as well as the United States, adds supporting evidence for the positive relationship between globalization and growth. This series of case studies showed that for an industry to be on the leading edge of technology, global competition is required; purely domestic competition, however intense, is not enough.[2] It is not surprising, then, that U.S. productivity growth has been fastest in manufacturing, whose products are or easily could be traded, and slowest in services, which are traded to a much lesser, although increasing, extent.

Finally, a number of studies conducted by the World Bank and other international organizations have yielded similar conclusions: that industrializing countries with outward-looking, market-oriented policy environments have, in general, grown significantly faster than those with a more inward-looking and protectionist policy approach.[3]

TRADE PROTECTION AND LABOR MARKETS

The empirical evidence summarized in the preceding paragraphs provides a strong underpinning for the near-universal view among economists that an open trading system has a positive effect on both a nation's level of income and its rate of economic growth. But these benefits tend to be small relative to the total size of the economy and widely diffused. The impact on the domestic distribution of income, however, is likely to be more significant and more concentrated, since the intertwined processes of trade and foreign direct investment are bound to create winners and losers. And it is these distributional effects that tend to be most visible and politically vulnerable.

By far the most prominent of these distributional effects is the impact of trade and investment flows on wages and/or employment in particular industries, communities, regions, and income or occupational groups. For those in the "losers" category these dislocation effects can be substantial. Some studies have found that workers displaced by trade bear a heavier burden of adjustment, in the form of longer periods of unemployment and larger permanent earning losses, than workers displaced by other shifts in the economy.

The political responses to such developments show up in patterns of trade protection. A survey of a large number of studies of trade protection in advanced industrial countries, with a primary focus on the United States, found that countries with a large number of labor-intensive, low-skill, low-wage industries beset by high or increasing import penetration tend to pursue protectionist policies.[4]

This set of characteristics suggests strongly that a major function of trade protection is to ameliorate, or perhaps delay, the costs of trade-related adjustments in labor markets. That is, protection appears to be focused on labor reallocations that are likely to be large, relatively expensive, or both. Protection also appears to be biased in favor of individuals who are most vulnerable and least able to bear the costs of adjustment, that is, low-skill low-wage workers in threatened or declining industries. Some of the studies, however, suggest that those who are most likely to receive protection are low-skill, relatively high-wage workers (who presumably have the most to lose).

The fact that the politics of trade and trade policy tend to focus on the labor-market or "jobs" aspect of such policies is nothing new. Several developments have intensified this focus in recent years, however. One is the increasingly unfettered nature of the other major factors of production—capital and technology—along with the steady increase in economic openness, as measured by the share of exports and imports in total economic activity of the United States and Western Europe. Another is the recent deteriorating performance of labor markets in virtually all industrialized nations, including a near-universal slowdown in inflation-adjusted earnings. Along with these developments has come either a substantial increase in unemployment or underemployment in Europe and Japan, respectively, or a substantial increase in wage dispersion and income inequality in the United States and other non-European, English-speaking nations.

In the United States and other leading industrialized nations, an increasing reliance on *external* (between-firm) rather than *internal* (within-firm) mechanisms to reallocate labor in response to market signals may also be intensifying the relationship between labor-market adjustments and attitudes toward trade and trade policies. The United States has long been at one end of this particular spectrum; in geographic mobility, job turnover, relative volume of job accessions and separations, and short average duration of unemployment, it leads the industrialized world. Japan, with its low rate of labor turnover, policies of lifetime employment, use of a wide range of alternatives to layoffs, and the tendency of its firms to adapt to changing market signals through internal diversification, lies at the other end of the spectrum. The nations of Western Europe fall somewhere in between the two.

Regardless of these intercountry differences, the major industrialized nations all appear to be moving toward greater reliance on external or market mechanisms for labor reallocation. A weakening of employment stability in many of these nations is one manifestation of this shift. Another is the tendency, at least in the United States, for manufacturing firms to become smaller and more specialized, suggesting a reduced enthusiasm for internal diversification and a move away from vertical-integration toward outsourcing parts of the production process.

Probably the most striking manifestation of a heavier reliance on external rather than internal adjustment mechanisms, however, is the increased use of a peripheral or contingent workforce consisting of temporary or part-time workers or contract services. In the United States, while the proportion of the workforce consisting of part-time or self-employed workers has remained relatively stable, the share of temporary employees and business services has tripled over the decade 1982–92, albeit from a very small base; today, this group comprises the nation's fastest-growing job category.

This shift toward a greater reliance on external, as opposed to internal, processes of labor-market adjustment appears to be a rational response to changes in the economic environment of the industrialized nations since 1973. Among these changes are the slowdown in aggregate growth rates, which demand greater flexibility for downward adjustments, and the intensified pressure from global competition to increase competitiveness by reducing labor costs, both of which increase the need to substitute the "hard" disciplines of the marketplace for "softer" internal ones. The increased number of large and unanticipated economic shocks has also played a role. Even the most enthusiastic supporters of internal labor markets recognize that, because custom exerts a strong inertial pull in these markets, their efficiencies are greater when change is gradual and predictable, less so when it is radical and unexpected. Finally, rapid changes in information technology, by reducing the costs of coordination among nonintegrated firms, have reinforced the trend toward outsourcing and have reduced vertical integration, as mentioned earlier.

However much this shift toward increased reliance on external rather than on internal labor reallocation, a rational response to changes in the external environment it has the effect of shifting some of the costs of adjustment away from firms and toward workers, making them more visible and politically sensitive. This fact, together with the labor-market difficulties experienced in the United States and other countries since 1973 and the bias that trade restrictions are cushioning or postponing the transitional costs of job shifts, all point to an enhanced vulnerability to protectionist pressures. And this suggests, in turn, the importance of domestic policies that reduce friction and enhance job security in labor markets, as well as policies directed toward reducing the growing inequality in earnings between skilled and unskilled workers.

COMBINING ECONOMIC FLEXIBILITY AND ECONOMIC SECURITY

Three elements are essential if we are to improve the functioning of American labor markets by combining economy-wide flexibility with an acceptable level of individual economic security. One is education and training to enhance the work-related skills people will need to insure their employability in a world where several changes of jobs and even occupations over a lifetime is rapidly becoming the norm. The second is the ability to maintain pension rights and health insurance when changing employers or moving in and out of the workforce. Third, and most important, the higher the sustainable growth rate of the U.S. economy, the greater the likelihood that people displaced by economic change will land on their feet, and the less likely they are to fear that such change will endanger their own and their families' economic future.

On the education front, no one has the answer as to why the United States—with the best system of higher education in the world—does such a relatively poor job of preparing students who are not college-bound for the workforce. But the very fact that education vouchers and charter schools have entered the political debate suggests an interest in experimentation and innovation that should yield valuable insights into how to improve our performance. As for lifelong training, both on and off the job, the private sector has been forging ahead on its own. The number of people over 35 years of age attending college has increased significantly in recent years, and more and more firms are providing or subsidizing ongoing training for their employees, either voluntarily or as the result of collective bargaining.

Policies to increase the effectiveness of basic education, improve the efficiency of the school-to-work transition, and provide for lifelong skill enhancement through training both on and off the job are also high on the list of measures that might narrow the earnings gap among Americans with different skill levels. Education and training are at best long-range propositions, however, and their effectiveness will vary widely among individuals. Some form of wage subsidy for those at the bottom of the skill and income scale would have a more immediate impact, suggesting that the Earned Income Tax Credit (EITC) program should be reformed, but not scrapped—as many in Congress believed. In addition the updating and improved integration of unemployment benefits and reemployment programs are needed to take into account the fact that a smaller proportion of unemployment than in the past is purely cyclical, with the result that fewer of the unemployed can expect to return to their previous jobs. Such changes would be particularly important to those who, because of low skills and/or poverty, have the most frequent and acute need for such services.

Although recent legislation has increased the portability of health insurance for working Americans, further improvements are still needed. Legislative and regulatory changes have also reduced the period of time required before an individual's contingent pension rights become permanent (known as vesting) and have increased the reliability of such vesting; but it is the ongoing shift among companies from defined-benefit to defined-contribution pension arrangements that has done the most to enhance portability. Finally, the increasing number of workers engaged in various nontraditional employment relationships, including temporary, part-time and self-employment, have contributed to the flexibility of the American economy. But if such people are not to be second-class citizens in the workplace, it is important that pensions, health care, and unemployment insurance be extended to them on a proportionate basis.

RESTORING THE VIRTUOUS CIRCLE OF GROWTH AND FREE TRADE

Whatever specific measures are taken to prepare people for job transitions and make the process easier, the most important factor in improving employment prospects and alleviating anxiety in the face of change is economic growth. It is not surprising, therefore, that a low growth rate is one of the most important factors associated with both the demand for and the actual supply of trade protection. By the same token, policies directed toward accelerating the economy's long-run growth rate can, if successful, play an important role in promoting trade liberalization.

In 1996, organized labor and some business groups called on the Federal Reserve to loosen the strings of monetary policy in order to push interest rates down and the growth rate up. But current levels of unemployment and capacity utilization indicate that there is little or no slack in the U.S. economy and that further easing by the Fed would serve only to raise inflationary expectations and long-term interest rates rather than increase the real growth of the economy. Given this situation, it is to the credit of both 1996 presidential candidates that neither engaged in the populist sport of Fed-bashing.

The focus, then, has to be on increasing the growth capacity of the U.S. economy—what have come to be called supply-side measures. A sustained increase in our real growth rate and in the compensation of our workers will require a reversal of the still-unexplained post-1973 slowdown in the growth of aggregate productivity. Because no one knows why the slowdown occurred, there are no clear-cut prescriptions for how to reverse it. Virtually all observers agree, however, that policies to encourage increasing the low rates of savings and net investment that have characterized the United States in recent decades would be a good place to start.

In addition to the interest-rate-lowering impact associated with deficit reduction, changes on both the taxing and the spending sides of the government budget would provide stimulus in the desired direction. The taxation side would require a shift from the current emphasis on tax cuts per se to a focus on structural changes in the taxation system that would bias it in the direction of encouraging savings and productivity-increasing investment. This tendency would require shifting a greater share of the tax burden onto consumption; the United States currently imposes a larger share of the tax burden on capital and a smaller share on consumption than almost any other major industrialized country. Such a shift, unfortunately, is as politically unpopular as it is economically desirable. On the government spending side, in the words of a recent report from the Committee on Economic Development, the need is to "... redirect public expenditures toward productive investment by reforming and restraining entitlement transfers (which enlarge private consumption) and redesigning or curtailing activities that are 'investments' in name only."[5]

Regulatory reform could also play a useful role in stimulating growth. Regulatory measures that make use of market-based incentives, employ risk-based and cost-benefit standards in establishing priorities, and focus on outcomes while giving regulators and firms broad latitude in achieving those outcomes would go far toward alleviating the increases in costs and constraints on innovation imposed by many current regulatory approaches. This easing would occur without attenuating the underlying social goals toward which the regulations are directed. In addition, legal reforms that reduced the costs and uncertainties generated by our present litigation system could have a similar beneficial effect.

Finally, government should take every opportunity to encourage a shift from private-sector downsizing as the major route to increasing profitability, to a greater emphasis on innovation and growth—a shift that may in fact already be underway. Aside from generating publicity (look what the Baldridge awards have done to encourage a private-sector focus on quality), our government should maintain its support for the sort of basic research and development that has traditionally generated positive externalities for private-sector growth but that is currently on the endangered-species list. And, while resisting any temptation to try to "pick winners and losers" via industrial policies, the government should support the initiatives of the Commerce Department's National Institute of Standards and Technology (NIST) to encourage the diffusion of new technologies, particularly to small and medium-sized firms that might otherwise not have access to them.

Many of the steps just mentioned as possible stimuli to the aggregate growth rate of the U.S. economy are discussed in greater detail elsewhere in this volume, and none appears to be a magic pill that can release the secret of faster sustainable growth. The difficulty of the search, however, underlines the desirability of restoring a virtuous circle in which a healthy aggregate growth rate reduces protectionist pressures and thereby contributes to preserving or expanding economic openness, which in turn largely stimulates the growth of productivity and aggregate economic activity. Such a virtuous circle would ultimately benefit the economic well-being of the American people.

NOTES

1. A.B. Bernard and J.B. Jensen, "Exporters, Jobs and Wages in U.S. Manufacturing 1976–87," *Brookings Papers on Economic Activity: Microeconomics* (1995), 67–112; Lawrence Katz and Lawrence Summers, "Industry Rents: Evidence and Implications," *Brookings Papers on Economic Activity: Microeconomics* (1989), 209–290.

2. Martin L. Baily and Hans Gersbach, "Efficiency in Manufacturing and the Need for Global Competition," *Brookings Papers on Economic Activity: Microeconomics* (1995), 307–358.

3. For a review and citations of this literature, see: Sebastian Edwards, "Openness, Trade Liberalization, and Growth in Developing Countries," *Journal of Economic Literature* XXXI-3 (September 1993), 1358-1393.

4. Dani Rodrick, "What Does the Political Economy Literature on Trade Policy (Not) Tell Us That We Ought to Know?," Working Paper no. 1039, National Bureau of Economic Research, 1996.

5. Committee for Economic Development, *American Workers and Economic Change*, (New York and Washington, D.C.: CED 1996), 10.

7

Government Can Boost Growth

Supply-Side Policies for Boosting Growth

ROBERT J. BARRO, ROBERT C.
WAGGNER PROFESSOR OF
ECONOMICS, HARVARD UNIVERSITY,
AND SENIOR FELLOW AT THE
HOOVER INSTITUTION

There is little doubt that an economy prospers when government policies focus on long-run growth. To learn which policies foster economic growth, I have studied a broad array of countries. Since 1960, reasonably good information on economic variables and social indicators exists for about 100 countries, representing a range of incomes from the poorest nations of Africa to the richest members of the Organization of

Economic Cooperation and Development. Although a study of such a diverse group involves numerous challenging concepts and data, it also provides a broad range of experience that is necessary to isolate the effects of alternative government policies.

LESSONS ON GROWTH FROM OTHER COUNTRIES

In a general sense, the results from this cross-country data are not surprising. One of the conclusions I reached was that growth of GDP per person is fostered by better maintenance of property rights and the rule of law, fewer market distortions, less nonproductive government spending, and price stability. Also helpful are high levels of human capital in the forms of education and health, low fertility rates (which correspond in the long run to low rates of population growth), and improvements in the terms of trade.

In some parts of the world, the interplay between a democratic government and growth is a major political issue. The level of democracy, measured by the subjective indicator of the electoral rights of citizens, turns out not to have a strong effect on subsequent growth. At low levels of political freedom, an expansion of democracy stimulates growth. However, once a moderate amount of political freedom has been attained, any further expansion actually has a small negative effect on growth.

For given values of these growth determinants, a country's growth rate is inversely related to its level of per-capita GDP. Or, to put it another way, if a poor country can stabilize its public institutions and human capital, then it tends to move fairly quickly toward the richer countries. In practice, however, the typical less developed country has low income precisely because of its past bad policies and low levels of human capital. Consequently, poor countries usually do not grow faster than rich ones, and no general pattern of income convergence appears in the data.

The cross-country evidence provides good and bad news for the growth prospects of the United States and other advanced countries. On the positive side, their basic institutions and policies are more favorable to growth than those of less developed countries. In particular, their legal systems and public bureaucracies function reasonably well, their markets and price systems are allowed to operate, freely and high inflation is unusual.

The population is also highly educated, reasonably healthy, and rich. The bad news behind these factors, however, is that it is hard to get the long-run per-capita growth rate in the advanced countries much above 1.5% to 2% per year. The notion that tax or other policy changes could double the long-term U.S. growth rate therefore looks unrealistic.

The basic problem is that successful countries cannot grow rapidly by filling the vacuum of nonworking public institutions or by absorbing the technologies and ideas that have been developed elsewhere. In addition, because the levels of physical and human capital are already high, further accumulations are subject to diminishing returns.

Sustained growth in advanced countries depends on technological innovations that lead to new products and better methods of production. The rate of technological progress is responsive to policies that shape the economic environment. However, the empirical evidence suggests that feasible policies will not improve technology rapidly enough to raise the long-term per-capita growth above the range of 1.5% to 2% per year. Since World War II, U.S. per-capita growth exceeded 2% only in the 1960s, but not for any other sustained period (if the Korean War years are excluded).

The numbers should, in any case, be kept in longer-term perspective: the average growth rate of U.S. output per person since 1870 is only 1.8% per year and has not shown clearly varying trends within this time. Although this growth rate looks unspectacular, it was high enough to make the United States in 1996 the richest country in the world (in terms of purchasing-power-adjusted GDP per capita).

SUPPLY-SIDE POLICIES FOR BOOSTING LONG-RUN GROWTH

The good news from the cross-country evidence is that some policy changes can be identified that would enhance long-term growth by a few tenths of a percentage point. Such changes would affect long-run standards of living a great deal. For example, based on the cross-country findings, I estimate that a shift in the United States to a flat-rate consumption tax would raise the long-term growth rate by about 0.3 percentage points per year, resulting in an increase of U.S. real GDP by about $300 billion after 10 years. On the down side, if price stability were abandoned and average annual inflation were to rise by 5 percentage points, I estimate that the long-run growth rate would decline by about 0.2 percentage points. In this case, the level of U.S. real GDP would decrease by about $200 billion after 10 years.

Aside from basic tax reform and price stability maintenance, other new policies would be important for long-term U.S. growth. Some promising suggestions include improvements in educational quality, notably those that would be stimulated by school-choice programs; privatization of Social Security along Chilean lines; reduced regulation of labor and other markets; and overhaul of the legal system to limit product-liability awards. Unfortunately, the cross-country growth research is not yet at a stage to yield precise estimates for the effects of all these reforms on the long-term growth rate.

Spending cuts are also essential for long-term U.S. growth. If spending declines along with taxes, the economy benefits from the switch of resources to private use and from the effects of permanently reduced tax distortions. My estimate from the cross-country studies is that a 10% cut in the size of government—that is, in spending *and* taxes—would raise the long-term growth rate by about 0.1% per year. Although this growth effect seems small, it means that U.S. real GDP would be higher by about $8 billion in the first year and $41 billion after 5 years. More substantial growth effects—perhaps as much as 0.3%–0.5% per year—could be expected from implementation of basic tax reform, a school-choice experiment, reduced government regulation, and changes in the legal system. The school-choice idea may be the best welfare program that has ever been conceived.

The so-called greedy 1980s saw impressive economic developments, especially after the 1982 recession, which may have been connected with the end of inflation. The Reagan tax cuts in 1981 and 1986 appear to have contributed to the economic good times, and the resulting budget deficits had the virtue of restraining federal spending outside of defense and the main entitlement programs. Although budget deficits are never welcome, we did not see the feared surge in interest rates and the contraction of investment. Additional benefits came from the move to-ward a more efficient tax system, especially with the reforms of 1986 (other than the rise in the capital-gains rate). Since 1990, however, the federal deficit has been used mainly as an excuse to raise or maintain taxes rates. In this light, proposed tax cuts mark a welcome return to the Reagan agenda of using revenue starvation to force a downsizing of the government.

What is most needed is a thorough series of reforms that call for taxing consumption rather than income, lowering marginal tax rates by flattening the rate structure, eliminating a variety of deductions, and simplifying the overall system. A number of good plans exist, such as the one proposed by Robert Hall and Alvin Rabushka of the Hoover Institution. One attractive feature of their plan is that it permits a shift to consumption taxation while allowing for any desired structure of tax rates on wage in-come, including a generous family allowance.[1]

If a more efficient tax system is inevitable, then it makes good economic sense to have a tax cut immediately—even if it causes a temporary budget deficit—in order to reduce the amount of taxes collected from the old, inefficient system. Budget deficits are sometimes warranted as part of an effective public-finance policy.

Other tax proposals should be evaluated in terms of whether they move the system closer to the desired reform. The $500-per-child tax credit seems to be popular with both political parties, but its only incentive seems to be as subsidy for having children. A focus on economic growth suggests that other forms of tax cuts would be more productive.

Another frequent suggestion—income-tax deductions for Social-Security "contributions"—would shift collections from a flat-rate payroll tax to a graduated-rate levy on all income. Al-though some business groups support this tax change as a way to reduce labor costs, the suggestion is bad because it would play into the worst features of the existing system: average mar-ginal tax rates would rise, and rates on capital income would increase relative to those on labor income. The Social Security system is problematic in many ways, but its form of finance—essentially a flat-rate levy on wages—is remarkably efficient. After all, the revenue to pay for government spending has to be raised somehow.

Cutting capital-gains rates, expanding IRAs, and subsidizing education and training are generally favorable measures, but are only partial steps toward a consumption-based system in which all saving is exempted from taxation. It would be far better to correct the overall system than to erect more piecemeal provisions that favor designated kinds of investment and are politically difficult to eliminate later on. Some of these provisions—though not the capital-gains cut—complicate the system and create distortions among types of investments.

It may be useful to relate this discussion to *supply-side economics*, a phrase that critics of President Reagan and his intellectual followers tried to ridicule in applying it to the extreme proposition that tax cuts pay for themselves by generating a sufficiently dramatic expansion of the tax base. (This view may be correct in certain cases, for example, historical cuts in the top marginal income-tax rate, for elimination of the luxury tax on boats, and, more conjecturally, for reductions in capital-gains rates.) It may actually be too conservative to estimate that only about 27% of the static revenue loss from a cut in marginal rates would be recouped over 6 years by increases in the tax base.

For me, supply-side economics encompasses a variety of influences on an economy's ability and willingness to produce goods and services. Among such influences are increases in stocks of physical capital, education, training, and health; incentives to invest and work from low tax rates and institutions that maintain property rights and foster free markets; stimulants to technological progress; and provision of core infrastructure services. The supply-side approach was a reaction to the narrow concentration on aggregate demand in the standard Keynesian model of the macroeconomy. To put it bluntly, no one believes the United States is richer than Ethiopia because the United States has engaged in better management of aggregate demand. We are richer because we embrace—although not tightly enough—some form of supply-side economics.

NOTES

1. Robert E. Hall and Alvin Rabushka, *The Flat Tax*, 2d ed. (Hoover Institution Press, Stanford CA, 1995).

A Progrowth Fiscal System

ROBERT A. MUNDELL, PROFESSOR OF
ECONOMICS, COLUMBIA UNIVERSITY

Several countries have experienced su-
pergrowth at particular times in their history. Western Europe
experienced rapid growth in the early post-World War II decades. The East Asian tigers astounded the world with their
soaring development: in the past 2 decades, China has grown at
2-digit rates, matching Japan's phenomenal "sudden economic
rise" between 1955 and 1970.

Yet the conventional wisdom argues that the United States is
doomed to grow at 2.3% or less. Is this view correct? I believe
not. The stakes are high. Growth at 2.3% means that GDP doubles every 31 years, while growth at 4% doubles GDP in 18 years.
Higher growth would make the future economy much larger,
creating fundamental changes in everybody's "most-wanted
list" of government activities, such as tax reductions, debt reduction, solvency of entitlement programs, welfare supplements,
medical research, and defense.

GROWTH EXPERIENCES

Apart from the spectacular instances of growth noted above, the
history of growth shows a wide disparity of results. Table 7.1
shows growth rates of the G–7 countries over 3 recent decades.
In the first period, growth rates ranged from a low of 2.9% in the
United Kingdom to a high of 9.7% in Japan, with 6 of the 7 countries experiencing growth rates above 4%. The spreads were
much lower in the next-decade as growth collapsed under the
weight of the international monetary system breakdown, oil
shocks, and rampant inflation. Spreads between growth rates
continued to narrow in the most recent decade as growth recovered and inflation subsided.

Much more information is now available about growth over
longer periods of time as a result of the work of Angus Maddison
and others. Table 7.2 shows growth rates for selected periods

Table 7.1.   G–7 Growth Rates, Selected Periods

	1963–1972	1973–1982	1983–1992
United States	4.8	1.6	2.6
Japan	9.7	3.5	4.1
Germany*	4.3	1.9	2.7
France	5.3	2.5	2.4
Italy	4.6	3.0	2.5
U.K.	2.9	0.8	2.1
Canada	5.3	3.0	2.7

WEFA World Economic Service. *Historical Data.* June 1993 and June 1995.
*West Germany, except for 1985–1994, which includes a 16.4% increment in 1990 due to the accession of Eastern Germany.

Table 7.2.   GDP Growth Rates, Selected Periods, 1820–1992

	U.S.	France	Germany	U.K.	Japan
1820–1870	4.22	1.27	2.00	2.04	0.31
1870–1913	3.94	1.63	2.81	1.90	2.34
1913–1950	2.84	1.15	1.06	1.19	2.24
1950–1973	3.92	5.02	5.99	2.96	9.25
1973–1992	2.39	2.26	2.30	1.59	3.76

Angus Maddison, *Monitoring the World Economy* (Paris: OECD Development Centre Studies, 1995).

from 1820 to 1992 for the G–5 advanced countries. Growth in the United States ranged from a high of 4.22% during the half-century before 1870 (a period that included the devastation of the Civil War) to a low of 2.4% from 1973 to 1992; in all other periods, growth was above or close to 3%. For all countries except Japan, the slowest growth rates occurred between 1913 and 1950, the period that included the two world wars. For Japan the slowest growth occurred before 1870, before the Meiji reforms, and its most spectacular growth took place between 1950 and 1973. Except for the United States and the United Kingdom, who were in some sense technological leaders, growth tended to be much lower in the early periods than in the post-war decades. But there is sufficient diversity to confirm that there are no "growth laws" restraining growth to a 2.3% speed limit.

As noted earlier, some countries, most notably in the Pacific Rim, have had more spectacular results: over the decades 1975–84 and 1985–94, the annual average growth rate of China was 7.6% and 9.4%, South Korea 7.8% and 8.6%, Taiwan 7.7% and 7.9%, Singapore 7.8% and 6.9%, and Malaysia 7.1% and 6.6%.

HUMAN CAPITAL

Human capital can be increased by education, training, and practice, and can be measured by, for example, years of schooling and on-the-job training; once human capital is taken into account, the unexplained residual declines dramatically. Because labor is of little use without learned skills, if land is counted as capital, and if entrepreneurship is included in human capital, it may be convenient for some purposes to relate output to capital in its broadest sense. In this case, growth can be conceived of as the sum of the rate of growth of capital and the rate of growth of capital's productivity.

In the special case where the productivity of capital is constant, the rate of growth of output would be equal to the rate of growth of the capital stock, which is itself equal to the fraction of income saved and invested, multiplied by the productivity of capital. If, for example, the rate of investment and saving is one-tenth of income, and income is one-quarter of the capital stock, the rate of growth would be $.1 \times .25 = .025$, or 2.5%.

Looked at in this way, there are two ways of increasing growth. One is to increase the supply of capital—including human capital and entrepreneurship—through changes in the rate of investment and saving. The other is to increase the ratio between output and capital, i.e. the productivity of capital.

INCREASE GROWTH THROUGH INVESTMENT AND SAVING

In order to determine how investment and saving increase growth, we must examine their economic characteristics. Saving, an activity of households, is the excess of the flow of income over consumption and has its counterpart in the demand for financial assets. Investment, an activity of firms, is the rate at which firms are increasing their capital stock and has its counterpart in the supply of financial assets. Although motivated by different considerations, saving and investment are brought into equality by changes in prices, interest rates, and incomes. Over the business cycle, discrepancies between investment and saving lead to expansions and contractions. Despite the equality of saving and investment in equilibrium, however, it is necessary to examine both the forces determining the propensity to save and the forces governing the incentive to invest.

Changes in investment and saving, expressed as a percentage of GDP, can have a large effect on the growth rate. An increase in the rate of saving by 5% of income (GDP), say from 10% of income to 15%, would increase the rate of growth by 50%, i.e., from 2.5% to 3.75%. What factors then are likely to increase investment and saving?

Saving is motivated by the need for future assets to meet the needs of liquidity, contingencies, retirement income, and bequests. Demographics, wealth, government policy, and the growth rate are variables that affect the propensity and ability to save.[1] When private households bear the responsibility of saving for retirement income, their claims are anticipated by the higher capital stock that prior capital formation yields. Government provisions for Social Security not only diminished the urgency for private saving, but also squandered, via government consumption and budget deficits, the trust funds that would have augmented the size of the economy under a privately organized pension system.

Investment is motivated by after-tax profits from investment relative to the interest rate. When there is an increase in prospective profits from capital, such as that occasioned by a new discovery or invention, or when there is a decrease in the interest rate, such as that caused by an increase in voluntary saving, entrepreneurs take advantage of the opportunity, using the capital market for funds to finance additional investment and higher growth. At the new equilibrium, the rate of return over cost will be again brought into equilibrium with the rate of interest at a higher rate of investment, saving, and growth.

Most of the examples of very rapid growth in economic history have been achieved in countries where the economic surplus of society—the excess of output over traditional subsistence—has been channeled into investment. This was the case with many of the Western European countries and Japan after World War II where the share of wages in national income was comparatively low and where growth "miracles" were common. By contrast, when surplus had been appropriated by labor or used up by high taxation to finance heavy military spending or welfare-entitlement programs, economies tended to stagnate. Spending programs that were initiated at favorable stages in the demographic cycle have often proved to be unsustainable when demography became unfavorable to growth.

INCREASE GROWTH BY INCREASING THE PRODUCTIVITY OF CAPITAL

The second way to increase growth involves changes in the productivity of capital. Changes in the rate of growth of productivity affects growth in two ways: through its *rate of change* and its *level*. If the saving rate is 10% and the productivity of capital is 25% and *constant*, the growth rate would be, as before, 2.5%. But if it is *initially* at that level but *rising* at the rate of, say, 1.8% a year, the growth rate would be, *initially*, equal to $.02 + .1 \times .25 = .045$, or 4.5%. Productivity growth of x% adds x percentage points to the growth rate.

This is not all, however. If productivity is changing—even at a constant rate—the growth rate will itself be changing. The 2% annual productivity increase lifts the growth rate from 2.5% to 4.5%, but the growth rate of 4.5% continues to increase as the productivity of capital becomes higher. Suppose the productivity of capital increases at the rate of 2% a year for 10 years. After that, the productivity of capital would have risen to 31.94% and the growth rate would be 5.19%. If at that time the increase in the productivity of capital ceased, the rate of growth would drop back to a new level of 3.19%; this is higher than the original 2.5% because the *level* of productivity is higher and therefore saving is more effective.

What determines the productivity of capital? For one thing, capacity utilization and employment: higher utilization of labor and human capital with a given capital stock means a higher productivity of capital, resulting in the procyclical movement of real interest rates. Europe's experience is indicative: low unemployment in the 1950s and 1960s was matched with rapid growth, whereas high unemployment from the 1970s to the 1990s was matched with low growth. Coincident with this increase in unemployment and decline in the growth rate has been a stunning increase in the share of GDP accounted for by government.

More important than the productivity of capital over the long run is the pace of invention and innovation. There is a major difference between technological pioneers, who pay for their groundbreaking work by research and development, and imitators, who can adapt existing technology from elsewhere, often at a small fraction of the cost of initial development. A certain educational level, however, is required to utilize advanced technology; Europe and Japan in the early post-war period achieved this critical level and the capacity to absorb American technology.

New consumer products increase the value of final output; because their development often requires a one-time investment, discoveries typically lead eventually to a higher output-capital ratio. The same argument holds for innovations in equipment. The pace of invention is largely determined by R & D investment and is itself a function of the level and rate of improvement in education. Most of the research in applied areas can be carried out by the private sector, but government policy fosters the scientific climate for pure research that benefits the entire society.

GOVERNMENT SPENDING, FISCAL POLICY, AND TAXATION

Government affects growth by the character of its spending, its fiscal policy, and the sources through which it is financed. In principle, government spending on investment adds to the capital stock and can increase growth. If rates of return were identical for both, an increase in public spending at the expense of private spending would raise or lower the growth rate according to whether the share of investment in spending was, respectively, higher or lower in the public sector than in the private sector.

Reality, however, is very different. In noncommunist countries, government spending has typically been taken up by government consumption and transfer payments; very little is left over for investment. In the OECD countries in recent years, only a tiny (and, in some cases, negative) fraction of government expenditure has been devoted to investment.[2] The positive output effects of government spending have therefore been minimal. In addition, the very rapid expansion of the government sector in the past 4 decades,[3] to the extent that it has been at the expense of private investment, has reduced economic growth.

Government spending must be financed by taxes, bonds, or money creation. Current taxes finance the bulk of government spending; but along with the social revolution that brought about a tremendous increase in the government sector, debt finance has also soared. In 1960, OECD debt averaged 25.2% of GDP; in 1990, it had grown to 76.4%.[4] Although this debt is an asset of bondholders, it is matched by liabilities of taxpayers and does not constitute *net* wealth; an issue of government bonds, for example, financed by an increase in the tax on profits, would decrease the value of private stock to the same extent that it raised the outstanding level of government bonds.[5]

Both current taxes and future taxes (to finance interest on the debt) have allocative effects that influence the decisions of entrepreneurs to produce and invest. The entrepreneur is the profit-seeking factor that assumes risk, hires and coordinates the factors of production, establishes production and investment plans, sets production in motion, arranges for inventory replenishment, raises finance for investment, determines prices and outputs, and introduces new techniques. The reward of the entrepreneur is profits—after-tax profits—the beacon that guides production and investment along the lines where it can be most efficiently used. The tax and regulatory system of an economy has its biggest impact on growth through its effect on entrepreneurial decisions. If taxes and regulations have been given short shrift in academic discussions of growth policy, it is because the entrepreneur does not explicitly appear in growth theory!

Lump-sum is the phrase describing taxes that in discussions of theory have no distorting effects. But in reality such effects do not exist: all taxes have distorting side effects that involve waste. A tax on labor income drives a wedge between the productivity and rewards of effort; a tax on profits drives a wedge between what capital produces and what savers earn; a poll tax alters population growth; and so on.

Taxes are, nevertheless, required to finance needed government expenditure. The problem is to find the revenue along with the taxes that produce the least wasteful side effects. A pattern of taxes is most likely to be efficient when it raises revenue without artificially altering the relative prices on which individuals and firms formulate their consumption, production, and investment plans.[6]

The law of diminishing returns applies here. At very low tax rates, the revenue per unit of waste is high relative to the waste; but the higher the tax, the less the benefit and the higher the waste. For this reason, punitively high taxes on particular sources of income are likely to be especially distorting and will at some point produce less rather than more revenue. Other things equal, low tax rates spread broadly are preferable to high tax rates spread narrowly.

A PROGROWTH FISCAL SYSTEM

Japan pioneered the use of periodic tax rates as a means of promoting growth in the miracle years between 1955 and 1970, when its economy grew at 2-digit levels and it became again a major economic power. In the 1960s, the Kennedy-Johnson tax cuts, combined with a monetary policy designed to protect the dollar and avoid inflation, similarly propelled the U.S. economy toward one of the longest economic expansions in its history.

In the 1970s, the breakdown of the international monetary system and the emergence of stagflation brought to the fore the economic ideas associated with supply-side economics. High and steeply progressive income taxes, combined with inflationary monetary policies, clogged the arteries of profit, depressing employment and stalling growth. Supply-side economists advocated lower marginal tax rates to spur employment and growth, the indexing of tax brackets to offset "bracket creep," and tighter monetary policy to restore stability of the price-level and exchange rates.

Reaganomics borrowed from both the Kennedy-Johnson administrations and supply-side theory to get the economy moving and lower inflation. Top marginal tax rates were lowered at the federal level from 70% to 28%, and tax brackets were indexed for inflation to create an inflation-immune tax structure. Although some recidivism took place on tax rates during the Bush and Clinton administrations, not even the most die-hard critics of supply-side economics have advocated a return to the prohibitive tax rates that characterized the half century spanning the Roosevelt and Carter administrations.

The supply-side policy mix in the 1980s not only brought inflation under control, but also, like the Kennedy-Johnson tax cuts of the 1960s, had a magnificent effect on employment and growth. Despite a nine-month recession that started in 1990, the expansion of employment and growth has continued through the Bush and Clinton administrations. From 1982 to 1996, 34 million jobs were created, an *increase* in U.S. employment in 15 years matching the *total* employed labor force in Germany, the third largest economy in the world!

Although some critics argue that Reaganomics was a failure because the tax cuts and increased military spending in the 1980s produced a huge budget and trade deficits, they cannot deny the success of these policies in expanding the economy and ending the Cold War![7] The budget deficits increased because military spending increased between 1981 and 1989 by a cumulative amount of $779 billion, compared with a cumulative increase in the deficit of $806 billion over the same years.[8] The cost in terms of debt buildup was high, but U.S. debt at 63% of GDP is still lower than that of the European Union's debt of 73% of GDP. In addition, who would deny that ending the Cold War in victory justified the cost?

CONCLUSION: THE CASE FOR AN ACTIVE GROWTH POLICY

The case for an active growth policy is a strong one. History has shown that growth rates substantially above 2.3% can be and have been sustained for long periods in the United States and other countries. Monetary policy cannot be the engine of higher noninflationary growth. But fiscal policy—both levers of it—can be. With every tax-and-spend fiscal system is associated a differ-ent growth potential. The U.S. tax-and-spend system reduces po-tential growth because it penalizes success and rewards failure; it discriminates against the efficient corporate form of enterprise; it penalizes risk and innovation; and it inhibits human and mate-rial capital-deepening. The tax systems of many European coun-tries are even worse than the U.S. system.

Growth is sensitive to the division between productive and unproductive government spending and the structure of the tax system. A lower *level* of government spending would make more of the surplus of society available for capital formation and growth. A *shift* in government priorities from consumption and redistribution to social overhead capital, improved education, and investment in scientific and medical research would go far in raising the productivity of capital with a permanent effect on growth. On the tax side, reducing top marginal income tax rates to the levels of the Reagan years, slashing of the capital-gains tax, and eliminating or drastically reducing the corporate-income tax would be major steps toward a tax system that could propel the economy considerably beyond the 2.3% growth speed limit that past misguided policies have set as a standard.

Notes

1. In earlier societies, before wealth could be built up in the form of durable goods, children were the traditional way households handled the need for re-tirement income. Investment in children was implicitly repaid in the three-generation family by the socially mandated duty of children to look after their retired parents. When, as in China, population policy imposed the one-child-per-family rule, household saving soared as households were deprived of their traditional social-security system.

2. See, for example, *OECD Economies at a Glance: Structural Indicators* (n.p., 1996) 101, table 7.9.

3. "Unemployment, Competitiveness and the Welfare State," *Rivista di Po-litica Economica* 84 (November 1994): 127–192. Table 14 on page 155 shows the changes in the "tax wedge," measured by the share of government expenditure in GDP, between 1963 and 1993. Between these years, the share of government spending in GDP rose from 13.6% to 26.3% in Japan, from 27.5% to 34.4% in the United States, from 30.1% to 40.6% in the U.K., from 24.7% to 48.7% in Canada, from 30.4% to 46.6% in Germany, from 33.5% to 51.2% in France, from 26.8% to 51.6% in Italy. In several other countries, the share of government increased to

above 50% and even 60% of GDP. The full implications of this revolution in the sphere of government have hardly begun to be understood.

4. *OECD Structural Indicators* (1996), table 7.1.

5. Robert J. Barro, "The Public Debt, Corporate Income Taxes and the Rate of Interest," *Journal of Political Economy* 68 (December 1960): 622–26; and Robert J. Barro, "Are Government Bonds Net Wealth?" *Journal of Political Economy* 1974: 1095–1117.

6. Even lump-sum taxes change prices insofar as the transfer of income from the private to the public sector alters the global pattern of demand.

7. In a recent paper from the Cato Institute, Niskanen and Moore have shown that the deficits were due mainly to the increased military spending, not the cuts in tax rates. Revenues rose between 1982 and 1989 by 24.1%. This can be compared with the effects of the tax increases in the Bush and Clinton administrations, when revenues between 1990 and 1997 (based on forecasts) rose by only 19.3%. See Niskanen and Moore, "Supply Side Cuts and the Truth about the Reagan Record," *Policy Analysis*, 22 October 1996. In other words revenues rose by a higher percentage during the years of the Reagan tax cuts than they did during the years of the subsequent Bush and Clinton tax increases!

8. Niskanen and Moore.

Fiscal and Monetary Policies for Growth

BENJAMIN M. FRIEDMAN, WILLIAM
JOSEPH MAIER PROFESSOR OF
POLITICAL ECONOMY HARVARD
UNIVERSITY

Increasing the nation's rate of ongoing economic expansion is an objective that practically all Americans favor, and in recent years the subject has taken on renewed urgency.

Much of the discussion of potential public-policy actions to stimulate more robust growth have focused on issues other than monetary and fiscal policy. Economic growth, after all, comes from increasing the quantity and quality of inputs to the production process (labor, capital, knowledge, and so on); from allocating these inputs more efficiently across different potential uses; and from combining them in more efficient ways within any given use. More specific policies for educating and training the workforce, enhancing the development and application of new technologies, strengthening incentives and reducing disincentives to work and invest, and removing impediments to efficient production (due either to governmental interference or to market failure) have often been at the center of the discussion of ways to support superior long-run growth.

THE IMPORTANCE OF FISCAL AND MONETARY POLICIES

Monetary and fiscal policies significantly impact the growth process in at least three ways, however. First, the experience of many countries clearly shows that rapid and volatile price inflation impedes economic growth; and there is no lack of cogent explanations for why this is so. As a result, a major responsibility of demand-management policy, and of monetary policy in particular, is to maintain sufficient price stability to allow sustained growth to proceed.

Since the early 1980s, the United States has had a good record on this front. According to the U.S. government, price increases over the last 10 years have averaged 3.5% per annum at the consumer level and 2.0% at the producer level. Each figure is well within the low-inflation range that indicates there is little or no negative effect on economic growth. In addition, recent inflation has been even more modest (for example, 2.5% for consumer prices in 1995).[1] The Federal Reserve Board deserves high praise for this record. In order to avoid retarding real economic growth, maintaining comparable performance into the future is a high priority—but there is no need for new policies in this regard.

Second, maintaining full utilization of the economy's labor and capital resources, another traditional responsibility of demand-management policies, stimulates labor-force participation and creates new physical capital. Ample evidence shows that unemployed workers often do not seek employment when jobs are scarce. Similarly, idle factories are a deterrent to new investment. Most of these two types of situations are probably only temporary, but some may become permanent and result in slower economic growth, possibly on an ongoing basis.

The United States has been quite successful in maintaining high employment for over a decade. Only one business recession, and that fairly short and shallow, has punctuated relatively full employment since the mid 1980s. Government statistics indicate that unemployment has averaged 6.2% of the labor force over the past 10 years, and use of plant capacity has likewise stayed at or near convential full-employment benchmarks.[2] Although changing degrees of fiscal stimulus might sometimes contribute to this kind of success in principle, in fact much of the credit for maintaining full employment over this period again goes to monetary policy. Maintaining comparable performance in the future is a priority—in this case presumably more for other reasons than for the direct connection to long-run economic growth—but there is no apparent need for new monetary policies.

The third way in which growth is spurred is through fiscal policy in particular, and more specifically the relationship between what the government spends and what it takes in from taxes and other revenues. Such policy is important for the growth process because of the crowding out of private capital formation resulting from whatever borrowing the government must do to finance its budget deficit. This borrowing absorbs saving that would otherwise be available to finance firms' investment in new factories and machinery, thereby making workers more productive. The larger the government's deficit, the more it borrows; and the less of the economy's scarce saving is available for private businesses and individuals to deploy in productivity-enhancing investment.

Of course, if American private saving were sufficient, financing both a large government deficit and ample private capital formation would present no problem. The same would be true if there were no long-run disadvantages inherent in a trade deficit so as to supplement American saving with large amounts of saving borrowed from abroad. Large government deficits also would not be a factor if families and individuals increased their private saving as the government's deficit grew; or if the government itself were running a deficit mostly because of enlarged expenditures on infrastructure or other productivity-enhancing public capital.

Unfortunately, none of these hypothetical situations accurately describes the recent experience of the United States. The U.S. private saving rate has always been lower than in most other major industrial countries, and in recent years it has fallen lower still. The United States has already become a net-debtor country and is steadily becoming more so (even in relation to the growing size of the U.S. economy). Neither U.S. individuals nor businesses showed much tendency to adjust their saving in response to even very large movements in the government's deficit. And the surge of large deficits in the 1980s accompanied a decline, not an increase, in the share of government expenditures for nondefense capital formation.

America's record in preventing government borrowing from impeding private capital formation has been far from uniformly good over the past 15 years. Enlarged during the early 1980s by a combination of tax cuts and defense-spending increases, together with the government's unwillingness to cut high-cost nondefense programs like Social Security and Medicare, the federal budget deficit in the 1980s averaged 4.1% of national income, compared to 0.8% in the 1960s and 2.3% in the 1970s. (After adjustment to allow for the influence of recessions versus full employment, the "structural" deficit averaged 3.2% of national income in the 1980s versus 1.5% and 2.2% in the 1960s and 1970s, respectively.)[3] Interest rates on short-term business borrowing rose to 4.26% above the inflation rate on average in the 1980s, compared to 1.85% in the 1960s and 1970s. Private net investment in new factories and machinery declined from 3.2% of national income on average in the 1960s and 1970s to 2.5% in the 1980s.

Such policies have lasting effects, including those on future government budgets as well as on future economic growth. Deficits that run year to year do not simply go away. They accumulate into debt outstanding. The government still owes that debt and must pay interest on it, even if it succeeds in reducing the current deficit to zero. Investments in factories and machines made in any year do not simply go away either. They accumulate into the nation's stock of productive capital, which business can continue to use long after the initial investment. Conversely, when investment is inadequate, the result is a capital stock that remains shrunken even after yearly investment has recovered to a more satisfactory rate.

In recent years the amount of capital per worker in the United States has grown much more slowly than it did in the postwar era, despite the fact that the labor force has grown more slowly since the baby-boomers reached adulthood, with the result that maintaining the growth of capital per worker should have been easier. At year-end 1994 (the most recent date for which comprehensive capital-stock data are available), U.S. business had $62,900 of plant and equipment for every worker employed in the private sector. If, during the period 1981–94, the United States had simply continued to devote the same 3.2% of national income to net new investment that it had invested on average in the 1960s and 1970s, the private capital stock would have had $73,500 per worker by 1994 (even without any allowance for the additional output that the capital would have produced)—a difference of almost 17%. Even with conservative estimates of how much physical capital adds to workers' productivity, this large difference is a major reason why U.S. economic growth has been disappointing during this period. With an elasticity of 1/3 (a fairly standard estimate), a capital stock that was 17% larger by 1994 would have meant nearly 6% in additional output. And so the average growth rate between 1980 and 1994 would have been greater by 0.4% per annum.[4]

THE BUDGET DEFICIT REDUCTION

The good news is that the nation has lately made very substantial progress in narrowing the budget deficit from the record levels of the recent past. In fiscal year 1992 the deficit was $290 billion, or 4.9% of the national income. In fiscal 1996 the deficit was down to $107 billion, or just 1.4% of national income—the smallest federal deficit compared to national income since 1974. Part of this improvement has been the result of the spending cuts (mostly on defense) and tax increases (mostly on high income taxpayers) that Congress adopted at President Clinton's urging in 1993. Another part has been due to restraint on nondefense spending pushed by the new Republican congressional majority elected in 1994. The rest reflects the improvement in the economy since 1992. The decline in the structural deficit has been about 2% of national income.

The fact that the American economy has moved to lower unemployment and greater capacity utilization since 1992, even as the federal government has cut its deficit by more than two-thirds compared to the national income, illustrates an important point about the relationship between fiscal and monetary policies. Large and growing deficits are not a precondition for maintaining full employment and reducing the deficit need not lead to recession. True, raising taxes and cutting government spending reduces aggregate demand if all else is equal. But the role of monetary policy in such circumstances is precisely to make other things *not* equal. With appropriately stimulative monetary policy to offset the fiscal contraction, there is no need for deficit reduction to depress aggregate economic activity.

At the same time, the combination of tighter fiscal policy and easier monetary policy does alter the composition of aggregate demand—which, after all, is the whole point of reducing the deficit in the first place. The American economy has remained at full employment since 1992, but with lower interest rates and a higher investment rate than would presumably have emerged in the absence of the changed monetary-fiscal mix. By 1994 net investment in plant and equipment as a share of national income had at least recovered somewhat from the postwar record lows of the 1991–92 period, when investment was also depressed by recession and its immediate aftermath, but when net investment still remained small even compared to the 1980s. Net-investment data are not yet available for 1995 or 1996, but gross investment in plant and equipment has risen from 9.6% of national income in 1994 (and only 8.9% in 1992) to 10.2% in 1995 and 10.3% in the first half of 1996. The net-investment rate has presumably continued to rise as well.

TWO BUDGET DEFICIT PROBLEMS THAT REMAIN

The narrowing of the government's deficit over the last 4 years is a major accomplishment, which bodes well for the nation's future economic growth. But two major problems remain. First, as most budget analysts in and out of government agree, under current tax and spending policies the deficit will widen almost continually from now on. The challenge today is therefore to change these policies in order to, at least, prevent this reversal and, better yet, keep the deficit shrinking.

The challenge in meeting this objective has become harder over time. Last year, defense, Social Security, Medicare, and interest payments on the national debt accounted for 67% of all federal spending.[5] Literally everything else that the government does—law enforcement, air-traffic control, hurricane tracking, scientific research, space exploration, interstate highways, welfare programs, disaster relief, disease control, and all the rest—added up to only one-third of the total. By contrast, as recently as 15 years ago the three large "sacred cow" programs, including interest payments, amounted to only 57% of the budget. Finding politically acceptable spending cuts on a scale sufficient to keep the deficit from rising in the face of the country's growing elderly population is therefore ever harder. And the public clearly has little appetite for tax increases.

The second major problem is that the private saving rate has steadily fallen over almost the past 2 decades. To be sure, some ways of measuring private saving—in particular, those including capital gains on holdings of equity securities—show less of a decline. The rally of stock prices, however, does not by itself provide financing for new capital formation. This happens only when the higher value of existing capital induces firms to pay more to attract financing for new capital, which would appear as a new flow of saving. It is this saving from the private sector that has now declined from an average 8.2% of national income in the 1950s, 1960s, and 1970s to 7.2% in the 1980s, and just 5.6% thus far in the 1990s.

What is important about total investment for the nation as a whole (including the positive or negative balance of net investment abroad) is total national saving, including private saving plus any government surplus or minus any government deficit. From this perspective, a rise in private saving of 1% of national income, therefore, is equivalent to reducing the government deficit—that is, government dissaving—by the same 1% of national income. And a decline in private saving is equivalent to an increase in the government deficit.

In the 1980s the declining private saving rate increased the growing federal deficit. In the first half of the 1990s, this continuing decline prevented national saving from rising significantly, despite substantial progress in reducing the deficit. As of 1996 the deficit as a share of national income is back down to about the average level of the late 1960s or early 1970s, but net national saving as a share of national income is lower by about 3%.

CONTINUE REDUCING THE DEFICIT

In this situation as in others, however, what is true at the average does not dictate what matters at the margin. As of 1996 it is no longer true that a larger federal deficit, compared to a quarter century ago, is depressing U.S. capital formation and economic growth. This does not mean, however that further narrowing of the deficit, or even eliminating the government's imbalance altogether, would not help the American economy grow faster in the future. Similarly, although many of the reasons why the U.S. growth rate has slowed in recent years have nothing directly to do with deficits and capital formation, fiscal policy can still be helpful in fostering future growth.

Challenging though it may be, the continued reduction of government dissaving is a major American public-policy priority. A smaller deficit remains the surest way to increase the nation's capital formation, which in turn is one important ingredient of the growth process.

NOTES

1. Data on consumer and producer prices are from the U.S. Department of Labor, Bureau of Labor Statistics.

2. Data on unemployment are from the U.S. Department of Labor, Bureau of Labor Statistics; data on capacity utilization are from The Board of Governors of the Federal Reserve System.

3. Data on federal budget deficit (National Income and Product Accounts basis) and national income are from the U.S. Department of Commerce, Bureau of Economic Analysis; data on federal budget deficit (structural basis) are from the Congressional Budget Office.

4. Data on private sector capital stock, net investment, and national income are from the U.S. Department of Commerce, Bureau of Economic Analysis; data on private sector employment are from the U.S. Department of Labor, Bureau of Labor Statistics.

5. Data on federal spending are from the Executive Office of the President, Office of Management and Budget.

The Growth Burden of Federal Regulation

WILLIAM A. NISKANEN, CHAIRMAN
OF THE CATO INSTITUTE, FORMER
EDITOR OF *REGULATION* MAGAZINE,
AND A FORMER ECONOMIC ADVISER
TO PRESIDENT REAGAN

F ederal regulations now impose direct compliance costs of about $500 billion a year on the private sector.[1] This represents an annual cost of about $5,000 per private sector employee, with relatively higher costs per employee in manufacturing and in smaller firms.

The cost of federal regulation has been a relatively stable share of GDP in recent years, but this apparent stability masks two contrary trends. One is the loosening of federal economic regulation for about the last 20 years, including the substantial deregulation of transportation, energy, finance, more recently agriculture and telecommunications, and electricity, in the near future; there has also been a continued reduction of barriers to international trade. Over this same period, however, the cost of regulation of health, safety, and the environment has been increasing sharply. Figure 7.1 presents my estimate of the total direct cost of federal regulation and the contrary trends of the two major types of regulation from 1977 through 1996. A reduction of the relative burden of federal regulation will require a continued effort to reduce the remaining economic regulations; major changes in the legislative authority for the regulation of health, safety, and the environment; and much more effective administrative and congressional review of both existing and proposed regulations.

REGULATION AND ECONOMIC GROWTH

The total cost of federal regulation, of course, is substantially larger than the direct compliance cost. The indirect cost of regulations includes the labor diverted from creative tasks, capital di-

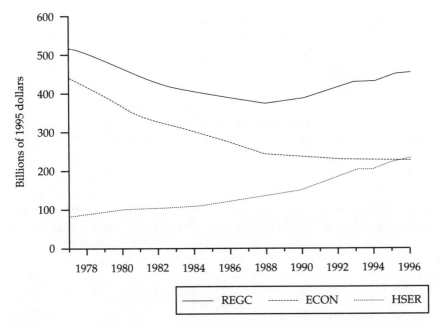

Figure 7.1.   Annual costs of federal regulation (RECG = total regulation cost, the sum of ECON and HSER; ECON = economic regulation; HSER = health, safety, and environmental regulation).

verted from productivity-enhancing investments, undeveloped new products, and goods not offered to American consumers. Most of these indirect effects of regulation are reflected in the level of productivity in the business sector, where the measured productivity growth rate has been generally low for over 30 years. These regulatory impacts must be separated from the other conditions that affect productivity.[2] There is no one good measure of the aggregate magnitude of these effects on productivity, but there are a number of valuable studies that provide selective estimates of these effects.

Most of the available studies estimate the effects of a specific set of regulations on a specific industry.[2] Frank Gallop and Mark Roberts (1983), for example, conclude that environmental regulation explains a substantial part of the decline in productivity in the fossil-fueled generation of electric power. Studies by Ann Bartel and Lucy Thomas (1987) and by Wayne Gray (1991) conclude that EPA and OSHA regulations substantially reduced the growth of productivity in manufacturing.

The most important of these studies provides general equilibrium estimates of the long-term effects of environmental policy on labor supply, savings and investment, and output. Dale Jorgenson and Peter Wilcoxen (1990) estimate that the final costs of environmental regulation—the loss in GDP relative to trend—are substantially higher than the direct compliance costs. A similar study by Michael Hazilla and Raymond Kopp (1990) estimates that the total costs of environmental regulation again higher than the direct compliance costs by an order of magnitude. A more recent study by Wayne Gray and Ronald Shadbegian (1993)—which focuses on the effects of environmental regulation on the oil, paper, and steel industries—estimates that total-factor productivity in these industries was reduced by three to four dollars for each dollar of compliance costs. These studies are more suggestive than conclusive because they focus on specific regulations and specific industries, but they suggest that the total cost of regulation may be much higher than the direct compliance cost.

The few studies of the economywide effects of regulation provide a wide range of estimates and are less analytically satisfactory. Studies by Gregory Christiansen and Robert Haveman (1981) and by Edward Denison (1983) conclude that increased regulation explained only a small part of the general reduction in productivity growth in the late 1970s. For the present, my best judgment is that there is no plausible estimate of the total cost of regulation, but that it is probably much higher than the direct compliance cost.

A REGULATORY AGENDA TO INCREASE ECONOMIC GROWTH

This inadequate understanding of the total cost of regulation should not be an excuse for inaction. Market economies did quite well before the development of modern national-income accounts and econometrics. Measured U.S. productivity growth is now extraordinarily low (a 0.4% annual rate during Clinton's watch so far), and average real wages have been stagnant for some years. Changes in regulation must be part of any growth agenda. The first step in regulatory changes to increase economic growth is clear, although we do not yet know the appropriate last steps.

Economic Regulation

The most obvious first step is to continue to reduce the remaining pockets of price and entry controls. The goals of this initial action should be to:

- Eliminate the monopoly-service areas for the supply of electric power;
- Eliminate restrictions prohibiting foreign flag carriers from providing shipping between American ports;
- Eliminate the restrictions that prohibit banks from providing securities and insurance services;
- Eliminate the Postal Service's monopoly of first-class mail.

The second round of steps should include a major review of the complex web of occupational licensing by the states. This system has long restricted the efficient division of labor and now threatens to restrict the potential for telemedicine, telelegal services, etc. A continuing effort will be required to ensure that the generally deregulatory new telecommunications law is not used to restrict the entry of firms or services or to bias the choice of technology to provide specific services.

Health, Safety, and Environmental Regulation

The present major regulatory threat to economic growth is the almost unrestrained pursuit of infinitesimal risks. Federal health, safety, and environmental regulations now impose direct compliance costs of about $250 billion a year with very little to show for them. U.S. vital statistics show a continued increase in most measures of health, safety, and life expectancy, but not at a higher rate than prior to all this regulation.

The reason why federal regulations have so little effect on these conditions should be more broadly understood. An example of this is the connection between industrial chemicals and cancer. Studies have shown that they cause no more than 3% of all cancer cases, and the true number may be closer to zero.[3] Based on animal tests, many chemicals have been identified as carcinogens, but there is no objective way to extrapolate these results to the effects of very low doses on humans. One leading scholar recommends that all such risk estimates, except those that are confirmed by epidemiological studies, be rejected (Wildavsky 1996). So far, however, none of these findings seems to have restrained the EPA. A recent study (Viscusi and Hamilton 1996) estimates that the Superfund program spends $3.6 billion for every cancer it prevents.

The incentive for employers to reduce risk-based-wage and worker-compensation premiums overwhelms any effect of OSHA regulations on workplace safety and health, fortunately, because any potential effect of OSHA is inherently limited. OSHA inspects about 1% of the nation's workplaces each year and levies small fines on about one-third of the firms inspected. In addition, the leading causes of work-related deaths are now motor-vehicle accidents and murders—conditions beyond OSHA's capacity to regulate effectively. OSHA regulations now cost about $11 billion a year (in addition to considerable irritation), with little or no significant effect on workplace injuries and fatalities (Kniesner and Leeth 1995).

Similar conditions affect the National Health and Transportation Safety Administration, the Consumer Product Safety Commission, and the other federal safety-regulation agencies created since the late 1960s. The record of the Food and Drug Administration, which has been in existence much longer, is effective but costly; it has prohibited the use of a small number of unsafe drugs at the cost of considerable delays in the introduction of safe and effective ones. The most recent FDA initiative is to regulate the marketing of cigarettes, a measure for which they have no obvious statutory authority.

Such a body of regulation must be restrained as part of an effective agenda for economic growth. The increasing direct and indirect costs of regulations these types are now widely recognized, but the general public is not aware that many of them have little effect on the quality of our health and the environment. Improved scientific and economic analysis of these regulations will help inform the public about their efforts and costs, but a major revision of the legislation that authorizes these regulations is necessary to stop this costly pursuit of tiny risks.

Some changes need to be made in these laws in order that certain federal agencies stop regulating:

- Risks for which adults bear the full cost of their own choices;
- Risks of interpersonal relationships that are better handled by contract or tort law;
- Activities for which there are no significant risks across state borders;
- Potential risks based on animal studies, but not confirmed by epidemiological studies;
- Risks for which the costs are more than about $200,000 per year of *healthy life extended.*

Eliminating these from federal risk regulation would leave it with an important but very limited role to play. A much better understanding of the problems caused by such regulation on the part of the public and the policy community, however, is necessary to effect such major legislative changes.

PROCEDURES FOR CHANGE

The regulatory reform movement has been dominated by the quest for some silver bullet—a set of standards and procedures that would stop bad regulation. For several reasons, this quest has been elusive. The net-benefit standard is not a sufficient basis for redistributing income, taking private property to provide a public benefit, or restricting the activities of individuals and firms that bear the full cost of their choices. Judicial review provides no protection against bad analysis; the courts will not accept the role of evaluating scientific and economic studies. And Congress will not accept the regimen of an automatic sunset rule.

There is only one effective solution: Congress must assume greater responsibility for the rules that are made with its authority. The necessary first step is careful drafting of substantive and effective legislation because bad regulation is often a faithful interpretation of bad legislation. If Congress is the problem, only a political or constitutional challenge can stop bad regulation.

One general rule would make both Congress and the agencies more responsible: The Fifth Amendment guarantee of just compensation should be broadened to include all property owners who are required by law to provide a public benefit. No compensation would be required, of course, for the costs of meeting regulations to reduce a public harm originating on the property. The distinction between providing a public benefit and reducing a public harm is one that courts had made for many years and it should be restored. A requirement to compensate property owners who provide a habitat for endangered species, for example, would enormously improve the incentives of both property owners and the government.

In many cases, however, final rules go well beyond the intent of Congress; and Congress now has no effective procedure to veto them. After a brief preamble, the first words of the Constitution are that "All legislative Powers herein granted shall be vested in . . . Congress." For 60 years or so, however, Congress has delegated the authority to approve final rules to regulatory agencies, subject only to the constraints of the substantive legislation and the Administrative Procedures Act. Since the 1983 *Chadha* decision, Congress may veto an agency rule by enacting a new law; agency-made rules, then, become law even if endorsed only by the president and one-third of either house. The Constitution has been turned upside down.

One way or another, Congress must restore its authority to approve all final rules. A little-noticed amendment to the 1996 debt-limit bill permits Congress to delay a final rule for 60 legislative days, but overriding the rule still requires a new law. The 105th Congress should first test this new authority by very carefully selecting some pending rules to delay, with the objective of using the delay to organize a sufficient coalition to override these rules. Congress should also consider a resolution opposing the *Chadha* decision and some instrument to challenge it; the reasoning of the Court in this decision is about as dumb as any decision it has made in the past 20 years, and there is a reason to hope that the Court will change its position.[4]

Congress may soon be ready for a more radical reassertion of its constitutional authority to approve all pending rules before they become law. Several bills with this objective were introduced in the 104th Congress and should be reconsidered. Even with a revamped system, Congress could continue to delegate the *drafting* of rules to the regulatory agencies, but would require an affirmative vote for approving a final rule. As a consequence, the regulatory agencies would be transformed from rule-making and rule-enforcing agencies into rule-drafting and rule-enforcing bodies. And the constitutional separation of powers would be restored.[5]

A case has been made that this procedure would overload Congress, since it would not be willing to address as many new rules as are now approved every year. But the number of new rules is neither optimal nor preordained. New regulations, like any other types of new laws, should be limited to those that Congress thinks need to be addressed. Given the enormous impact of regulations on economic growth, more congressional responsibility not only will improve the quality of the regulation, but also help all Americans achieve economic prosperity.

REFERENCES

Bartel, Ann P., and Lucy Glenn Thomas. 1987. Predation through regulation: The wage and profit effects of the Occupational Safety and Health Administration and the Environmental Protection Agency. *Journal of Law and Economics* (October).

Christiansen, Gregory B., and Robert H. Haveman. 1981. Public regulations and the slowdown in productivity growth. *American Economic Review* (May).

Denison, Edward F. 1983. The interruption of productivity growth in the United States. *Economic Journal* (March).

Gallop, Frank M., and Mark J. Roberts. 1983. Environmental regulation and productivity growth: The case of fossil-fueled electric power generation. *Journal of Political Economy* (August).

Gough, Michael, and Steven Millov. 1996. The environmental cancer epidemic that never was. *Regulation*, no. 2.

Gray, Wayne B. 1991. The impact of OSHA and EPA regulation on productivity growth. *Journal of Regulation and Social Costs.* (June).

Gray, Wayne B., and Ronald J. Shadbegian. 1993. *Environmental regulation and manufacturing productivity at the plant level.* National Bureau of Economic Research Working Paper, no. 4321. (April).

Hazilla, Michael, and Raymond J. Kopp. 1990. Social cost of environmental quality regulations: A general equilibrium analysis. *Journal of Political Economy*, no. 4.

Hopkins, Thomas D. 1996. *Regulatory costs in profile.* Center for the Study of American Business Policy Study, no. 132 (August).

Jorgenson, Dale W., and Peter J. Wilcoxen. 1990. Environmental regulation and U.S. economic growth. *RAND Journal of Economics* (Summer).

Kniesner, Thomas J., and John D. Leeth. 1995. Abolishing OSHA. *Regulation*, no. 4.

Shapiro, Martin. 1996. A golden anniversary? The Administrative Procedures Act of 1946. *Regulation*, no. 3.

Schoenbrod, David. 1993. *Power Without Responsibility: How Congress Abuses the People through Delegation*. New Haven: Yale University Press.

Viscusi, W. Kip, and James T. Hamilton. 1996. Cleaning up Superfund. *The Public Interest* (Summer).

Wildavsky, Aaron. 1996. Regulation of carcinogens: Are animal tests a sound foundation? *The Independent Review* (Spring).

NOTES

1. For several years, these estimates have been prepared by Thomas Hopkins, a professor at the Rochester Institute of Technology. For the most recent estimates, see Hopkins (1996). This estimate does *not* include the cost of federal financial regulation, civil rights, antitrust laws, mandates on state and locate governments, and any new regulations (such as the minimum wage) enacted since 1994; the budgets of the federal regulatory agencies; and the cost of state and local regulation. No plausible estimate of the total compliance cost of regulation has been prepared.

2. These studies provide estimates of the effects of selective regulation on the business sector *net* of any benefits to the business sector from these regulations. The net cost to the American population of these regulations will be smaller than the cost to the business sector to the extent that the benefits of regulations are not measured by our economic accounts.

3. This estimate, from the monumental study by Sir Richard Doll and Richard Peto published in 1981, was confirmed by the EPA in 1987. For a good summary of this issue, see Gough and Milloy (1996).

4. On this issue, see Shapiro (1996).

5. On this issue, see Schoenbrod (1993).

The Growth-Boosting Power of a Consumption Tax

DALE W. JORGENSON, CHAIRMAN, DEPARTMENT OF ECONOMICS AND FREDERIC EATON ABBA PROFESSOR OF ECONOMICS, HARVARD UNIVERSITY

This section will consider the economic impact of a tax on consumption for corporate and individual income taxes at federal, state and local levels. I will limit this discussion to a revenue-neutral submission—one that would leave the government deficit unchanged—and to the impact of this tax reform on economic growth. The benefits of such a tax are these:

1. An immediate and powerful impact on the level of economic activity;

2. A sharply higher tax rate on consumer goods and services;

3. Individuals would sharply curtail consumption of both goods and leisure, which would produce a dramatic jump in savings and a substantial rise in labor supply;

4. A radical shift away from consumption toward investment; real investment would leap upward by a staggering 80%;

5. Holding net foreign investment consistent, exports would jump to 29% while imports would rise only slightly; the initial export boom would gradually subside, while remaining around 15% higher than under the current tax system;

6. Since producers would no longer pay taxes on profits or other forms of income from capital and, since workers would no longer pay taxes on wages, prices received by producers would fall by an average of 20%; and industry outputs would rise by an average of 20% with substantial relative gains for investment-goods producers.

7. In the long run, producers' prices would fall by almost 25% relative to prices under an income tax. The shift in the composition of economic activity toward investment and away from consumption would dramatically redistribute economic activity. Production would increase in all industries, but the rise in production of investment goods would be much more dramatic.

IMPLEMENTATION OF A CONSUMPTION TAX

In hearings on replacing the federal income tax held by the Committee on Ways and Means in June 1995, testimony focused on alternative methods for implementing a consumption tax. The consumption-tax base can be defined in three alternative and equivalent ways. First, subtracting investment from value added produces consumption as a tax base, where value added is the sum of capital and labor incomes. A second definition is the difference between business receipts and all purchases from other businesses, including purchases in investment goods. A third definition of the tax base is retail sales to consumers.

The three principal methods for implementing a consumption tax that correspond to these three definitions are:

1. The subtraction method. Business purchases from other businesses, including investment goods, would be subtracted from business receipts, including proceeds from the sale of assets. This method could be implemented within the framework of the existing tax system by integrating individual- and corporate-income taxes, as proposed by the U.S. Treasury in 1994. In this approach all businesses would be treated as partnerships or "subchapter S" corporations. The second step would be to allow full expensing of investment goods purchased in the year of acquisition. If no business receipts were excluded and no deductions and tax credits were permitted, the tax return could be reduced to the now familiar postcard size, as in the flat-tax proposal of Majority Leader Dick Armey and Senator Richard Shelby in 1995.[1] Enforcement problems could be reduced by drastically simplifying the tax rules, but the principal method of enforcement, the auditing of taxpayer records by the Internal Revenue Service, would remain.

2. The credit method. Business purchases would produce a credit against tax liabilities for value-added taxes paid on goods and services received. This method is used in Canada and all European countries that impose a value-added tax. From the point of view of tax administration, the credit method has the advantage that both purchases and sales generate records of all tax credits. The idea of substituting a value-added tax for existing income taxes is a novel one. European and Canadian value-added taxes were added to preexisting income taxes. In Canada and many other countries the value-added tax replaced an earlier and more complex system of retail- and wholesale-sales taxes. The credit method would require substantial modification of collection procedures, but decades of experience in Europe have ironed out many of the bugs.

3. National retail-sales tax. Like existing state sales taxes, national retail-sales tax would be collected by retail establishments, including service providers and real-estate developers. This method would also require a new system for tax administration, possibly subcontracting the actual collection to existing state agencies. Enforcement procedures would be similar to those used by the states, and the Internal Revenue Service could be transformed into an agency that would subcontract collections. Alternatively, a new agency could be created for this purpose and the IRS abolished.

The crucial point is that all three methods for implementing a consumption tax could be based on the same definition of the tax base. This concept greatly simplifies the tax economist's job, since the economic impact would be the same for all three approaches. The concept also leaves important issues to be resolved by other tax professionals, especially tax lawyers who would write the legislation and the implementing regulations in accounting practice and advise economic decision makers about their implications.

From an economic point of view, the definition of consumption is contained in the Personal Consumption Expenditures (PCE) defined in the U.S. national income and product accounts. However, the taxation of services poses important administrative problems, which were reviewed in a U.S. Treasury monograph (Jorgenson and Yun 1984) on the value-added tax. First,

PCE includes the rental-equivalent value of the services of owner-occupied housing, but does not include the services of consumers' durables. Both are substantial in magnitude, but could be taxed by the prepayment method described by David Bradford (1986). In this approach, taxes on the consumption of the services would be prepaid by including investment rather than consumption in the definition of the tax base.

The prepayment of taxes on services of owner-occupied housing would remove an important political obstacle to the substitution of a consumption tax for existing income taxes. At the time the substitution takes place, all owner-occupiers would be treated as having prepaid all future taxes on the services of their dwellings. This is equivalent to excluding not only mortgage interest from the tax base, but also returns to equity, which might be taxed upon the sale of a residence with no corresponding purchase of residential property of equal or greater value. Of course, this argument is open to the criticism that home owners should be allowed to take the mortgage-interest deduction twice—once when the substitution occurs and again when consumption-tax liabilities are assessed.

Under the prepayment method, purchases of consumers' durables by households for their own use would be subject to tax. These would include automobiles, appliances, home furnishings, and so on. In addition, new construction of owner-occupied housing would be subject to tax, as would sales of existing renter-occupied housing to owner-occupiers. These are politically sensitive issues and it is important to be clear about the implications of prepayment as the debate proceeds. Housing and consumers' durables must be included in the tax base in order to reap the substantial economic benefits of putting household and business capital onto the same footing.[2]

Other purchases of services especially problematical under a consumption tax would include those provided by nonprofit institutions such as school and colleges, hospitals, and religious and eleemosynary institutions. The traditional tax-favored status of these forms of consumption would be defended tenaciously by recipients of the services and even more tenaciously by the providers. Elegant and, in some cases, persuasive arguments should be made that schools and colleges provide services that represent investment in human capital rather than con-

sumption. However, consumption of the resulting enhance-
ments in human capital often takes the form of leisure time,
which would remain as the principal untaxed form of consumption. Taxes could, however, be prepaid by including educational
services in the tax base.

Finally, any definition of a consumption-tax base will have to
distinguish between consumption for personal and business
purposes. Ongoing disputes over exclusion of home offices,
business-provided automobiles, equipment, and clothing, and
business-related lodging, entertainment, and meals would continue to plague tax officials, the entertainment and hospitality industries, and holders of expense accounts. In short, substitution
of a consumption tax for the federal income-tax system would
not eliminate all the practical problems that arise from the neces-
sity of distinguishing between business and personal activities
in defining consumption. However, these issues are common to
both tax systems.

NEXT STEPS

Under any one of the three approaches, the substitution of a consumption tax for existing individual and corporate income taxes
would be the most drastic change in federal-tax policy since the
introduction of the income tax in 1913. It should not be surprising that the dimensions of the economic impact would be truly
staggering. As Americans become more fully apprised of the
manifold ramifications of fundamental tax reform, it is easy to
forecast that Gucci Gulch[3] will be transformed into the political
equivalent of the Grand Canyon.

The coming debate over tax reform is both a challenge and an
opportunity for economists. It is a challenge because the impact
of fundamental tax reform will involve almost every aspect of
economic life. Economists who have spent their lives preoccu-
pied by the latest debating points in professional journals read
only by other economists will suddenly find themselves swept
up in the journalistic maelstrom of American political life. The
fine points that dominate scholarly discussions will be subjected
to the fire of media exposure and public scrutiny. While transla-
tion of professional debating points into sound bites requires

considerable talent and experience, a substantial number of economists have acquired the requisite skills.

The debate will nonetheless be a wonderful opportunity for economists because economic research has generated an enormous amount of valuable information about the impacts of tax policy. Provided that the economic debate can be properly focused, economists and policy makers will learn a great deal about the U.S. economy and its potential for achieving a higher level of performance. I am personally very gratified that the Joint Committee on Taxation has convened a group of leading tax economists to began serious work on shaping the professional discussion. I will close this section with the recommendations I will make at the beginning of this landmark debate.

The first issue that will surface is progressivity or use of the federal tax system to redistribute resources. My recommendation is that this issue be set aside at the outset. Fiscal economists of varying persuasions agree that progressivity or the lack of it should be used to characterize all government activity, including both taxes and expenditures. Policies to achieve progressivity could and should be limited to the expenditure side of the government budget. This initial policy stance would immeasurably simplify the debate over the economic impact of fundamental tax reform. I view this radical simplification as essential to intellectual progress, since there is no agreed-upon economic methodology for trading off efficiency and equity in tax policy or anything else.

The second issue to be debated is fiscal federalism or the role of state and local governments. Since state and local income taxes usually employ the same tax bases as the corresponding federal taxes, it is reasonable to assume that substitution of consumption at the state and local level will have the same impact as on the federal level. For simplicity, I propose to consider the economic impact of substitution at all levels simultaneously. Since an important advantage of fundamental tax reform is the possibility, at least at the outset, of radically simplifying tax rules, it does not make much sense to assume that these rules would continue to govern state and local income taxes, even if the federal income tax were abolished.

The third issue in the debate will be the economic impact of the federal deficit. Nearly two decades of economic dispute over this issue has failed to produce resolution. No doubt this dispute could continue well into the next century and preoccupy the next generation of fiscal economists, as it has the previous generation. An effective rhetorical device for insolating the discussion of fundamental tax reform from the budget debate is to limit the consideration to deficit-neutral proposals. This device was critical to the eventual enactment of the Tax Reform Act of 1986 and is, I believe, essential to progress in the debate over fundamental tax reform.

REFERENCES

Birnbuam, Jeffery H., and Alan S. Murray. 1987. *Showdown at Gucci Gulch: Lawmakers, lobbyists, and the unlikely triumph of tax reform.* New York: Random House.

Bradford, David. 1986. *Untangling the income tax.* Cambridge: Harvard University Press.

Hall, Robert E., and Alvin Rabushka. 1995. *The flat tax.* 2d ed. Stanford, Cal.: The Hoover Institution.

Jorgenson, Dale W., and Peter J. Wilcoxen. 1993. Energy, the environment, and economic growth. In *Handbook of natural resource and energy economics.* Edited by A. V. Kneese and J. Sweeney. Amsterdam: North—Holland.

Jorgenson, Dale W., and Kun-Young Yun. 1984. *Tax reform for fairness, simplicity, and economic growth.* Washington, D.C.: U.S. Government Printing Office.

———. 1992. *Taxing business income once.* Washington, D.C.: U.S. Government Printing Office.

U.S. Congress. 1995. *The Freedom and Fairness Restoration Act.* 104th Cong. 1st sess.

U.S. House. 1996. Committee on Ways and Means. *Hearings on Replacing the Federal Income Tax.* 104th Cong. 1st sess.

NOTES

1. Economists will recognize the flat-tax proposal as a variant of the consumption-based value-added tax proposed by Robert Hall and Alvin Rabushka (1995).

2. See, for example, my testimony before the Committee on Ways and Means of June 6, 1995.

3. A colloquial expression for the corridor outside the hearing room of the Committee on Ways and Means, it appeared in the title of the definitive journalistic account of the Tax Reform Act of 1986, by Jeffrey H. Birnbaum and Alan S. Murray (1987).

Privatizing Social Security Can Boost Growth

Lessons from Chile

JOSÉ PIÑERA, PRESIDENT OF THE
INTERNATIONAL CENTER FOR
PENSION REFORM, COCHAIRMAN OF
THE CATO PROJECT ON SOCIAL
SECURITY PRIVATIZATION, AS
FORMER CHILEAN MINISTER OF
LABOR AND SOCIAL SECURITY

In 1980, Chile replaced a government-run pension system with a revolutionary innovation: a privately administered, national system of Pension Savings Accounts. After 15 years of operation, the results speak for themselves. Pensions in the new private system already are 50% to 100% higher—depending on whether they are old-age, disability, or survivor pensions—than they were in the pay-as-you-go system. The resources administered by the private pension funds amount to around 42% of Chile's GNP. By improving the functioning of both the capital and the labor markets, pension privatization has been one of the key initiatives that, in conjunction with other free-market-oriented structural reforms, has increased the growth rate of the economy from the historical 3% a year to 7.0% on average during the last 12 years. A persuasive case can be made that privatizing Social Security in the United States could also boost economic growth, perhaps substantially.

Sebastian Edwards (1996) has stated that "pension reform has had important effects on the overall functioning of the economy. Perhaps one of the most important effects is that it has contributed to the phenomenal increase in the country's saving rate, from less than 10% in 1986 to almost 29% in 1996." He goes on to say that "pension reform has also had an important effect on the functioning of the labor market. First, by reducing the total rate of social security contributions it has reduced the cost of labor.

Second, by relying on a capitalization system it has eliminated the labor tax component of the retirement system."

The success of the Chilean private pension system has led three other South American countries to follow suit. In recent years, Argentina (1994), Peru (1993), and Colombia (1994) undertook a similar reform. Both Mexico and Bolivia will move in 1997 to pension schemes that follow the Chilean model.

The Chilean experience can be instructive not only to developing countries but also to the mature economies of the developed world. In many of them, demographic trends will create enormous deficits in their pay-as-you-go systems. Even though the transition in countries with chronic budget deficits will not be easy, gradual and *ad hoc* rules can be defined so as to make the transition viable (Piñera 1996).

THE CHILEAN PSA SYSTEM

Under Chile's *Pension Savings Account* (PSA) system, what determines workers' pension level is the amount of money they accumulated during their working years. Neither workers nor employers pay a social security tax to the state. In addition, workers do not collect a government-funded pension. Instead, during their working life, 10% of their wages are automatically deposited by employers in the workers own individual PSA each month. A worker may contribute an additional 10% of wages each month, which is also deductible from taxable income, as a form of voluntary savings.

Workers choose one of the private Pension Fund Administration companies, Administradoras de Fondos de Pensiones (AFPs) to manage their PSAs. These companies cannot engage in any other activities and are subject to government regulation intended to guarantee a diversified and low-risk portfolio and to prevent theft or fraud. A separate government entity, a highly technical AFP Superintendency, provides oversight. Of course, there is free entry to the AFP industry.

Each AFP operates the equivalent of a mutual fund that invests in stocks and bonds, with Investment decisions being made by the AFP. Government regulation sets only maximum percentage limits both for specific types of instruments and for the overall mix of the portfolio; and in the spirit of reform, is that the government regulation will constantly loosen these regulations as the AFP companies gain experience. There is no obligation whatsoever to invest in government or other types of bonds. Legally, the AFP company and the mutual fund that it administers are two separate entities. Then, should an AFP go under, the assets of the mutual fund—that is, the workers' investments— are not affected.

Workers are free to change from one AFP company to another. For this reason, the companies compete to provide a higher return on investment, better customer service, and a lower commission. Each worker is given a PSA passbook and receives a regular statement every three months stating how much money has accumulated in the retirement account and how well the investment fund has performed. The accounts bear the workers' names, are their property, and will be used to pay their old-age pension (with a provision for survivors' benefits).

As should be expected, individual preferences about how to live after retirement differ as much as lifestyle preferences when one is young. The previous pay-as-you-go system did not have the flexibility to fit individual retirement plans and situations, except through collective pressure to allow, for example, an early retirement for certain politically powerful constituencies. It was a one-size-fits-all scheme that was inequitable and ineffective.

The PSA system, on the other hand, allows workers to make independent decisions about their retirement benefits. In the branch offices of many AFPs, workers use computers to calculate the expected value of their pensions, based on the amount of money in the account and the expected year of retirement. Workers can also specify the pension amount they hope to receive and use the computer to determine the amount they need to deposit each month to retire at a certain age. Workers can then instruct their employers to withdraw the new amount from their salary. Of course, the amount can be changed periodically, depending on the yield of the pension fund or changes in life expectancy. The bottom line is that workers can determine the amount of the expected pension and retirement age in the same way they can order a tailor-made suit.

As noted, worker contributions are deductible for income tax purposes, and the return on the PSA is tax free. Upon retirement, when funds are withdrawn, taxes are paid according to the income tax bracket at that time.

The Chilean PSA system includes both private and public sector employees. The only individuals excluded are members of the police and armed forces, whose pension systems, as in other countries, are built into their compensation system. (In my opinion—but not theirs yet—they would also be better off with a PSA.) All other employed workers must have a PSA. If they wish, self-employed workers may enter the system, creating a way for these workers to join the formal economy.

Workers who have contributed to the fund for at least 20 years, but whose pension amount, upon reaching retirement age, is below the legally defined minimum, receive the pension from the state once their PSA has been depleted. What should be stressed here is that no one is defined as "poor" before his or her working life has ended. Only after it has ended and the PSA has been depleted, does a poor pensioner receive a government subsidy. (Those without 20 years of contributions can apply for a welfare-like pension with a much lower amount.)

The PSA system also includes insurance against premature death and disability. Each AFP provides this service to its clients by taking out group-life and disability coverage from private life-insurance companies. This coverage is paid for by an additional worker contribution of about 2.9% of salary, which includes the commission to the AFP.

The mandatory minimum savings level of 10% was calculated on the assumption of a 4% average net yield during the whole working life, so that typical workers would have sufficient money in their PSA to fund a pension equal to 70% of their final salary.

Upon retiring, a worker may choose from two general payout options. In one case, retirees may use the capital in their PSA to purchase an annuity from any private life-insurance company. The annuity guarantees a constant monthly income for life, indexed to inflation (there are indexed bonds available in the Chilean capital market so that companies can invest accordingly), plus survivors' benefits for the worker's dependents. Alternatively, retirees may leave their funds in the PSA and make programmed withdrawals, subject to limits based on the life expectancy of the retiree and dependents. In the latter case, if a retiree dies, the remaining funds in the account form a part of his or her estate. In both cases, retirees can withdraw as a lump-sum the capital in excess of that needed to obtain an annuity or programmed withdrawal equal to 70% of their last wages.

The PSA system solves the typical problem presented by pay-as-you-go systems with respect to labor demographics: in an aging population the number of workers per retiree decreases. In contrast to pay-as-you-go, under the PSA system, the working population does not pay for the retired population; and the potential for intergenerational conflict and eventual bankruptcy is avoided. The problem that many countries face—unfunded pension liabilities—does not exist under the PSA system.

In contrast to company-based private pension systems that generally impose costs on workers who leave before a certain number of years and that sometimes end in bankruptcy—depriving workers of their jobs and their pension rights—the PSA system is completely independent of the company. Since the PSA is tied to the worker, not the company, the account is fully portable. Given that the funds must be invested in tradable securities, the PSA has a daily value and therefore is easy to transfer from one AFP to another. In addition, because it does not hinder labor mobility, both nationally and internationally, the PSA system helps create labor market flexibility and does not subsidize or penalize immigrants.

A PSA system is also much more efficient in promoting a flexible labor market. The system allows people to work part time or temporarily leave the labor force, which is especially attractive to women and young people. In pay-as-you-go systems, these flexible employment styles create gaps in contributions that have to be filled in some way. Not so in a PSA scheme, where stop-and-go contributions are acceptable.

THE TRANSITION

There are several challenges that have to be faced in the PSA system. One is defining a permanent system. Another, in countries that have a pay-as-you-go system, is managing the transition to the new system. Of course, the transition has to take into account the particular characteristics of each country, especially constraints posed by the budget.

In Chile we set three basic rules for the transition:

1. The government guaranteed those already receiving a pension that their pensions would be unaffected by the reform. This rule was important because the social security authority would cease to receive the contributions from workers who moved to the new system. The authority would continue paying pensioners with existing tax revenues, since it would be unfair to the elderly to change their benefits or expectations at this point in their lives.

2. Every worker already contributing to the pay-as-you-go system was given the choice of staying in that system or moving to the new PSA system. Those who left the old system were given a recognition bond that was deposited in their new PSAs. (The bond was indexed and carried a 4% real interest rate.) Bonds are paid by the government only when the worker reaches the legal retirement age, and they are traded in secondary markets, so as to allow them to be used for early retirement. This system took into account the amount of money workers had already acquired in the pay-as-you-go system, so workers that did not have to start at zero when they entered the new system.

3. All new entrants to the labor force were required to join the PSA system, thereby closing the door on the pay-as-you-go system. It will end once the last worker in it reaches retirement age (from then on, and during a limited period of time, the government has only to pay pensions to retirees of the old system).

After several months of national debate on the proposed reforms and a communication and educational effort to explain it to the people (Piñera 1991), the pension reform law was approved on November 4, 1980.

As part of the new system, all gross wages were redefined to include most of the employer's contribution to the old system. (The rest of the employer's contribution was converted to a temporary tax on the use of labor to help the financing of the transition; once the tax was completely phased out, as established in

the pension reform law, the cost to the employer of hiring workers decreased.) The worker's contribution was deducted from
the increased gross wage. Because the total contribution was
lower in the new system than in the old, net salaries for those
who moved to the new system increased by around 5%.

In this way, we ended the belief that both the employer and
the worker contribute to social security, a system that allows political manipulation of *tax rates*. From an economic standpoint,
all the contributions are ultimately paid from the worker's marginal productivity, because employers take into account all labor
costs—whether called salary or social security contributions—in
making their hiring and pay decisions. By renaming the employer's contribution, the system makes it evident that all contributions are made by the worker. In this scenario, of course, the
final wage level is determined by the interplay of market forces.

The financing of the transition is a complex technical issue,
which each country must address according to its own circumstances. The implicit pay-as-you-go debt of the Chilean system
in 1980 has been estimated by a World Bank study (1994) at
around 80% of GDP. (The value of the debt had been reduced by
a reform of the old system in 1978, especially by the rationalization of indexing, the elimination of special regimes, and the raising of the retirement age.) The study stated that "Chile shows
that a country with a reasonably competitive banking system, a
well-functioning debt market, and a fair degree of macroeconomic stability can finance large transition deficits without large
interest rate repercussions."

Chile used five methods to finance the fiscal costs of changing
to a PSA system.

1. In the state's balance sheet (in which each government
should show its assets and liabilities), state pension obligations
were offset to some extent by the value of state-owned enterprises and other types of assets. Therefore privatization was not
only the way to finance the transition, but also to increase efficiency, spread ownership, and depoliticize the economy.

2. Since the contribution needed in a capitalization system to finance adequate pension levels is generally lower than the current payroll taxes, a fraction of the difference between them can

be used as a temporary transition tax without reducing net wages or increasing the cost of labor to the employer.

3.   Using debt, the transition cost can be shared by future generations. In Chile, roughly 40% of the cost has been financed by government bonds issued at market rates of interest. These bonds have been bought mainly by the AFPs as part of their investment portfolios, and the "bridge debt" should be completely redeemed when all the pensioners of the old system have died.

4.   The need to finance the transition was a powerful incentive to reduce wasteful government spending. For years, the budget director has been able to use this argument to kill unjustified new spending or to reduce wasteful government programs.

5.   The increased economic growth that the PSA system promoted substantially increased tax revenues, especially those from the value-added tax. Only 15 years after the pension reform, Chile is running budget surpluses.

THE RESULTS

The PSAs have already accumulated an investment fund of $28 billion, an unusually large pool of internally generated capital for a developing country of 14 million people and a GDP of $65 billion.

This long-term investment capital has not only helped fund economic growth, but has also spurred the development of efficient financial markets and institutions. The decision to create the PSA system first, and then privatize the large state-owned companies second, resulted in a virtuous circle. It gave workers the opportunity of benefiting handsomely from the enormous increase in productivity of the privatized companies by allowing workers, through higher stock prices that increased the yield of their PSAs, to capture a large share of the wealth created by privatization.

One of the key results of the new system has been to increase the productivity of capital and thus the rate of economic growth in Chile. The PSA system has made the capital market more efficient and influenced its growth over the last 15 years. The vast resources administered by the AFPs have encouraged the creation of new kinds of financial instruments, while enhancing others that are underdeveloped. Another of Chile's pension-reform contributions to the sound operation and transparency of the capital market has been the creation of a domestic risk-rating industry and the improvement of corporate governance. (The AFPs, for example, appoint outside directors in the companies in which they own shares.)

Since the system began to operate on May 1, 1981, the average real return on investment has been 12% per year (more than three times higher than the anticipated yield of 4%). Of course, the annual yield—ranging from −3% to 30% in real terms—has reflected the oscillations that are intrinsic to the free market but the important yield is the average one over the long term.

Pensions under the new system have been significantly higher than under the old state-administered system, which required a total payroll tax of around 25%. According to a recent study (Baeza 1995), the average AFP retiree receives a pension equal to 78% of his or her mean annual income over the previous 10 years of working life. As mentioned, upon retirement workers may withdraw in a lump sum their "excess savings" (above the 70%-of-salary threshold). If this money were included in calculating the value of the pension, the total value would be nearly 84% of working income. Recipients of disability pensions also receive, on average, 70% of their working income.

The new pension system, therefore, has made a significant contribution to the reduction of poverty by increasing the size and certainty of old-age, survivors, and disability pensions, and by the indirect but very powerful effect of promoting economic growth and employment.

When the PSA was inaugurated in 1981, one-fourth of the eligible workforce joined the new system in its first month of operation alone. Today, more than 93% of Chilean workers are in the new system.

As the state pension system disappears, politicians will no longer decide whether pension checks need to be increased and in what amount or for which groups; pensions are no longer a key source of political conflict. Now, people's retirement income depends on their own work and on the success of the economy, not on the government or on the pressures brought by special interest groups.

For Chileans, pension-savings accounts now represent real and visible property rights—they are the primary sources of security for retirement. After 15 years under the new system, in fact, the main asset of typical Chilean workers is not their used car or small house (which is probably still mortgaged), but the capital in their PSA.

Finally, the private pension system has had a very important political and cultural consequence, indeed, by giving Chileans a personal stake in the economy; typical Chilean workers are therefore not indifferent to the behavior of the stock market or interest rates. Intuitively they know that their old age security depends on the well-being of the companies that represent the backbone of the economy.

WHY NOT THE UNITED STATES?

The Social Security system of the United States is facing a profound crisis. According to the latest report of its board of trustees, the system will be insolvent by 2029, which was revised from 2030 in last year's report, the eighth time in the last 10 years that the insolvency date has been lowered.

That fact, however, does not provide the full story of Social Security's looming crisis. The important date is 2012. Social Security taxes currently bring in more revenue than the system pays out in benefits, a surplus that theoretically accumulates in the Social Security trust fund. However, in 2012 the situation will reverse, as Social Security will begin paying out more in benefits than what it collects in revenues. To continue meeting its obligations, it will have to begin drawing on the surplus in the trust fund, which, unfortunately, is really little more than a polite fiction. For years, the federal government has used the trust fund to disguise the actual size of its budget deficit, borrowing money from the trust fund to pay current operating expenses and replacing the money with government bonds.

Even if Congress can find a way to redeem the bonds, the trust fund will be completely exhausted by 2029, at which point, Social Security will have to rely solely on revenue from the payroll tax. But such revenues will not be sufficient to pay all promised benefits. Either payroll taxes will have to be increased—to between 28% and 40%, according to various estimates by the trustees—or benefits will have to be reduced by as much as one-third.

Even if Social Security's financial difficulties can be fixed, the system remains a problem for most Americans, a situation that is growing worse for today's young workers. Payroll taxes are already so high that even if today's young workers receive the promised benefits, they will amount to a below-market return on those taxes. While today's retirees will generally get back all they paid into Social Security (including the employer's portion), plus a modest return on their investment, when today's young workers retire, they will actually receive a negative rate of return—resulting in payments less than what they put in. Young workers today would actually be better off stuffing their Social Security taxes in a mattress than counting on benefits from the program.

What would happen to economic growth if the United States were to privatize its Social Security system? I believe that the benefits would be substantial. Harvard professor Martin Feldstein (1996), for example, estimates that "the combination of the improved labor market incentives and the higher real return on savings [of moving to a fully funded Social Security system] has a net present value gain of more than $15 trillion, an amount equivalent to 3% of each future year's GDP forever."

And, most important, today's young workers would be assured that when they retire, they would be able to do so with dignity and security.

REFERENCES

Baeza, S. 1995. *Quince años después. Una mirada al sistema privado de pensiones.* Santiago, Chile: Centro de Estudios Públicos.

Edwards, S. 1996. The Chilean pension reform: A pioneering program. Paper presented at NBER Conference, Privatizing Social Security Conference, 1–2 August.

Feldstein, M. 1996. The missing piece in the policy analysis: Social Security reform. Paper presented at the annual meeting of the American Economics Association, 5 January.

Piñera, J. 1991. *El cascabel al gato.* Santiago, Chile: Editorial Zig Zag.

Piñera, J. 1996. *Una propuesta de reforma del sistema de pensiones de España.* Madrid: Círculo de Empresarios.

World Bank. 1994. *Averting the old age crisis.* New York: Oxford University Press.

Epilogue

The Rising Tide

JERRY J. JASINOWSKI

This book has featured seven chapters of articles by some of America's most successful and brilliant industrialists, policy makers, and economists. Imagine your reaction, however, if the government allowed you to read only five of these chapters, because the ideas in the rest of them were beyond the bounds of conventional thinking.

That is the situation in which the American economy finds itself today—growing and thriving, the envy of the world, yet restricted by a political and bureaucratic mind-set that does not realize how the global economy has changed the economic rules in the past decade.

The authors in *The Rising Tide* have proposed many creative new ideas about how to enhance the growth of the U.S. economy through both private initiative and public policy. I would suggest that what we need most, especially in the nation's capital, is *a new way of thinking* about our economy.

Why a new way of thinking? Because America has a whole new way of doing business, driven by technology, free trade, a competitive spirit, and a team-oriented approach in the workplace. Today, we can compete with anybody in the world, given a level playing field.

We need government to recognize these changes and to reconsider its own role in this American success story. Because while we have a new economy, policy makers are still playing by the old rules.

Too many policy decisions in the United States are made on a short-term, piecemeal basis, mired in outdated concepts. We raise interest rates to head off inflation, based on old formulas about how the economy reacts to growth. Despite the 1997 agreement between Congress and the White House lowering the capital-gains tax, overall tax policy discourages productive investment.

We promise every year to balance the budget—but we refuse to deal with the *real* budget issues: costly entitlement programs like Medicare and Social Security. We talk about tax reform without addressing one of the most regressive taxes—the payroll tax. We threaten unilateral sanctions against trading partners for emotional reasons that have little effect on their policies but that harm our international trade. We try to micromanage the world's largest, most diverse economy by tinkering with interest rates on almost a month-by-month basis, a process that does little except to satisfy Wall Street's obsession for short-term results.

You could describe these policies as management by increment. And policy makers—especially the Federal Reserve Board—cling to that incremental approach because of some bedrock beliefs about the American economy: in particular, that growth must be limited to x, and unemployment has a "natural" level of y, because otherwise inflation will rise to z.

I believe, and so do many others who have contributed to this book, that those beliefs are obsolete. It is finally becoming widely recognized that achieving higher growth without triggering inflation is possible.

Consider, for example, the following "x, y and z" news about what we could describe as the new U.S. economic order, all from the summer of 1997:

- The U.S. economy grew by over 3% from mid-1996 to mid-1997.
- The unemployment rate in June was at 4.8%, a 24-year low.

Conventional wisdom would say these trends were alarming—a sure harbinger of an overheated economy. But, in fact, they were no such thing:

- Prices at the producer level *dropped* for six consecutive months—the longest such stretch since the government began tracking these prices in 1947.
- Inflation, as measured by the consumer price index for all urban consumers, rose only 1.4% in the first half of the year—the lowest rate in 11 years. Said Janet Yellen, chair of the president's Council of Economic Advisers: "Today's consumer price numbers indicate that the expansion is continuing at a sustainable rate with no apparent pressure on prices."
- The employment cost index, which tracks total compensation (wages and benefits) in the private sector, rose only 2.9% at an annualized rate in the first six months of 1997, indicating that wages were not rising at unhealthy rates. When productivity is subtracted, the inflation rate plunges to less than 2%.

These results should demonstrate that the American economy has changed its spots and become an entirely different animal.

If the rules have changed—and, clearly, most of the authors in this book believe they have—then strategy and policy at the government level must change too. Otherwise, as Jack Kemp put it in chapter 1, "Once again, theoretical impossibilities seem to loom in the way of human progress."

I must emphasize, again, the central theses of *A Rising Tide:* First, America is creating a new economy that is more competitive than ever in terms of technology, productivity, worker compensation, and pricing. But, we can do better. That's the second point. The economy should be allowed to grow faster because *it can safely do so* without inflation accelerating and because growth will create greater prosperity for everyone.

We can grow faster, safely, for several reasons that the existing "rules" of policy do not reflect:

1. With the end of the Cold War, we are part of a truly global, intensely competitive economy that produces a tremendous volume of goods and holds down prices. U.S. companies literally cannot raise prices that trigger inflation, because of this global competition; instead, profits can—and do—come from improving productivity and increasing sales. Somebody, somewhere in the world, can always make a product more cheaply than we can; we can succeed by making it better, producing it more quickly, and marketing it better.

2. The technological revolution in computers, communications, and manufacturing is creating productivity improvements, for example, just-in-time manufacturing, statistical quality control, and CAD/CAM, that are not reflected by conventional measures. By the turn of the century, we will see a massive shift to digital technology, especially in the communications field, from phones to cameras to televisions, resulting in another surge of productivity.

3. After a sometimes wrenching transition, U.S. industrial companies are better managed than ever before. Costs have been cut. Manufacturing processes are more efficient. Workers have been empowered to take responsibility. We are using new technology, especially the overwhelming numbers of personal computers, to manage faster and better, to use more information more efficiently.

4. We can achieve lower unemployment without inflation accelerating because we are moving toward compensation systems based on improvements in output, quality, and productivity. We are linking pay to performance. Firms are now relying on alternative forms of compensation, such as bonuses, stock options and pay-for-performance schemes, instead of increases in hourly wages. As a result, total compensation to labor can increase without triggering wage inflation, because it is more closely linked to the profitability of firms.

These changes require creative thinking and more entrepreneurship in the private sector. America's most successful firms have met the challenge through innovative product development, increased speed, greater flexibility, and, in some cases, top-to-bottom structural changes. Whole layers of middle management have been eliminated; workers have more input in how their jobs are performed; many companies can change product lines and services quickly to match the changing tastes of the marketplace. The widespread purchase and use of new technologies—a huge investment—has enabled the U.S. to outpace its principal Asian and European rivals three years in a row, according to the World Economic Forum.

Now we need to match these changes with a new role for government—including a determination to support the emerging consensus that, in most areas, less is more.

For the past half-century, the federal government has gobbled up large chunks of what was once the province of business, communities, and individuals. It's taken onto itself the role of rule maker and goal setter.

We need to change that thinking. We need to make government a customer of American workers and American industry. We need government to ask how it can be customer-sensitive. Instead of government telling us what it *can* do, it should be asking us what it *should* do.

The recent agreement to balance the federal budget by 2002 is a step, but only a small step, in the right direction. While Congress and the White House agreed to rein in the worst antiinvestment excesses of the alternative minimum tax, which penalizes firms that make productive investments when profits are low, and agreed to make cuts in the capital-gains tax, the budget agreement did little to overhaul the tax system to stimulate the additional savings and investment required to achieve higher growth.

For instance, Washington has done little to address the potential demographic catastrophe awaiting Medicare and Social Security. Allowing workers to manage at least part of their own retirement dollars by investing in the stock market would ensure the availability of funds for the 75 million baby boomers while providing needed resources for private sector investment. Similarly, taxes are still too high and much too complex. We can only reach our full growth potential if the federal government agrees to leave more money in the pockets of its citizens.

Washington must also free Americans from some of the unnecessary regulations that stifle growth, investment, and job creation. One study estimated that current federal regulations impose direct compliance costs to business of $500 billion per year, or about $5,000 per employee. While some of these regulations are important and necessary, they should all be subject to rigorous cost-benefit analysis, and the private sector should be given the flexibility to efficiently meet the goals set by regulators.

Perhaps our most urgent mission is improving the education and training of the American workforce. While education is primarily local, Washington can provide communities the tools necessary to makes their schools succeed. Washington should allow parents to determine how best to educate their children through the use of vouchers and the creation of charter schools. Public schools, like their private counterparts, should be forced to compete for their education dollars. Nothing short of radical educational reform will allow the U.S. to stay ahead of global competition in a variety of areas.

All these reforms are worthwhile in their own right, but we should not lose sight of the ultimate goal: a higher standard of living and a better quality of life for America and, ultimately, the world.

Two centuries ago, improvements in tools and transportation brought on by the industrial revolution triggered economic growth on an unprecedented scale and the first great surge in the human standard of living. Today, the tools are our own brains, amplified by the marvelous technology of computers and communications. If we rise to the challenges that this new way of thinking has created, and if we establish government policies that reflect and support the rapidity of change in today's world, we are ready for another great improvement in the human condition.

About the Editor

Jerry J. Jasinowski is president and CEO of the National Association of Manufacturers, the largest industry trade group in the country. He is also vice chairman of The Manufacturing Institute, the education and research affiliate of the NAM, and is one of the nation's most frequently quoted authorities on political, economic, and manufacturing trends and new developments.

He has addressed audiences across the country—from The Commonwealth Club of California to the National Press Club in Washington, D.C.—as:

- an astute analyst who understands the rapid changes creating a new global economy and their impact on business and workers
- a CEO who runs a first-class operation and has written a book on how manufacturing companies have regained their competitive edge, *Making It in America: Proven Paths to Success from 50 Top Companies* (Simon & Schuster, 1995)
- a player in the political game whom *Washingtonian* magazine calls industry's "most powerful advocate on Capitol Hill."

Under Jasinowski's leadership, the NAM has been hailed as Washington's most influential and respected business group, helping to shape national policy on a broad range of issues from taxes to trade. He currently is calling for a national strategy to boost economic growth and improve opportunities for employees through empowerment, education, and wealth creation. He also has written and lectured on what companies should do to increase their growth, particularly in terms of factory floor productivity, going global, and empowering and educating workers.

Jasinowski is widely quoted in the media and has appeared on almost every major national network and public-affairs program, including ABC's *Good Morning America, Nightline,* and *This Week with David Brinkley;* NBC's *Today, Meet the Press,* and *The McLaughlin Group;* CBS's *Face the Nation,* CNN's *Crossfire* and *Moneyline,* PBS's *Firing Line,* C-Span, and the evening network news shows. His opinion editorials have run in the *New York Times, Washington Post, Chicago Tribune, Harvard Business Review,* and other major publications.

Jasinowski became president of the NAM in January 1990, after serving as the association's executive vice president and chief economist for 10 years. The NAM is the largest and oldest broad-based industrial trade association in the United States. Its more than 14,000 member companies and affiliates, including approximately 10,000 small firms, employ 18 million, are in every state, and account for roughly 85% of U.S. manufactured goods.

A one-time factory worker, Jasinowski joined the U.S. Air Force as an intelligence officer, serving in the Far East in the mid-1960s. He went on to become assistant professor of economics at the U.S. Air Force Academy. In the early 1970s, Jasinowski came to Washington to manage research and legislative activities for the Joint Economic Committee of Congress. In 1976, he served as director of the Carter administration's economic transition team for the departments of Treasury, Commerce, Labor, the Council of Economic Advisors, and the Federal Reserve. He later was appointed assistant secretary for policy at the U.S. Department of Commerce.

A native of LaPorte, Indiana, Jasinowski received his B.A. in economics from Indiana University, his master's degree in economics from Columbia University, and is a graduate of the Harvard Business School's Advanced Management Program. He serves on the board of directors for Phoenix Home Life and Atwood Richards. In 1997, Jasinowski was awarded the Anti-Defamation League's Person of the Year Award for his leadership role in advancing more inclusive policies for the workforce, including immigration.

Jasinowski has three children and resides in Washington, D.C. with his wife, vice president of government relations for The Goodyear Tire and Rubber Company.

About the Contributors

Robert J. Barro is the Robert C. Waggoner Professor of Economics at Harvard University and a Senior Fellow of the Hoover Institution. He is also a contributing editor of the *Wall Street Journal* and a contributing author for IntellectualCapital.com.

His books include *Getting It Right: Markets and Choices in A Free Society; Economic Growth* (coauthored with Xavier Sala-i-Martin); *Macroeconomics; Modern Business Cycle Theory;* and *Money, Expectations, and Business Cycles.* In February 1996, he was the Lionel Robbins Lecturer at the London School of Economics. The lectures, "Determinants of Economic Growth: A Cross-Country Empirical Study," were published in 1997.

Dr. Barro also writes extensively in professional journals.

Michael J. Boskin is T.M. Friedman Professor of Economics and Senior Fellow at the Hoover Institution, Stanford University. He is a research associate of the National Bureau of Economic Research and adjunct scholar of the American Enterprise Institute. A recipient of numerous professional awards, Dr. Boskin focuses his research and consulting on world economic growth, tax and budget theory and policy, U.S. saving and consumption patterns, and the implications of changing technology and demography on capital, labor, and product markets.

From 1989 to 1993, he served as chairman of the Council of Economic Advisers (CEA) and has recently chaired the Congressional Advisory Commission on the Consumer Price Index.

Anthony P. Carnevale is an internationally recognized authority on education, training, and employment. He currently serves as vice president for public leadership at the Educational Testing Service. Since its creation in 1947, ETS has been the world leader in the development and delivery of instruments for assessing individual competencies, the assessment and certification of competencies in particular occupations, and tools for individual career guidance and planning.

Before coming to ETS, Mr. Carnevale served as vice president and director of human resources studies at the Committee for Economic Development, a business think tank that is led by nearly 250 trustees who are also chief executive officers of a broad range of the nation's business organizations.

In August of 1993, President Clinton appointed Mr. Carnevale as chair of the National Commission of Employment Policy. Carnevale also serves on numerous other boards and commissions, including the Board of Overseers for the Malcolm Baldrige Quality Award; the Kellogg Commission on Lifelong Learning; the human resources committee of the U.S. Council on Competitiveness; the congressional U.S. Competitiveness Policy Council; the National Alliance of Business Workforce Excellence Advisory Council; the Twentieth Century Fund Task Force on Worker Retrainings; and the Hudson Institute Advisory Board on Workforce 2000.

Mr. Carnevale has written numerous books and articles on competitiveness and human resources. His most recent books are *The American Mosaic: An In-depth Report on the Future of Diversity at Work*, published in 1995, and *Tools and Activities for a Diverse Work Force*. His other books include *America and the New Economy: How New Competitive Standards Are Radically Changing American Workplaces; Jobs for the Nation: Challenges for a Society Based on Work; Workplace Basics: The Essential Skills Employers Want; Training in America: The Organization and Strategic Role of Training; and Training the Technical Workforce*.

Before joining CED, he served as the president of the Institute for Workbased Learning, an applied research center affiliated with the American Society for Training and Development, a professional association for human resource specialists in private companies. Before joining ASTD, Mr. Carnevale served as senior economist for the Senate Democratic Policy Committee; government affairs director for the American Federation of State, County, and Municipal Employees; staff director for employment, education, training, and social service programs for the U.S. Senate Committee on the Budget; senior staff economist for the Government Operations Committee in the U.S. House of Representatives; and senior policy analyst in the Office of the Secretary in the Department of Health, Education, and Welfare.

Prior to coming to Washington, he worked as a research economist with the Syracuse University Research Corporation, where he was involved in the reform of school financing and was a coauthor of the principal affidavit in *Rodriguez* v. *San Antonio*, a U.S. Supreme Court action to remedy unequal tax burdens and education benefits. He was also a psychiatric social worker and high-school teacher in his home state of Maine.

Mr. Carnevale received his B.A. from Colby College in Waterville, Maine, and his Ph.D., with a concentration in public finance economics, from the Maxell School at Syracuse University.

Richard M. Cyert, President Emeritus and Richard M. and Margaret S. Cyert Professor of Economics and Management of Carnegie Mellon University, is internationally recognized for his work in economics, behavioral science, and management.

He became Carnegie Mellon's sixth president in 1972 and served for 18 years. Through his leadership, Carnegie Mellon became financially solvent and enhanced its reputation as one of the nation's leading educational and research institutions.

Dr. Cyert was described by the *New York Times* as "the archetype of the new breed of leaders at American universities . . . an economist and management theorist."

Donna M. Desrochers is a senior economist, specializing in skill and employment issues, at the Educational Testing Service. Her research efforts are focused on employer-provided training, public job training for disadvantaged and dislocated workers, and skill and literacy issues that involve workforce training. Ms. Desrochers received her M.A., with a concentration in labor economics, from Northeastern University.

Robert Eisner, the William R. Kenan Professor of Economics Emeritus at Northwestern University, is a past president of the American Economic Association and a Fellow of the American Academy of Arts and Sciences and of the Econometric Society.

Dr. Eisner's most recent works are *The Great Deficit Scares: Social Security, Trade and the Federal Deficit* and *The Misunderstood Economy: What Counts and How to Count It.* His other books include *Factors in Business Investment, How Real Is the Federal Deficit?,* and *The Total Incomes System of Accounts.* He has published extensively in leading professional journals, writes regularly for the *Los Angeles Times,* has been a frequent contributor to the *Wall Street Journal,* the *New York Times,* and other major newspapers, and has appeared on a variety of national television programs.

Stuart W. Elliott is a research fellow at Carnegie Mellon University and a visiting scholar at the Russell Sage Foundation. His background includes a Ph.D. in economics from MIT and postdoctoral work in cognitive psychology at Carnegie Mellon. Elliott's thesis and work in psychology focused on the relation between rational and psychological models of choice in a changing environment. More recently his research has focused on the long-term impact of computers on the economy. This work involves understanding the economic relationship between future technology and human skills.

Audrey Freedman is the author of over 50 reports and articles covering a wide variety of human resource subjects. Her articles have appeared in university business journals such as the *Harvard Business Review,* and in Congressional hearing reports and conference proceedings. Several have been translated and published in French, Japanese, and German.

Her recent observations about economic and workforce issues include her 1994 testimony to the House Budget Committee about the causes of wage moderation in a booming economy; her April 1995 article about contradictory policy objectives for minimum wages and welfare; her article on the skills employers value most; and several of her published articles on contingent workers, including "Contingent Work and the Role of Labor Market Intermediaries," in *Of Heart and Mind* (edited by Garth Mangum and Stephen Mangum, and published by the Upjohn Institute for Employment Research in 1996).

Mrs. Freedman is a member of the board of directors and the compensation committee of Manpower Inc., a company providing staffing services to businesses in over 40 countries, employing one-and-a-half million people. She works with several industry associations as well as the U.S. Bureau of Labor Statistics, where she was chairperson of the Business Research Advisory Council, 1992–1994. Mrs. Freedman is also an independent advisor to the International Labour Review.

After receiving her B.A. in economics from Wellesley College, Mrs. Freedman was a research assistant at the Graduate School of Public Administration at Harvard University. In 1960, she joined the U.S. Department of Labor. While serving as a supervising economist at the Bureau of Labor Statistics, she published a number of studies of technological change and its effects on productivity, skill requirements, and the response of union organizations to changing conditions within industries. From 1967 through 1970, she managed experimental projects that relocated workers from depressed areas to growth centers in 38 states.

During phase one and two of President Nixon's economic controls, Mrs. Freedman was with the Cost of Living Council and the Pay Board, in policy development. She was subsequently an economist at the Conference Board for 16 years.

Mrs. Freedman speaks to industry association gatherings, advises and leads discussions at internal corporate-planning sessions, and provides background data and commentary to the electronic and print media.

Benjamin M. Friedman is the William Joseph Maier Professor of Political Economy, and formerly chairman of the Department of Economics, at Harvard University. His research and writing have primarily focused on economic policy, in particular the role of the financial markets in shaping how monetary and fiscal policies affect overall economic activity. His best known book is *Day of Reckoning: The Consequences of American Economic Policy Under Reagan and After.* He is also the author of articles on monetary economics, macroeconomics, and monetary and fiscal policy published in numerous journals. Professor Friedman's other current professional activities include serving as a director of the Private Export Funding Corporation, a trustee of the Standish Investment Trust, and an adviser to the Federal Reserve Bank of New York. He is also a member of the Brookings Panel on Economic Activity and the Council on Foreign Relations, and a director of the American Friends of Cambridge University.

Richard A. Fry is a senior economist at the Educational Testing Service. His research focuses on the quantitative analysis of U.S. schools and labor markets, particularly the participation and outcomes of ethnic and immigrant populations. Mr. Fry has published articles in several journals, including *Industrial Relations, Contemporary Economic Policy,* the *Quarterly Review of Economics and Finance,* and *Population Research and Policy Review.* He received his Ph.D. in economics from the University of Michigan.

John Haltiwanger, professor of economics at the University of Maryland, received his Ph.D. in economics from the Johns Hopkins University in 1981. After serving on the faculty at UCLA and Johns Hopkins, he joined the Maryland faculty in 1987. He has written more than 40 articles for leading economics journals and other publications, including recent articles in the *American Economic Review,* the *Quarterly Journal of Economics,* the *NBER Macroeconomics Annual,* the *Brookings Papers on Economic Activity,* and the *Economic Journal.* He is a research associate of the Center for Economic Studies at the Bureau of the Census and of the National Bureau of Economic Research. His current research exploits the recently created longitudinal establishment databases at the Bureau of the Census. This research focuses on job creation, job destruction, restructuring, and lumpy investment activity at the plant level and the connection to aggregate fluctuations in employment, investment, and productivity. His recently published book, *Job Creation and Destruction* (MIT Press, 1996, coauthored with Steven Davis and Scott Schuh), presents a comprehensive analysis of job creation and destruction in the U.S. manufacturing sector over the last two decades. His research and commentary on these issues have been cited numerous times in leading newspapers and magazines, including

Business Week, The Economist, Fortune, the *New York Times, U.S. News and World Report,* and the *Wall Street Journal.*

William Hudson, as the CEO of AMP Incorporated, the world's leading manufacturer of electrical and electronic connectors and interconnection systems, is an outspoken proponent of global free trade.

He has had a wealth of international business experience as well as expertise in the international public-policy arena. He was recently named by President Clinton to the U.S. Advisory Committee on Trade Policy and Negotiation. In addition, Mr. Hudson chairs the National Association of Manufacturers' International Economic Policy Committee, which is responsible for developing the association's positions on U.S. trade and investment policy.

He is also a director of the Pacific Basin Economic Council (PBEC), the leading private-sector counterpart of the Asia Pacific Economic Cooperation Forum (APEC), and in January 1997 assumed the chairmanship of PBEC-US.

Mr. Hudson cochaired the investment working group of the 1995 Transatlantic Business Dialogue in Seville and the 1996 Transatlantic Business Dialogue in Chicago, sponsored by the U.S. Department of Commerce.

He is a member of the Global Business Policy Council, the Conference Board, the Executive Committee and Board of the U.S. Council for International Business; the Business Roundtable; the U.S. Chamber of Commerce; and American Trader Initiative Advisory Council of the Heritage Foundation. In addition, he is on the Executive Committee and a governor of the National Electrical Manufacturers Association, and is a director of the National Association of Manufacturers. He serves on the boards of AMP Incorporated, Goodyear Tire and Rubber Company, and Carpenter Technology Corporation.

He earned a bachelor's degree and a master's certificate in electrical engineering at Cornell University. In addition, he holds 12 U.S. patents.

Dale W. Jorgenson is Frederic Eaton Abbe Professor of Economics at Harvard University. He has been a professor in the department of economics since 1969 and Director of the Program on Technology and Economic Policy at the Kennedy School of Government since 1984.

Professor Jorgenson received the prestigious John Bates Clark Medal of the American Economic Association, awarded every two years for excellence in research. The citation for this award reads in part:

> Dale Jorgenson has left his mark with great distinction on pure economic theory (with, for example, his work on the growth of a dual economy); and equally on statistical method (with, for example, his development of estimation methods for rational distributed lags). But he is preeminently a master of the territory between economics and statistics, where both have to be applied to the study of concrete problems. His prolonged exploration of the determinants of investment spending, whatever its ultimate lessons, will certainly long stand as one of the finest examples in the marriage of theory and practice in economics.

Professor Jorgenson is the author and coauthor of more than 200 articles and the author and editor of 18 books in economics. His most recent books, *Aggregate Consumer Behavior* and *Measuring Social Welfare*, were published by the MIT Press in 1997.

Jack Kemp is a codirector of Empower America, a public policy and advocacy organization he cofounded in 1993 with William Bennett and Ambassador Jeane Kirkpatrick. Empower America is dedicated to three founding principles: expanding freedom and democratic capitalism; promoting policies to expand economic growth and entrepreneurship for our nation; and advancing social policies that empower people, not government bureaucracies.

Prior to founding Empower America, Jack Kemp served for four years as secretary of Housing and Urban Development. He was the first and strongest advocate of enterprise zones to encourage entrepreneurship and job creation in urban America and of expanding home ownership among the poor through resident management and ownership of public housing.

Secretary Kemp received the Republican Party's nomination for vice president in 1996. In the prior year, Senator Bob Dole and Speaker of the House Newt Gingrich put Secretary Kemp at the center of the tax and economic debate for the 1996 presidential campaign by naming him chairman of the National Commission on Economic Growth and Tax Reform to study how major restructuring of our tax code can help unleash the entrepreneurial spirit of Americans, grow the economy without inflation, and create greater opportunity for people to escape poverty.

Before his appointment to the Cabinet, then-Representative Kemp represented the Buffalo area and western New York in the House of Representatives from 1971 to 1989. He served for seven years in the Republican leadership as chairman of the House Republican Conference.

Lawrence R. Klein received a bachelor's degree from the University of California, Berkeley, and a Ph.D. from the Massachusetts Institute of Technology. He has served on the faculties of the University of Chicago, University of Michigan, Oxford University, and the University of Pennsylvania. He was the Benjamin Franklin Professor of Economics and Finance at Pennsylvania, where he taught for 33 years, and is now Benjamin Franklin Professor Emeritus.

Professor Klein is an econometrician and has constructed several statistical models of the United States and various other countries. At Pennsylvania, he founded Wharton Econometric Forecasting Associates and was a principal investigator of Project LINK, which combined models from countries throughout the world for studying international trade, payments, and global economic activity.

He has served as president of many learned societies, edited scholarly journals, and advised governments on economic policy. In 1976 he coordinated Jimmy Carter's economic task force in a successful campaign for the U.S. presidency. In 1980 he was awarded the Nobel Prize in economics.

Y. Kumasaka is chief economist at NLI Research Institute, New York.

Frank R. Lichtenberg is Courtney C. Brown Professor of Business at the Columbia University Graduate School of Business, and a research associate of the National Bureau of Economic Research. He received a B.A., with honors in history, from the University of Chicago, and an M.A. and Ph.D. in economics from the University of Pennsylvania.

Mr. Lichtenberg previously taught at Harvard University and the University of Pennsylvania; worked at the Brookings Institution and several U.S. government agencies; and has been a visiting scholar at the Wissenschaftszentrum Berlin, the University of Munich, and elsewhere.

Some of Professor Lichtenberg's research has examined how the introduction of new technology arising from research and development affects the productivity of companies, industries, and nations. Recently, he has performed studies of the impact of new drugs on hospitalization rates, the effect of computers on productivity in business and government organizations, and the consequences of takeovers and leveraged buyouts for efficiency and employment. His articles have been published in numerous scholarly journals and in the popular press, and his book *Corporate Takeovers and Productivity* has been published by MIT Press.

Professor Lichtenberg has been awarded research fellowships and grants by the National Science Foundation, the Fulbright Commission, the Brookings Institution, the Alfred P. Sloan Foundation, the German Marshall Fund, and other organizations. He has served as a consultant to private organizations and government agencies, including the Securities Industry Association, Pfizer, Inc., the Community Preservation Corporation, the RAND Institute, the Bureau of the Census, the New York City Water Board, Touche Ross and Co., the Walt Disney Company, and the National Pharmaceutical Council.

Robert A. Lutz was named vice chairman of Chrysler Corporation in December 1996. He is also a director of the company, focusing primarily on Chrysler's product development activities. As a member of the office of the chairman, he is involved in all major decisions and acts as a coach and advisor.

Prior to becoming vice chairman, Mr. Lutz was president and chief operating officer responsible for Chrysler's car and truck operations worldwide, including international operations. He led all of Chrysler's automotive activities including sales, marketing, product development, manufacturing, and procurement and supply. He was president of Chrysler from January 1991 to December 1996. He joined Chrysler in 1986 as executive vice president and was elected to the corporation's board of directors the same year.

Prior to Chrysler, Lutz spent 12 years at Ford Motor Company where he had been executive vice president of truck operations. Before that, he served as chairman of Ford of Europe and executive vice president of Ford's international operations. He was a member of Ford's board of directors from 1982 to 1986.

Lutz started his automotive career at General Motors Corporation, where he held a variety of senior positions in Europe. Later he served three years as executive vice president of sales at BMW and as a member of that company's board of management.

Lutz is a member of the board of directors of Northrop Grumman, ASCOM, a Swiss telecommunications and electronics company, and Silicon Graphics, Inc. He is also a member (and former chairman) of the American Highway Users Alliance and serves on the advisory board of the Walter A. Haas School of Business at the University of California, Berkeley. He is a trustee of the Michigan Cancer Foundation and serves as a member of the executive committee of the National association of Manufacturers. He also serves on the board of trustees of the U.S. Marine Corps University Foundation and the Marine Military Academy in Harlingen, Texas, and is a member of the advisory board of Creditanstalt Bank in Vienna, Austria.

Mr. Lutz received his B.S. from the University of California, Berkeley, in 1961, and was elected to Phi Beta Kappa. He received his M.B.A., with highest honors, from the same school in 1962.

He served as an aviator in the United States Marine Corps from 1954 to 1959, attaining the rank of captain.

Rosabeth Moss Kanter holds the Class of 1960 Chair as Professor of Business Administration at the Harvard Business School. Her book, *World Class: Thriving Locally in the Global Economy*, about the impact of globalization on businesses, workplaces, and communities, shows how "collaborative advantage" produces success in the new economy. Her latest book is *Rosabeth Moss Kanter on the Frontiers of Management*.

She also wrote *When Giants Learn to Dance: Mastering the Challenges of Strategy, Management and Careers in the 1990s,* which received the Johnson, Smith & Knisely Award for New Perspectives on Executive Leadership and was translated into 10 languages. Other books include *The Challenge of Organizational Change* (1992), *The Change Masters: Innovation and Entrepreneurship in the American Corporation* (1983), and *Men and Women of the Corporation* (1977), winner of the C. Wright Mills Award for the year's best book on social issues. She has published 12 books and over 150 articles. Her awards for best article include a McKinsey Award from the *Harvard Business Review.*

Robert A. Mundell has been professor of economics at Columbia University since 1974. After studying at M.I.T. and the London School of Economics, he received his Ph.D. from M.I.T. in 1956, and was the Post-Doctoral Fellow in political economy at the University of Chicago in 1956–57. He taught at Stanford University and The Johns Hopkins Bologna Center of Advanced International Studies before joining the staff of the International Monetary Fund in 1961. From 1966 to 1971, he was a professor of economics at the University of Chicago and Editor of the *Journal of Political Economy;* he was concurrently summer professor of international economics at the Graduate Institute of International Studies in Geneva, Switzerland.

Professor Mundell has been an adviser to a number of international agencies and organizations, including the United Nations, the IMF, the World Bank, several governments in Latin America and Europe, the Federal Reserve Board, the U.S. Treasury, and the government of Canada. In 1970, he was a consultant to the Monetary Committee of the European Economic Commission, and in 1972–73 a member of the Study Group on Economic and Monetary Union in Europe. He was a member of the Bellagio-Princeton Study Group on International Monetary Reform from 1964 to 1978, and chairman of the Santa Colomba Conferences on International Monetary Reform between 1971 and 1987.

The author of numerous works and articles on the theory of international economics, Professor Mundell prepared one of the first plans for monetary union in Europe and is known as the father of the theory of optimum currency areas. He was a pioneer of the theory of the monetary and fiscal policy mix, the theory of inflation and interest, the monetary approach to the balance of payments, and a founder of supply-side economics. He has also written extensively on the history of the international monetary system.

Professor Mundell's writings include over 100 articles in academic journals and the following books: *The International Monetary System: Conflict and Reform* (1965); *Man and Economics* and *International Economics* (1968); *Monetary Theory: Interest, Inflation and Growth in the World Economy* (1971); he coedited *A Monetary Agenda for the World Economy* (1983); *Global Disequilibrium* (1990); *Debts, Deficits and Economic Performance* (1991); *Building the New Europe* (1992); and *Inflation and Growth in China* (1996).

Professor Mundell gave the Frank Graham Memorial Lecture at Princeton University in 1965 and the Marshall Lectures at Cambridge University in 1974. He was the first Rockefeller Research Professor of International Economics at the Brookings Institution in 1964–65; the Ford Foundation Research Professor of Economics at the University of Chicago in 1965–66; the Annenberg Professor of Communications at the University of Southern California in 1980; the Annenberg Professor of Communications at the University of Southern California in 1980; the Repap Professor of Economics at McGill University in 1989–90; the Richard Fox Professor of Economics at the University of Pennsylvania in 1990–91; and the Agip Professor of Economics at the Bologna Center in 1997–98. He received a Guggenheim Prize in 1971, the Jacques Rueff Medal and Prize in 1983, the *Docteur Honoris Causa* from the University of Paris in 1992, an honorary professorship at Renmin University in China, and the Distinguished Fellow Award from the American Economic Association in 1997.

William A. Niskanen, an economist, has been chairman of the Cato Institute since 1985. From 1990 through 1996, he was also editor of *Regulation* magazine. Mr. Niskanen previously served as a member and acting chairman of the Council of Economic Advisers, as director of economics at the Ford Motor Company, and in several prior academic and government positions.

He is the author of *Bureaucracy and Representative Government, Reaganomics,* and numerous articles on public policy and public choice. Mr. Niskanen received a B.A. from Harvard and an M.A. and Ph.D. from the University of Chicago.

J. Tracy O'Rourke, as chairman and chief executive officer of Varian Associates, Inc., heads an international technology electronics company with annual sales of approximately $1.6 billion. Headquartered in Palo Alto, Varian is a major producer of components and equipment for international health care, scientific, and industrial markets.

Mr. O'Rourke has held numerous leadership positions in business and civic organizations, including a recent term as chairman of the National Association of Manufacturers, America's largest trade organization for manufacturing companies. He presently chairs the 14,000-member group's finance committee. He also is currently on the boards of directors of General Instrument Corporation, National Semiconductor Corporation, and SRI International. In addition, he serves as a director and executive committee member of the San Francisco Bay Area Council, on the board of the Council for Competitiveness, and on the executive committee of the California Business Roundtable. Until recently, Mr. O'Rourke was also a member of the Defense Science Board of the U.S. Department of Defense.

Mr. O'Rourke has lectured worldwide at universities and at trade-association and government-sponsored meetings on the subjects of quality, computer integrated manufacturing, and global competitiveness. He has been broadly published and interviewed on these subjects by the print and electronic media in the U.S. and abroad. Mr. O'Rourke has received numerous awards, including that of International Industrialist of the Year from the Society of Manufacturing Engineers and recent election to the state of Alabama's Engineering Hall of Fame.

Jóse Piñera currently cochairs the Cato Institute's Project on Social Security Privatization. As Chile's Minister of Labor and Social Security, he was the architect of that country's successful pension reform. As founder and president of the International Center for Pension Reform, Dr. Piñera now advises governments all over the world as they establish privatized pension systems.

Dr. Piñera is a member of the team of economists who transformed the Chilean economy. As Minister of Labor and Social

Security (1978–1980), he was responsible for the labor reform that introduced flexibility to the labor market. As Minister of Mining (1981), he was also responsible for the mining reform that established property rights in this key sector of the Chilean economy.

Dr. Piñera has advised several Latin American governments on the process of economic liberalization, in particular the presidents of Argentina, Colombia, Bolivia, El Salvador, and Peru on their pension reforms based on the Chilean model. He is also chairman of Proyecto Chile 2010, a think tank that promotes free-market economic policies in Chile.

Dr. Piñera has published numerous articles and is the author of six books: *Una Propuesta de Reforma del Sistema de Pensiones en Espana* (Spain, 1996); *Sin Miedo al Futuro* (Spain, 1994, and Poland, 1996); *Camino Nuevo* (Chile, 1993); *El Cascabel al Gato* (Chile, 1991); *La Revolucion Laboral en Chile* (Chile, 1990); and *Fundamentos de la Ley Minera* (Chile, 1982). In addition, he is the editor and publisher of *Economia y Sociedad*, a quarterly journal of opinion.

Dr. Piñera holds an M.A. and a Ph.D. degree in economics from Harvard University.

Joel Popkin is the president of Joel Popkin and Company, an economic consulting firm established in 1978. He has been an analyst observing and predicting the U.S. economy for over 30 years. He specializes in the measurement, analysis, and forecasting of specific wages and prices and the overall rate of inflation. This specialization is a result of his earlier experience at the Bureau of Labor Statistics where he was assistant commissioner for prices and living conditions, responsible for the preparation and publication of the government's official consumer and producer price indexes. He also served as senior staff economist at the Council of Economic Advisers with responsibility for inflation analysis and forecasting during the wage and price controls of the early 1970s.

Felix Rohatyn, who lives in New York City, is internationally recognized as one of the preeminent experts in corporate mergers and acquisitions, public policy, and business economics. He retired this year as a managing director of the New York investment banking house of Lazard Freres & Co. LLC, which he joined in 1948, becoming a partner in 1960. Mr. Rohatyn was also chairman of the Municipal Assistance Corporation (MAC) for the city of New York from 1975–1993, and directed the negotiations that restructured the city's obligations during the fiscal crisis of the mid-1970s. He is a former governor of the New York Stock Exchange.

Mr. Rohatyn earned a B.A. in physics from Middlebury College in 1949 and has received honorary degrees from various universities. He is on the board of directors of Pfizer, Inc. and is a member of the Council on Foreign Relations and the American Academy of Arts and Sciences. He is a vice chairman of Carnegie Hall and is on the board of trustees of a number of other nonprofit organizations. He was awarded the Legion of Honor by the French Government in 1983 and was promoted to the rank of Commander in 1995. Mr. Rohatyn became ambassador to France in September, 1997.

He is married to Elizabeth Rohatyn, former chairman of the New York Public Library.

Jeffrey D. Sachs is the director of the Harvard Institute for International Development, and is the Galen L. Stone Professor of International Trade at Harvard University. He serves as an economic advisor to governments in Latin America, eastern Europe and the former Soviet Union, Asia, and Africa. He was cited in the *New York Times Magazine* as "probably the most important economist in the world" and in *Time* magazine's December 1994 issue on 50 promising young leaders as "the world's best-known economist." He is the author of many scholarly articles and books, including *Macroeconomics in the Global Economy* (coauthored) and *Poland's Jump to the Market Economy.*

Robert J. Shapiro is a founder and the vice president of the Progressive Policy Institute and the director of economic studies of the Progressive Foundation. He also is a contributing editor of the *New Republic, International Economy,* and Intellectual-Capital.com. Dr. Shapiro has been nominated by President Clinton to be the Undersecretary of Commerce for Economic Affairs.

Dr. Shapiro previously served as a principal economic advisor to Governor Clinton in the 1992 presidential campaign, senior adviser to the Clinton-Gore transition, consultant to members of congress and U.S. corporations, deputy national issues director for the Dukakis-Bentsen presidential campaign, associate editor of *U.S. News & World Report*, and legislative director to Senator Daniel P. Moynihan. Dr. Shapiro holds a doctorate from Harvard University, in addition to degrees from the University of Chicago and the London School of Economics.

James Tobin is Sterling Professor of Economics Emeritus at Yale University. He joined the Yale faculty in 1950 and formally retired in 1988.

Professor Tobin was born in Champaign, Illinois, and attended the University High School in Urbana. He graduated from Harvard College, summa cum laude, in 1939. His economics graduate study was interrupted by his service in the U.S. Navy as an officer on a destroyer from 1942 to 1946. He received his Ph.D. in economics from Harvard in 1947 and held a postdoctoral fellowship at Harvard and Cambridge University the next three years. In 1961 and 1962, while on leave from Yale, he served as a member of the Council of Economic Advisers to President Kennedy in Washington.

In 1955, the American Economic Association awarded Professor Tobin the John Bates Clark Medal for achievements as an economist under 40 years of age. He was elected to the National Academy of Sciences in 1972 and in 1981 he received the Nobel Prize in economics. He is author or editor of 16 books and more than 400 articles. His specialities are macroeconomics; monetary theory and policy; fiscal policy and public finance; consumption, saving and investment; unemployment and inflation; portfolio choice and asset markets; econometrics; inequality and poverty. He has written for the general public as well as for professional readers.

Marina Whitman is professor of business administration and public policy at the University of Michigan. From 1979 until 1992, she was an officer of the General Motors Corporation, first as vice president and chief economist and later as vice president and group executive for public affairs, which included the economics, environmental activities, industry-government relations, and public relations staffs.

Prior to her appointment at GM, Professor Whitman was on the faculty in the Department of Economics at the University of Pittsburgh, beginning as an instructor in 1962 and becoming

Distinguished Public Service Professor of Economics in 1973. She served as a member of the president's Council of Economic Advisers in 1972 and 1973 while on leave from the university.

Professor Whitman received a B.A. in government from Radcliffe College and her M.A. and Ph.D. degrees in economics from Columbia University. She is the recipient of numerous fellowships, honors, and awards, and holds honorary degrees from over 20 colleges and universities. She is a member of the boards of directors of five corporations (ALCOA, Browning-Ferris Industries, Chase Manhattan Corporation, Procter & Gamble, UNOCAL); and she has served as a trustee, director, or member of numerous educational, professional, and governmental organizations. She currently serves on the boards of the National Bureau of Economic Research and the Institute for International Economics. She is a former member of the boards of Harvard and Princeton Universities.

Professor Whitman is the author of several books, including *Reflections of Interdependence* (1979), and many articles including "Labor Market Adjustment and Trade: Their Interaction in the Triad," in *International Trade and Finance: New Frontiers for Research* (1997), edited by Benjamin Cohen; "Has Global Competition Killed the Socially Responsible Corporation?," in *Is the Good Corporation Dead? Social Responsibility in a Global Economy* (1996), edited by John W. Houck and Oliver F. Williams; "Using Board Guidelines As A Strategic Tool," in *The Corporate Board*, September/October 1995; and "Flexible Markets, Flexible Firms," in *The American Enterprise*, May-June 1994. As a member of the Michigan Board of Contributors to *The Detroit News*, she writes quarterly op-ed pieces, primarily on international economics. She has also moderated the television series *Economically Speaking*, carried on 200 PBS stations.

Index

DATE DUE
